THE POST-COLD WAR ORDER

THE POST-
COLD WAR ORDER

THE SPOILS OF PEACE

Ian Clark

OXFORD
UNIVERSITY PRESS

OXFORD

UNIVERSITY PRESS

Great Clarendon Street, Oxford OX2 6DP

Oxford University Press is a department of the University of Oxford.
It furthers the University's objective of excellence in research, scholarship,
and education by publishing worldwide in

Oxford New York

Athens Auckland Bangkok Bogotá Buenos Aires Cape Town
Chennai Dar es Salaam Delhi Florence Hong Kong Istanbul Karachi
Kolkata Kuala Lumpur Madrid Melbourne Mexico City Mumbai Nairobi
Paris São Paulo Shanghai Singapore Taipei Tokyo Toronto Warsaw

with associated companies in Berlin Ibadan

Oxford is a registered trade mark of Oxford University Press
in the UK and in certain other countries

Published in the United States
by Oxford University Press Inc., New York

© Ian Clark 2001

The moral rights of the author have been asserted
Database right Oxford University Press (maker)

First published 2001

British Library Cataloguing in Publication Data

Data available

Library of Congress Cataloging in Publication Data

Data available

ISBN 0–19–877633–0

1 3 5 7 9 10 8 6 4 2

Typeset in Adobe Minion
by RefineCatch Limited, Bungay, Suffolk
Printed in Great Britain by
T.J. International, Padstow, Cornwall

PREFACE

There is already a generation growing up for whom the period of the Cold War is not even a distant memory, and who regard the post-Cold War order as the normal state of affairs. To many others, who lived through part or all of the Cold War years, the sheer speed and drama with which the Cold War order collapsed remains a life-defining moment.

What both perspectives share is an overwhelming interest in, and perplexity about, what precisely it was that took the Cold War's place. For those growing to maturity in the 1990s and after, there is the natural desire to comprehend the features of their own world for its own sake. What are the major international forces shaping their lives, and how stable is this order likely to be? For those with Cold War memories, there is also a pressing need to judge whether the great hopes of 1989 have been fulfilled, or disappointed. Either way, the wish to make sense of the post-Cold War order remains strongly with us, but is as yet largely unsatisfied.

It is with the goal of contributing to this ongoing dialogue that the present book has come to be written. It is based on a central paradox. While all the rhetoric that developed after 1989 chose to emphasize the New World Order that arose in the aftermath of the Cold War, in fact the form of this order appeared to follow ancient historical precedents. At the end of all the great wars of the past, the new order has been framed by a post-war peace settlement. While large numbers of commentators have acknowledged the analogy between these historical settlements, and the ending of the Cold War, none has yet offered a detailed assessment of the nature of the post-Cold War peace settlement. How harsh or lenient a peace did it set in place, and with what likely results for the future stability of the present order? It is this agenda that animates the pages to follow.

I am delighted to have worked once more with the OUP team, and grateful for its support and encouragement of this project. The writing was made possible by a period of sabbatical leave granted by the University of Wales Aberystwyth, and I am much indebted to both the Department and the College for providing it. I owe particular thanks to Caroline Haste (even though it did not seem so at the time), for her inspired idea that the Department of International Politics should hold a series of public

'Millennium' lectures in Aberystwyth throughout 2000. The need for me to give one of these provided the momentum and focus that saw the writing of the book effectively launched. The work as a whole has benefited in innumerable small ways from exchanges with my departmental colleagues. The great privilege of working in this distinguished department is that many of the subject's leading lights can be found along its corridor. Michael Cox was particularly helpful in making sources available to me, and allowing me to benefit from his own challenging ideas about the topic. Many contributed to it directly by reading and commenting upon drafts. Tim Dunne, Andrew Linklater, and Nick Wheeler—to the extent that they did not share my conclusions overall—forced me to set them out more precisely and cautiously than would otherwise have been the case. On the historical side, Peter Jackson and Jenny Mathers generously gave me the benefit of their own expertise. I am deeply grateful to them all.

I.C.

Aberystwyth and Llanarmon Dyffryn Ceiriog

CONTENTS

CONTENTS

DETAILED CONTENTS

INTRODUCTION

The intent of this book is to reach some judgement about the essential features of the contemporary order. Such an exercise is, by its very nature, a comparative one. It is possible to see what is distinctive to the present order only by comparing it with what had gone before, both during the Cold War, and earlier. In turn, this compels us to engage in the historical analysis of the elements of continuity and discontinuity between these respective orders: what has changed with the end of the Cold War, and what has not. Briefly stated, the book develops two themes with regard to the contemporary order. The first is an enquiry into its operative principles or, more colloquially, what it is that 'makes it tick'. The second is an exploration of the novelty in this order. The post-Cold War order has been described by one author as a 'unique and quite extraordinary brew' (Hall 1996: 169). To the extent that this judgement is apposite, what is it that has changed that sets it apart from its predecessor? The answers to both sets of questions are, of course, interdependent: the degree of novelty will assuredly be a reflection of what is deemed to be distinctive in its substance. If, for example, one subscribes to the view of 'world order, old and new, as "codified international piracy"' (Chomsky 1997: 5), then the fundamental continuity thereby posited itself precludes any possibility of radical change.

What lends further point to the present endeavour is that the attempt to capture the contemporary order from, as it were, behind a veil of ignorance is precisely the task that has befallen those policy-makers who have had no option but to act in the midst of profound uncertainties. Perhaps it is thus not too outrageous for the historian to follow timidly where the policy-maker has already set foot. As will become apparent shortly, the comparison is an important one because this study is very much occupied with how policy-makers have sought to construct the present order. In that sense, it is proper for the historian to write from within the same limits of knowledge as those practitioners who have attempted to shape the world in which we now live. The policy-maker's is certainly not the only possible perspective, but it is one legitimate viewpoint amongst the others. It is no part of the argument of this book to suggest that *all* aspects of international order are under the effective control of states and their officials, but it is to those areas consciously shaped 'at the highest levels' that this analysis will devote its particular attention.

This book is an essay within the *genre* of contemporary history. To enter this field is, wittingly, to accept its attendant dangers. Ever since the end of the Cold War, there has been a complex and multifaceted debate about the contours of the world that has now taken its place. The debate has covered such matters as whether the successor to the Cold War is a more benign or a more turbulent world; to what extent the international distribution of power has shifted, and with what consequential impacts on stability; the degree to which habits and institutions of cooperation engendered during the Cold War had now become so deeply entrenched as to endure its passing; and whether, during its first decade or so, the aftermath of the Cold War constituted an actual order, or merely a transitory phase before a replacement order solidified and took its place.

It has proved exceptionally difficult to resolve these issues. Such consensus as there is does not extend much beyond the recognition that, if in 1989 'the world seemed beautifully simple', by the middle of the next decade 'complexity had replaced simplicity' (Reynolds 2000: 586). The problem derived, in part, from the fact that this *was* contemporary history—fast moving and seemingly shapeless—and that we were standing in the middle of it. No doubt there is a respectable body of historical opinion that, for this very reason, would counsel against any scholarly venture into the too recent past. And yet, Garton Ash is surely correct to deny the suggestion 'that you understand events better if you are further away from them' since, intuitively, 'this is actually a very odd idea' (2000: xvii). The justification for contemporary history of this kind is that, even if it is premature to expect it to yield definitive interpretations, we can bring to it the unique perspective resulting from our proximity.

Much of the commentary on the post-Cold War period has been directly concerned with the search for an understanding of the present order. As yet, however, we have no satisfactory overall framework within which to reach sensible conclusions. Although the events of 1989–91 are celebrated as a remarkable turning point in world affairs, we remain profoundly uncertain about how decisive these changes have been, and about what kind of order has emerged as a result.

How are we to grapple with the obvious elements of both continuity and discontinuity that are represented in the current era? Both change and continuity form part of all historical orders, but at some revolutionary moments the balance shifts between them. What this book sets out to advance is a particular framework that will permit a more precise engagement with that issue. This framework, and its historical antecedents, will be set out in greater detail in Chapter 3. For the moment, however, the reader requires some points of orientation to give an indication of the directions to be followed in the remainder of this study.

'Throughout modern European history', one distinguished student of contemporary history attests, 'periods of order have alternated with generally shorter ones of violent disorder, during which the political map is redrawn' (Garton Ash 2000: 466). Likening the closing decade of the twentieth century to such a period of redrawing, he then concludes that 'the main elements of a new order did seem to be in place by the end of the decade' (2000: 467). How did this come to pass? Unless the order emerged spontaneously, it was a work of contrivance and construction. This normal pattern, to which Garton Ash makes reference, is none other than that of periodic peacemaking, in the aftermath of the century's bloody and disruptive wars. New orders are crafted not by war alone—although these are consistently the predisposing agents—but by the process of peacemaking in its aftermath. Although he does not quite acknowledge this, his argument is fully consistent with the notion that the period of the post-Cold War world that we have just lived through has been, in function if not in form, an exercise in peacemaking. What then can we learn about the nature of that order if this is the perspective that we choose to adopt?

THE POST-COLD WAR ORDER
AS PEACEMAKING

The starting point for the argument is a very simple one. In depicting the period 1945–90 as the Cold War, we employ the language of war, and refer to it as a kind of war. To be sure this was no normal hot war, but a war of a kind nonetheless. If such was the case, it is instructive to pursue the logic of our own language, even if that reasoning is metaphoric. If the period that ended in 1990 was a form of war, then what has taken its place is a kind of peace. Or, to be more precise, what has come at the end of the Cold War is a phase of peacemaking. Since the Cold War was not a proper war, it is fitting that it should be brought to an end by a peace that is not a proper peace. If the Cold War was a functional substitute for a real war that was now too costly to wage, then the resulting peace was also a functional substitute for a settlement that was now too delicate to be formally negotiated. It was, however, the type of peace that the form of war itself demanded.

The central argument of this book is that, by so conceiving the post-Cold War order, we are better placed to understand some of the developments that have taken place within it. Above all, this provides us with a yardstick that can measure both the degree of change, as well as the degree of continuity. Furthermore, it can provide a plausible explanation for their joint presence, because both are essential features of classical phases of peacemaking in the aftermath of the great formative military contests of the modern era. Those settlements sought to make major changes, but they also aimed to conserve at the very least the fruits of the victory that had been won. Within this framework of peacemaking, we can thereby develop a set of concepts that helps make sense of the major ambiguities of the contemporary order.

A recent study into the making of peace in the aftermath of war poses the general question: 'When a war ends, how should victors treat the defeated in order to promote an enduring peace?' It also makes the significant observation that the 'geopolitical landscape is littered with military victories that never translated into stable political orders' (Kegley and Raymond 1999: 3). Reasoning metaphorically, we may pursue both trains of thought in relation to 1990. The former leads to an enquiry into how the victors have treated the defeated since the end of the Cold War. We need to review the elements of the peace settlement and, on that basis, reach judgements about how punitive or lenient its terms have been. The latter invites reflection on the prospects for the future. Has the peace settlement been developed in such a way that it holds promise of a stable and enduring order becoming established in its aftermath? In this respect, there is now a substantial body of historical wisdom about the precedents: this draws attention to those aspects of peace settlements that have contributed to durable peace in the past, and those that have tended to impede it. Remembrance of peace settlements past—such as Westphalia, Utrecht, Vienna, Brest-Litovsk, Versailles, Yalta/Potsdam, and San Francisco—can give us an insight into some of the essential qualities of the post Cold War order.

Seemingly at odds with this interpretation, one of the many accounts of the fragility of the post-Cold War order had rested its key diagnosis on the 'absence, seven years into the post-Cold War period, of a viable peace settlement' (Pierre and Trenin 1997: 7). This invites the query in turn: is this true? On what basis can we reach the conclusion that there has been no peace settlement to end the Cold War?

There are reasons for thinking that this is deeply misleading. Moreover, the cause of this misunderstanding may be found in a neglect of the real significance of the historical precedents. The last great failure to achieve a peace settlement was reportedly in 1945, at the end of the Second World War. The conventional understanding is that no peace could then be made because the allies fell out with each other, and a forty-five-year Cold War supervened instead.

More recently, we have been given an alternative interpretation. Central to Trachtenberg's (1999) thesis is that a post-war peace was eventually constructed during the course of the Cold War. The key year was to be 1963, because at that point 'the elements of a political system finally fell into place'. Even more significantly, 1963 was the great watershed since this 'system would provide the basis for a relatively stable peace for the balance of the Cold War period, and beyond' (1999: 352).

There are two ideas within this kind of argument that may be revealing for any attempt to understand the post-Cold War era. First, as his title suggests, Trachtenberg emphasizes that the peace settlement was *constructed* over time. Linked to this is the associated idea that peacemaking after 1945 was a *protracted* affair. Indeed, if we accept his argument, the peace settlement of 1945 was some eighteen years in the making and, arguably, may have taken even longer. In any case, what this suggests is that we already have a historical precedent for a phase of peacemaking that lasted over the long term. The days of holding a single Congress or Conference, such as at Vienna or Versailles, to *make* the peace may well have passed. Peacemaking has now to be thought of as a process, rather than as a singular event. As Sharp (1997: 5) has recalled, with a better eye for the historical antecedents, perhaps 'the age of the single, continuous peace conference, seeking to produce a universal settlement, had already passed by 1919'.

The connections between the 'peace' of 1945, and the 'peace' of 1990, may be even more intimate than this suggests. The ensuing argument will suggest two respects in which this was so. The first is that, in terms of substance, there was a striking continuity between the two periods of peacemaking. Indeed, they might plausibly be considered to be two phases of the same peace. This is recognized in Trachtenberg's admission that aspects of the political system constructed by 1963 (especially Germany's non-nuclear status, and the US military presence on German soil) persist into the post-Cold War era also (1999: 401). More pointedly, there is a sense in which it was only in 1990, at the end of the Cold War, that parts of the 1945 settlement were finally constructed: 'a true peace settlement of the scars of World War II', it has been claimed, 'was finally reached when the Berlin Wall was torn down in 1989' (Kegley and Raymond 1999: 196). On this reasoning, 1945 is not simply a good *model* for understanding the peace of 1990: more radically, the peace of 1990 was an actual *part* of the peace of 1945.

The second connection develops another important theme from a different direction. It challenges the claim that *no* peace was put in place in 1945. What happens to our understanding of the post-Cold War order if we deny the complete failure to make peace in 1945? And how might such an argument be developed? The common assertion that there was no peace settlement at all in 1945 is, at best, a half-truth. Fully to understand the import of this suggestion requires us to develop a more sophisticated conceptual understanding of what is entailed by peacemaking and, in Chapter 3, an attempt will be made to elaborate two essential dimensions of this. This scheme allows that there was a peace in 1945, albeit a partial one.

For the moment, the case can be made that considerable preparatory work for peace was already under way during the course of the Second World War itself. Even if the substance of the peace remained to be determined, the prosecution of the war was accompanied by a concerted effort 'to search for principles to underpin a stable postwar world order' (Kegley and Raymond 1999: 173). Instructively, this implies a possible distinction between the content of the substantive peace, and the *principles* that might be called upon to support it. Is it then true that no peace was put in place by 1945, if we think of that peace as being its constitutive principles, and not simply as the substantive implementation of them? What if some principles of the 1945 peace had indeed been put in place, and continued to be operative into the post-1990 order as well? One analysis of the situation in 1945 explains why that peace had to be unusually broad in its coverage. 'The postwar planners strove as much to eliminate the causes of economic crisis as international conflict', Maier (1996: 14) recalls, and draws his own conclusion that this contributed to 'a more robust settlement' in 1945 than in 1919. But how might such a positive verdict on 1945 be reconciled with the view that no settlement was produced at all? In short, the import of 1945 for 1990 is not that there was no peace at war's end, but more pertinently that part of the peace was already operative in the years after 1945: this was to persist as an important dimension of the post-1990 peace as well.

What is so perplexing is that, for all the appeal of 1990 as the ending of one of the great global wars, there has as yet been little systematic attempt to explore this image in any detail. The major exception to this is the recent work of Ikenberry (2000), on the subject of 'strategic restraint' after victory. There have been myriad commentaries on the end of the Cold War that have adopted the language of 'winning' and 'losing'. When this is juxtaposed to the argument that 1990 represents one of history's great landmarks, along with the likes of 1648, 1713, 1815, 1919, and 1945 (Gaddis 1992b), the implication that 1990 be understood as a form of peace settlement is very clear indeed. It has even been openly claimed that 'it was a cooperative settlement designed carefully by leaders in East and West' (Risse 1997: 184). And yet there is no detailed analysis extant of the 1990 peace settlement. How did it come to be negotiated? What were its terms, and how severe were they? Above all, what kind of order did the peace seek to construct?

There are two fundamental and interlinked reasons for the reluctance to investigate the post-Cold War order as an exercise in peacemaking. The first is that, since the Cold War has never been considered as a proper war, its ending has not been considered as requiring a proper peace. The assumption is that the Cold War was simply followed by little more than a Cold Peace, but without the formality of a settlement to mark the transition. Secondly, what has most impressed analysts about the end of the Cold War is precisely that it was resolved peacefully: the fact that it did not become hot at its dénouement reinforces the idea that there was no need for a peace to be made at its end. The logic at work here is that no peace is required when a conflict ends peacefully, as it is by then superfluous. But we should not confuse a peaceful ending with a peace settlement. The former refers simply to the means employed at the moment of resolution, and tells us little about the consequences for the 'belligerents' thereafter. It is, in fact, the peacemaking that defines the parameters of the subsequent relationship between them.

In short, the neglect of peacemaking as a key element of the post-Cold War order may seriously compromise our understanding of that order. It has been pointed out of the events surrounding 1990 that the 'transition from the first American world order to the second occurred without an intervening wave of large-scale war. The transition was relatively smooth' (Knutsen 1999: 292–3). This is, of course, literally true and helps explain the lack of a 'peacemaking' approach to the 1990s. Knutsen's claim seems plausible when the transition is looked at in the short term, and within the confines of 1989–91. But what if, by analogy with 1945, the peacemaking is understood to be protracted and may, in a sense, still be going on? Can we remain so confident about the smoothness of that transition? Can we be certain that victory in the Cold War, however peacefully accomplished, will issue in a stable political order thereafter?

The case for examining the recent order as a phase of peacemaking seems compelling. Because it offers us a way of dealing with the complex issues of continuity and discontinuity, it provides a suitable framework for understanding the ambiguous nature of the contemporary order. What defines the present order is that it is a phase of peacemaking that combines elements both old and new. The existing elements describe the balance of forces that contributed to the 'victory' of the West; the new elements describe the redistribution of forces that has resulted from victory and defeat. If it is the former that help us to understand why the 'peaceful' ending came to pass, it is the latter that give us an insight into the operation of the peace now in place.

While such an approach to the post-Cold War order is suggestive, it is not unproblematic. Most of these difficulties will be discussed in their appropriate contexts. But four general points are worth noting at the outset.

The contention that we gain some purchase on the post-Cold War order by regarding it as a phase of peacemaking seems to depend on an assumption that it is the very act of peacemaking that issues in the subsequent order. In this perspective, there is a causal instrumentality between the two, the settlement producing the order that emerges in its aftermath. However, this might be a false assumption and can be disputed on particular, as well as more general, grounds. Specifically, what seems to render the model inappropriate was the conscious decision in 1990 not to hold a 'single grand international conference to redraw the map of Europe'. In support of his verdict, Garton Ash is right to dismiss the Paris meeting of November 1990 as akin to little more than the expression of New Year's resolutions, rather than as any serious determinant of the ensuing order (Garton Ash 2000: 468). More generally, it might be argued that a peace settlement is symptom rather than cause. It reflects the distribution of power already in being, of which victory has been the consequence, and hence the peacemaking is merely symptomatic of the order already in place. Peacemaking possesses no causal efficacy of its own. This objection can be denied by appeal to historical examples, where the wisdom or ineptitude of peacemakers has been more or less decisive in converting military victory into sustainable political order. Importantly, however, it reminds us that peace settlements do not wipe slates clean, but are, by their intrinsic nature, embodiments of continuity as well as instruments of change. It is for this very reason that such a framework is helpful in teasing out the ambivalent quality of the post-Cold War order.

Secondly, it might be objected that the analogy with peacemaking is inappropriate to the end of the Cold War on the grounds that this resulted from negotiation rather than imposition. The Soviet Union did not lose the Cold War, and then suffer the indignity of its defeat in the peace settlement. Chronologically, it was instead the negotiation of the issues that lay at the heart of the Cold War that paved the way for its ending, and this created the basis for a new relationship between East and West. Paradoxically, it was the very manner of the ending of the Cold War that gave the Soviet leadership the confidence to proceed with its policies, reassured that the West would not take unilateral advantage of the changes that were being instigated (Ikenberry 2000: 5). To apply the language of peacemaking is then, it might be thought, to misconstrue profoundly both the nature of the relationship between the two protagonists at the Cold War's end, and also the sequence of events which helped bring it about. Essentially, the USSR had other choices but decided not to exercise them and, in that very important sense, agreed to the end of the Cold War. It was thus negotiated and not imposed. This is close to one analyst's conclusion that 'the Cold War's endgame is largely a story of reassurance rather than compellence or even coercion' (Risse 1997: 162). In short, what is wrong with the idea of peacemaking is that it misunderstands the end of the Cold War to be simply an effect of a dramatic shift in East–West relations, when it was actually a cause of that shift. There was no need for the USSR to suffer the extra punishment of a post-Cold War peace settlement, because the end of the Cold War was a means chosen by the Soviet leadership, and not a contingent outcome of military defeat. This objection, too, raises important issues that will be returned to in due course. But it fails as a rebuttal, in principle, of the peacemaking imagery since it disregards the element of negotiation that is present in all peace settlements, albeit to varying degrees.

Thirdly, there is the potential objection that while peacemaking might be considered an element within the post-Cold War order, the two cannot possibly be thought of as coextensive. At heart, the problem is that the present order defines the key regulative and allocative principles of the global system as a whole. No matter how significant was the Cold War, the measures required to bring it to an end do not amount to a settlement for the entire order. Indeed, much of that order required no settlement at all, since it was fundamentally untouched by either the Cold War or its ending. For example, the development of the global economy in the years since 1945 is a story that can be told without much reference to the Soviet Union, however much the existence of the Soviet Union facilitated its creation, or however much the Soviet Union was affected by it in turn. But, on the face of it, there was palpably no need for a new economic settlement in 1990, just because of the collapse of the USSR. 'Only part of the post-World War II order—the bipolar order—was destroyed by the dramatic events of 1989–1991', Ikenberry informs us. 'The order among the democratic industrial powers was still intact' (2000: 215). Peacemaking might then reveal something about what has happened since 1990, but it cannot be pretended that it tells us the whole story. Much of this argumentation can be readily admitted, but it requires one significant qualification: what it portrays as weakness is, in fact, the very strength of this framework. Where the objection goes adrift is in its misleading assessment of the historical function of peacemaking. Settlements are as important for what they seem not to 'settle', as for what they do. Accordingly, it is a misconception that, for example, the absence of any need to revise the global economy signifies that this was an area irrelevant to the post-Cold War peace. To suggest as much is to get the point entirely the wrong way round. It is a measure of its centrality to the settlement that it did not need to be adjusted by it.

Finally, the peacemaking framework might be subverted by pointing to the violence that seemingly resulted from the end of the Cold War. If there was a settlement at the end of the Cold War, then it resulted in a failed peace at best. How else are we to comprehend the agonies of the Yugoslav wars, and the wars of separatism in the former Soviet Union, such as that with Chechnya? There are, however, two counters to this objection. It is no part of the following argument that peace was imposed instantly and uniformly at the Cold War's end. Instead, the emphasis is upon a process or phase of peacemaking, of which these violent eruptions were to become an integral part. Secondly, peace settlements in the past have regularly been beset by bouts of violent disturbance in their wake. In this respect, there is little difference between the violence of the 1990s, and the various outbreaks of fighting, say, in the period 1919–22. Peace settlements are much harder to implement than to decree, and that following the end of the Cold War was no exception in this regard.

MAKING THE PEACE AND KEEPING THE PEACE

Insofar as international orders are the products of peace settlements, there are two aspects of the peace that shape the ensuing order, and this book is centrally concerned with the interrelationship between the two. The first is the content or the substance of the settlement, and is about the making of the peace. The second is the wider frameworks and systems of ideas that are required to keep the peace once it has been made. Often the latter may not appear to be a formal part of the settlement at all, but can nonetheless be critical to the viability of the peace in the longer term. Ikenberry has described a historical tendency to give greater prominence to such arrangements, and understands them as a trend towards an 'institutionalized' peace:

Most importantly, in the settlements of 1815, 1919, and 1945, the leading states made increasingly elaborate efforts to institutionalize the postwar security relations between the major powers. Rather than rely simply on balance-of-power strategies or preponderant power, they sought to restrain power, reassure weaker potential rivals, and establish commitments by creating various types of binding institutions. (2000: 8)

Moreover, the fact that these devices for keeping the peace are often part of the settlement, but at one remove, entails that they may not necessarily be new features at all—as the example of the global economy attests. What is then so intriguing about this second aspect of peace settlements is that it may often represent an element of continuity with the pre-war situation. In short, it would be erroneous to imagine that peace settlements are necessarily and exclusively about the creation of something new. While the substantial part of a settlement will often bring about new distributions—for example, as regards the territorial spoils—this second dimension can as readily take the form of a reaffirmation and rearticulation of existing principles and structures. Peace settlements are therefore instruments that deal explicitly with issues of continuity and change, and this is why they afford such an appealing framework for furthering our understanding of the post-Cold War order in particular.

How is peace, once made, best preserved? Essentially, this book explores two mechanisms through which that goal can be achieved. These can be presented, for the moment, as two separate and distinct ideal types. In reality, of course, actual practice tends to be a mixture of the two, and a great deal of our interest needs to focus on this inter-relationship. The first mechanism relies upon power, exaction, imposition, and enforcement. The second is based upon legitimacy, consensus, acquiescence, and compliance. For a durable peace, the balance between these two approaches needs to be carefully modulated. In order that the winner can economize on resort to the former, the latter needs to be developed and find acceptance; if the latter is suspect, there must be a willingness to employ the former to a sufficient degree. However, if the former is too obtrusive, it is likely in any case to subvert the latter. It is a delicate, and shifting, balance that has to be struck if the peace is to be sustainable.

How then did the post-Cold War peace seek to preserve itself, and what has been the balance between these two instruments? One clear verdict is that 'considerations of power are massively present' (Hall 1996: 174) within it, but there is more than this that can be said about the matter. Precisely because of the way in which the Cold War came to an end, there was a greater continuity into the post-Cold War period of ideological convictions and beliefs that had never been seriously challenged, either during the Cold War or at its end. Writers have thus pointed to the oddity of 1990 in that 'no war had been necessary for, ostensibly, the West's agenda to "win"' (A. J. Williams 1999: 59). This resulted in a greater potential for the persistence of the old order into the new. Hall himself accepts as much when he acknowledges that the 'current rules curiously combine old institutions with new realities' (1996: 164). It is the nature of this combination that we must seek to address if the post-Cold War order is to be fully comprehended for what it is.

The argument unfolds in the following stages. Chapters 1 and 2 take stock of the existing debate about the current order. While Chapter 1 directly confronts the issue of its novelty within the wider frame of twentieth-century history, Chapter 2 explores what it is that, distinctively, makes it tick. Chapter 3 then sets out in detail the framework and insights that attach to the notion of peacemaking, and provides a historical perspective upon them. This makes it possible, in turn, to apply that framework to the analysis of the post-Cold War order. This is done throughout the remainder of the book. Chapters 4 and 5 are about how the post-Cold War peace was made, both in Europe and globally. They review the main substantive provisions of that settlement, and the division of the spoils that resulted from it. Chapter 6 looks at the content of the peace through the different perspective of the division of the spoils associated with globalization.

Here onwards, the focus shifts somewhat. While it still deals with substantive aspects of the peace settlement, the content of these provisions has to be understood in terms of its contribution, not just to the making of the post-Cold War peace, but to the keeping of it. It was the dramatic changes associated with the spoils of 1990 that implied the emergence of a wholly new order. As against these, the subtle role of these other, less visible, spoils—concerning multilateral institutions and the global economy, a collectivization of security, and a liberal rights order—serves as a stark reminder of the considerable continuities with the old. These other dimensions of the peace settlement are surveyed in Chapters 7 to 9. In sum, they make the case that peace settlements are about much more than the allocation of territories and resources. In this respect, once more, the post-Cold War peace proved to be no exception.

I

POST-COLD WAR PERSPECTIVES

1

ORDERS OLD AND NEW

To what extent can we discern a genuine 'order' in today's post-Cold War world? The question, in turn, implies two others. First, is there a discernible order at all at the present time? Secondly, if there is, is it sufficiently distinct from what preceded it during the Cold War era? Commentators are divided in their response to the first question, and demonstrate degrees of scepticism about it. As to the second, it is most commonly taken for granted that the answer is in the affirmative: whatever we may now have—order or not, and for better or worse—it is demonstrably no longer the Cold War, and is therefore radically distinct from it.

How can we tell when, and whether, one order has replaced another? As this formulation implies, there are two interrelated dimensions to the problem. One is broadly chronological, whereas the other is substantive. The first requires us to map changes in time, and to make judgements about how to date the patterns of order that we are tracing. The other, and the crucial determinant of that chronology, is an engagement with the substance of these changes, and this entails judgements about what represents the most radical transformations to that order. Although the separation is artificial, this chapter deals with matters of chronology, and Chapter 2 with the substantive issues of order that underlie them.

This chapter, accordingly, confronts the question of continuity and discontinuity. It takes a wide historical perspective, and suggests that the problem of locating the post-1990 order is only a part of a wider problem of discerning the shape of twentieth-century history as a whole, and of the place of the Cold War within it. We cannot sensibly determine the novelty of the post-Cold War world without a more fundamental attempt to see where the Cold War period fits into the wider shape of twentieth-century history. The argument also focuses more specifically upon the debates about the nature of the Cold War, and about the dynamics thought to have brought it to an end. Understanding these dynamics is an integral part of unravelling the bases of the present order and, for that reason, the debate about why the Cold War came to an end is itself inseparable from the attempt to understand the contemporary order. This brings the question of continuity and discontinuity to the forefront, and suggests why it is that the answer to it is far less clear-cut than often supposed. We have been so impressed by the dramatic ending of the Cold War that we have failed to notice the substantial elements of continuity between the two periods. A richer historical perspective can be developed only by locating the period within a framework that spans the past sixty or so years. When this has been done, we will be better able to explore the historical significance of the peace settlement arrived at after the end of the Cold War.

As yet, there has been no fully adequate effort to trace the elements of continuity and discontinuity in the present order. Is it simply a mixture of previous orders? Does it oscillate between forms of unipolarity and forms of multipolarity, depending upon the issue involved? Alternatively, these traditional analytical concepts might no longer tell us much about how the present system works. Might the emerging order be *sui generis*, entailing a sharp break from previous historical forms, and thus rendering redundant existing theoretical frameworks as means of comprehending it? Hoffmann holds out such a prospect in his speculation that the 'world after the cold war will not resemble any world of the past' (1998: 121–2). Might it be so different because much of this order is transnational in nature, and dependent upon actors not controlled by states? Is it qualitatively new because of the effects of globalization? The pervasive resort to the imagery of a new medievalism—with the simultaneous realization of how inappropriate this model is to present global conditions—is illustrative of the puzzled search for meaningful terms of reference.

We need initially to explore the reasons for our ambivalent feelings about whether the contemporary world is 'orderly' or not. This involves standard issues about competing conceptions of order, made all the more problematic by the widening framework within which issues of order now tend to be discussed. We must begin with the issue of whether today's world represents any form of order at all.

THE PROBLEM OF ORDER

At the moment of the Cold War's ending, and during the next few years succeeding it, there emerged a mixed reaction to that event. There were initially the optimists who thought its historical significance lay in the new opportunity for developing an improved world order. This sentiment was embodied in the calls emanating from the United States, and from then President George Bush specifically, for a New World Order (NWO) that would achieve the goals of peace, stability, justice, rights, and the rule of law. The end of the Cold War created the necessary universal conditions, originally intimated in 1945 but stultified by the ensuing rivalry between the superpowers, that would make this possible. Now, once again, the prospects for international organization, collective security, and advancement of human rights shone brightly. 'The end of the Cold War', C. Brown (1999*b*: 42) reported, was seen in some quarters as 'ushering in an (indefinite) period of world dominance by forces which . . . could be seen as "liberal"'. Since liberalism had been the real victor in 1989, there would be a liberal peace to enshrine the historic significance of its achievement.

The pessimists, whose voice became more audible in the early 1990s, took a more dismal view of what had happened, and emphasized the dangers rather than the opportunities. For them, the release from the Cold War represented a loosening of restraints, and the likelihood of a regressive return to previous instabilities. There would be a re-emergence of the traditional agenda of international politics that had been concealed by the distracting overlay of the Cold War. The passing of the Cold War was therefore likely to unveil a new age of power politics, untrammelled by the checks and balances of the Cold War. As Skidelsky (1995: xi) was to express it, 'the collapse of the over-arching imperial structures of the Cold War would release not the cosmopolitan Utopia but the historical passions and enmities which the bipolar hegemony had kept under control'. This would once more set loose those demons of the 1930s that had since been thought securely laid to rest. The fear was of a new age of vicious national, ethnic, or civilizational conflict. According to these doom-laden predictions, 'the dismantling of Cold War security structures . . . would lead to another redivision of Europe' (Kaplan 2000: xii), rather than to a continent 'free and whole'.

Although the optimists and the pessimists differed sharply in their respective prognoses for the future, what was so remarkable was that they shared a common diagnosis. They both started from the assumption that, whether as a new dawn or as atavistic conflict, the post-Cold War era certainly marked a watershed: if they disagreed as to whether it would be better or worse, they were at least of a common opinion that it would not be the same.

But to assess whether the contemporary world is more or less orderly than its predecessor compels us to enquire into the fundamental nature of order itself. What constitutes an order? Can we speak of a single order in which all humanity participates, or is order inevitably always for someone and for something? Order then, like the curate's egg, may be deemed good in parts. It may seem better when viewed from the perspective of the minority 20 per cent who enjoy most of the world's material resources, than when viewed by the 80 per cent who do not. In turn, this raises profound questions about the normative basis of order. Do orders necessarily entail values, and which might these be? Is order concerned with peace, stability, justice, human rights, basic needs, fair distribution, environmental sustainability, or what? And if it embraces all of these, in which proportions and with what priority are they to be selected, should these principles clash as they must?

Hedley Bull's (1977) conception of order was as a condition that meets the basic goals of the members of international society: most fundamentally these are survival, security, and stability. To this has been added the suggestion by Hoffmann (1998: 203) that order should be thought of as 'a construct and a condition'. This reflects the ambivalent degrees of conscious intention, as opposed to incidental by-product, that might characterize any particular order. It also conveniently makes allowance for a distinction between order as a set of 'really existing' conditions, as against the notion that patterns of order are indeed constructed by human agents, and reflect real value choices. It is on these grounds that Smith challenges the idea that order deserves to enjoy primacy in the hierarchy of values (S. Smith 1999: 106).

These controversies expose the profound fault-lines that run through the discussion of order. How does an international order of states relate to a world order of human beings (Bull 1977)? In particular, it is commonplace to suggest that conceptions of *international* order assign priority not only to states but, implicitly, to those most powerful states at the apex of the hierarchy. It was for this reason that the United States' declarations of a New World Order were decried in the early 1990s as bearing only too clearly the stamp of their authors. '[A] genuine New World Order', it was surmised by one critic, 'would require a shift from a great power preferred order to one that reflects the interests of international society as a whole and which has regard for the justice due to individuals' (Keal 1993: 99). But how much 'regard' must it have? And what are the interests of international society as a whole? The basic dilemma, as Hoffmann has so powerfully argued, is that once we move beyond minimum conceptions of order, we are confronted by the stark reality of conflicting choices. This is true even within the limited confines of liberalism itself, and thus of a mere segment of international society. Liberalism's problem, Hoffmann complains, is that it wants to pursue four goods simultaneously: sovereignty, national self-determination, democracy, and human rights. The harsh reality is that it is 'extremely difficult to have all four' (1998: 61), and hence painful choices must be made amongst them.

It is thus evident that there is much scope for disagreement about whether or not an order exists, and about what are its real bases. In this respect, the post-Cold War period is no different from many others. Indeed, the very idea that there was once a Cold War order itself is thought self-contradictory by many, since this was a system of superpower control and management that infringed many of the values that might otherwise be thought integral to any conception of order.

For similar reasons, many analysts certainly dismiss any attribution of order to the present era. They do so on a variety of grounds: politically, because of its embodiment of Western hegemony (Chomsky 1997; R. W. Cox 1996; Gill 1997); normatively, because it enshrines inequality (Hurrell 1999: 291; Chubin 1995: 435), or represents a chaos of conflicting norms (Hoffmann 1998: 79); economically, because of its inner contradictions (Gray 1998); in terms of security, because it remains statist and is not emancipatory (Falk 1999; Booth 1991); and sociologically, because it is 'out of control' (Bauman 1998). Those who describe the contemporary order in terms of globalization are, thereby, as likely to regard it as 'the harbinger not of a new world order but of a new world *disorder*' (Cerny 1996: 619).

Nonetheless, and with appropriate qualifications, there remains substantial agreement that the Cold War order has indeed been replaced, not just by chaos, but by another pattern of order. The editors of one comprehensive survey of the problem conclude that 'it is with surprise that we note the emergence of a fairly widely shared view as to the orderly nature of the current global condition' (Hall and Paul 1999: 395). Not all agree on the constituents of that order, but most seem to accept that one assuredly exists.

But these all represent partial judgements at best. They lack any integrated historical perspective within which the assertions, or denials, of order might become fully intelligible. The following argument therefore shares one historian's claim: 'the most basic questions about the NWO . . . cannot in fact be answered without a fairly long historical perspective. Such a perspective is essential for understanding the nature of the contemporary international system by revealing how it developed and how it differs from previous counterparts' (Schroeder 1995: 367).

The argument of this book is that the post-Cold War order is, indeed, a distinctive form of order. However, contrary to the most common versions of this argument, its distinctiveness does not reside in its 'newness', in the fact that it represents a sharp break with the past. It is impossible to understand the post-Cold War order without due recognition being accorded to the elements of continuity as well. Like most orders, the post-Cold War version is a combination of continuity and discontinuity. What then is distinctive about it is that it is best understood as an extended phase of peacemaking, and possesses many of the characteristics of that *genre* of statecraft. But before this case can be made in detail, it is first of all necessary to place the argument in its wider historical context.

THE PROBLEM OF CONTINUITY

The early responses to the end of the Cold War tended to emphasize the radical change that it signified, and it was typically referred to as 'a historic divide' (Garthoff 1994: 1). More recently, the discussion has drawn attention to the points of continuity as well. That ambivalence is nicely summarized in the observation that the 'landscape in 1999 may look very different to 1989, but there are still some very familiar landmarks' (Cox,

Booth, and Dunne 1999*b*: 1). A few brief examples can be offered at this stage, and others will be examined in greater detail below.

An array of analysts point to an essential continuity in the role of American power, between what has been termed Pax Americana I and II. More specifically, there are institutions that were created during the Cold War, and which were almost defining attributes of it, but which still endure into the post-Cold War era. One thinks in particular of NATO. It is the persistence of such elements that leads one noted historian to conclude that 'the Cold War may have ended, but the Cold War political system remains largely intact' (Trachtenberg 1999: 402). Another structure that stands out prominently across both the Cold War and post-Cold War periods is the Western liberal order. Ikenberry tellingly insists that 'the post-Cold War order is really a continuation and extension of the Western order forged during and after World War II' (1996: 90). There are components of that which encourage a progressive view of the contemporary order, as Schroeder notes (1995: 369). But in making his claim that idealists are 'right to insist that a genuinely new and effective NWO has emerged in the last 50 years, especially the last decade', he implicitly elides the significance of the Cold War's ending, and endorses the view of continuity instead. The importance of the 1990s lies, on this account, in the deepening and widening of those very principles of order, already articulated in 1945. Similar, if less sanguine, interpretations can be constructed around globalization, environmental agendas, and economic immiseration in the South. All of these represent pronounced elements of continuity within which it is distorting to make claims for any salient transition around 1990. Whatever the end of the Cold War signified, it was not a radical break within these ongoing historical trends.

Consequently, the broader analytical context in which these issues need to be set is questions about the elements of continuity and discontinuity in post-1990 international politics. These, in turn, relate backwards to similar problems about the year 1945. They confront, in that sense, what is one of the key historiographical questions about twentieth-century international relations, namely the extent to which it is 1945 that represents the fundamental watershed. Was this the turning point when the major problems of the first half of the century were progressively resolved—the eclipse of the old balance of power, nuclear weapons and the obsolescence of great power war, international organization, a managed international economy, welfare states, human rights, decolonization, and the spread of liberal democracy? Many histories implicitly treat events in this fashion, and present 1945 as the point of radical discontinuity in the century. Typically, Mazower (1998: 406) claims that 'Europe's twentieth century divides sharply into two halves'.

Such a view of 1945 as representing some kind of absolute break arguably seemed more convincing when viewed from within the Cold War itself, but is less plausible in its aftermath. As an alternative to it, the Cold War period might be conceived as an aberration from a story that is now, in some respects, being resumed. It is for this reason that some claim that the pre-1945 world has moved much closer to the present, and seems much more relevant, than it did while the Cold War was still ongoing. The effect of the Cold War perspective, by emphasizing the fundamental transitions after 1945, was to 'distance' the pre-1945 world from the contemporary. This trick of perspective has been undone by the demise of the Cold War and, as a result, the continuities between the 1990s and the pre-Second World War period stand out more sharply. This is testified to, for example, in the assertion that the 'Balkan War is, if you like, the final consequence, the last by-product of the Great War' (Hobsbawm 2000: 7). Any balanced historical understanding of the contemporary phase requires us to see how it 'fits' into the shape of the wider century. Debates about whether peace is now deeply institutionalized (e.g. Jervis 1991/2)—and hence the peaceful ending of the Cold War itself—or whether the post-Cold War situation takes us back to earlier multipolar instabilities (e.g. Mearsheimer 1990) are implicitly reliant on these very judgements.

Classically, this kind of problem has been resolved by the historian's device of the 'long' or 'short' century—what Charles Townsend (1995: 200) has called the 'skidding century'. The sixteenth and nineteenth are traditionally presented as 'long' centuries, the latter running to 1914. There is now an emerging consensus (Hobsbawm 1994: Gaddis 1992b) that the twentieth will come to be seen as short, running from the First World War to 1989/90. A variation on the same position is the Danchev/Sontag thesis of the 'Sarajevo century'—where the century started in 1914, and also finished in 1993 (Danchev 1995b: ix–xiii).

What all such views share in common is the notion that there is a coherent historical framework unifying the 'short' century, basically the lifespan of the Soviet state, or the rise and fall of the Soviet–American antagonism. This approach — that the short twentieth century embraces a coherent theme, and can as such be treated as an analytic unity—is very much at odds with the above-mentioned view that the twentieth century fundamentally 'splits' in the middle. How are these various contentions to be reconciled, and what are their implications for understanding the post-Cold War order?

The explicit side effect of such analyses is, of course, to sever off the 1990s as not belonging to either story. The post-Cold War world does not fit into the short twentieth century, but neither is it akin to the pre-1945 era from which it remains detached by that revolutionary split in the middle. Formally, our period tends to be shoehorned into the twenty-first century, which is taken to have started in 1990. While this 'skid' is merely for the historian's convenience, and not to be taken overly seriously, more important issues of substance are raised by it. Its result is to create a radical separation, not just between the pre- and post-1990 worlds, but also between the post-1990 and the pre-1945 worlds. It is this procedure that is deeply problematic in terms of historical perspective. First, the period 1989–91 is presented as a fundamental historical break, what Gaddis (1992b: 22) has called one of the 'rare points of punctuation'. The danger with any such notion is that it neglects various dimensions of continuity: in the structure of power (Waltz 1993); in American foreign policy (M. Cox 1995); in the impact of globalization (Clark 1997); or in the construction of a liberal capitalist order (Ikenberry 1996). Secondly, the post-1990 order also seems, at least superficially, to have much in common with the first half of the century, a point which Hobsbawm (1990: 165) himself concedes in his own suggestion of the ethnic separatism of the early 1990s as the 'unfinished business' of 1919. In summary, one of the striking effects of the end of the Cold War has been to make the pre-1945 world seem less distant, and to focus attention instead on the elements of continuity stretching back to it. It is the Cold War period that then takes on the appearance of 'exceptionalism'.

Many analysts have been reluctant to describe the end of the Cold War as leading to radical change in world politics. They have, to that extent and for a variety of reasons, been inclined to emphasize instead the elements of continuity as between the 1990s and the Cold War period. Such a position can be illustrated with reference to three dimensions of world politics: the role and status of American power; conditions in the Third World; and processes of globalization.

As to the first, this has been at the heart of the debate about the nature of post-Cold War order, as it relates directly to issues of the polarity of the present system, as will be further discussed in the next chapter. There is a reasonable consensus that the United States remains central to the contemporary balance of power. In terms of size, there is remarkable continuity, as Heisbourg (1999/2000: 5) has noted: 'As an economic power, the post-Cold War US weighs just about what it weighed during the previous quarter of a century, approximately 22% of the world's gross domestic product (GDP).' But it is more than a matter of such statistical data alone. The leading—if variable—role played by Washington in the 1990s has placed it at the heart of the global security structure, and this represents a substantial element of continuity with the entire period since 1945. This note is struck explicitly in the comment that 'despite expectations of great transformations and new world orders, the half-century-old American order is still the dominant reality in world politics today' (Ikenberry 1999: 123). Others have joined the chorus in suggesting that, while the NWO united a distinctive conception of order with America's leadership, 'neither element was novel' (Tucker and Hendrickson 1992: 43). Wohlforth (1999: 39) too is of the opinion that 'unipolarity is nearing its tenth birthday . . . Calling the current period the true Pax Americana may offend some, but it reflects reality.' While this seemingly differs from Ikenberry's view, it also hints at substantial continuity because the present situation has now eventuated in a mature *Pax Americana* that existed only in embryo throughout the Cold War. This has created the conditions for an even greater unilateralism in Washington's approach to multilateralism (Tucker and Hendrickson 1992: 43).

To be sure, there has been heated debate about the stability and durability of this unipolarity. Wohlforth (1999: 8) insists, on the one side, that 'unipolarity is durable and peaceful'. This is set against the claim, on the other, that 'America's unipolar moment will not last long. To assume that international order can indefinitely rest on American hegemony is both illusory and dangerous' (Kupchan 1998: 40–1). What is at stake here is not disagreement about the current salience of American power, but whether or not this represents a transitional phase, as against a long-term structural feature of the system. Neither side takes issue with the fundamental notion that it is American power that shapes the current contours of the post-Cold War order, just as it did the world of the Cold War itself.

But these debates are possibly too much centred on the great powers, and take an unduly top-down view of the international order. A second illustration of continuity can be provided from beyond those European or Atlantic worlds. According to this perspective, the basic confusion arises from a failure to understand that the 'constructed' post-1945 peace had itself been largely confined to Europe. It was only there that the peace (eventually) took hold, and only there that it has recently become unravelled. Elsewhere, in much of the former Third World, there was little Cold War peacemaking in the first place, and less in consequence to dismantle after 1990. This makes sense of claims about the peripheral Cold War impact on the periphery: 'Nothing could reveal more clearly Western conceits and post-imperial perspectives than the idea that the end of the Cold War unleashed a whole new set of security problems in the Third World and that only Cold War competition had kept the Third World from exploding into chaos' (Holsti 1999: 291–2). Holsti's robust reprimand echoes Ravenhill's (1993: 71) earlier judgement: 'And the continuities between the characteristics of the periphery in the 1990s and those of the Cold War era give every reason to believe that the nature of security and conflict in the periphery will remain qualitatively different from that in the centre'. Essentially, the argument deployed by both writers is that the Cold War never shaped the basic features of Third World politics, since these remained largely indigenous in inspiration. Accordingly, the passing of the Cold War hardly represents a fundamental watershed for those large sections of the globe. If there is a 'coming anarchy' in those parts of the world, this has been developing for a long time, and for a variety of reasons, and it is misleadingly simplistic to attribute these trends to the ending of the Cold War.

The point deserves to be developed more fully and can be substantiated from positions that are themselves set widely apart. '[T]he writers in the main debate', says Fry (1993: 226), 'overestimate the relative significance of the Cold War international order as determinative of global order in the 1945–1990 period. And consequently, they also overstate the relative significance of the end of the Cold War as a watershed in world order.' The same kind of claim has been made, but from a radically different perspective. 'What is the new order?', asks Chubin (1995: 435), and answers: 'From the South, it looks like a new form of Western dominance, only more explicit and interventionist than in the past'. Equally, seen through Chomsky's eyes, the end of the Cold War signifies little for the South. The reason for this is that the Cold War itself must be viewed in longer-term perspective as little more than 'a particular phase in the five hundred-year European conquest of the world . . . now termed the "North–South confrontation"' (1997: 74). What seems to set them apart is that Fry diminishes the end of the Cold War by pointing to the limited impact the Cold War had on much of the South. For his part, Chomsky is unimpressed by the significance of 1990 because it has not brought about any radical changes in the under-lying relationship of power between North and South. But whether because the Cold War affected the periphery too little or too much, both are curiously agreed that little has changed with its passing.

The third great problem with the idea of 1990 as a watershed is that it makes no sense to think of the complex set of issues surrounding global-ization in these terms. To be sure, the end of the Cold War marked a symbolic extension of the potential field of the global economy. But it is certainly not the case that the end of the Cold War was a fundamental part of the 'causal' story of globalization. Globalization preceded the end of the Cold War. Indeed, in many respects, it was a significant contributory factor in bringing it to an end. It thus serves as a major element of continuity between the two periods (Falk 1999: 64). This is hardly surprising. What it reflects is a set of political and economic norms devised in response to the Great Depression of the 1930s. This jolts us into recognition of the Depres-sion as possibly the greatest formative event of twentieth-century history, and one that transcends the punctuation points of both 1945 and 1990. Its haunting presence still lingers into the new millennium, and much of the current quest to strengthen the architecture of global capitalism continues to reflect fears of its repetition. This is unquestionably an integral aspect of the post-Cold War order. And it is demonstrably not new.

THE COLD WAR: ORIGINS, ENDINGS, AND AFTERMATH

At the heart of these discussions about the novelty of the post-Cold War period lies a complex series of issues tied up with our understanding of the Cold War itself. This author has earlier noted (Clark 1997: 175–9) the striking parallel between the format of the debate about the origins of the Cold War, and the debate about why it came to an end. The same variety of interpretation is on display in both instances. This is not in the least surprising. The reason is simply that the debate about the causes of the Cold War was never focused narrowly on the causes alone but was, much more fundamentally, about the very nature of the Cold War. It was not that historians shared a common concept of the Cold War, but simply differed as to its causes. What separated them was the very phenomenon that they were seeking to explain. It followed logically, and in the same way, that different accounts of what the Cold War was should have evoked differing historical interpretations of the forces that brought it to an end. The view, for example, that the Cold War was essentially an abnormality in the balance of power was always likely to take a different explanatory form, both as to origin and termination, from one that saw it as an ideological and systemic contest.

This general point can now be extended to embrace the disagreements about how radically different is the order in the aftermath of the Cold War. The reason for this connection is straightforwardly that the competing interpretations why the previous order collapsed hold important implications for the substance of the order that has since replaced it. Insofar as these positions identify the forces prevalent in bringing the Cold War to an end, as well as their trajectories, they provide clues to the mainsprings of the order that has since ensued. An understanding of the dynamics of the end of the Cold War is therefore the logical first step in any attempt to gain insight into the forces that now shape its successor. What this implies is a profoundly integrated single debate—rather than three separate controversies—about the origins, endings, and aftermath of the Cold War. All three are unified by a shared conception of what the Cold War actually was, because only within its terms can we give a plausible account of what led to it, what brought it to a conclusion, and what are the consequences of its passing.

The point can be demonstrated most clearly by linking it to the discussion of when it was that the Cold War came to an end. Most famously, Lynch (1992) made the claim that the Cold War seemed to have come to an end on a number of occasions, but certainly before 1989, largely as a result of the instances of détente in the 1960s and 1970s. He was thus able to make the suggestion, in the words of one reviewer, that what came to an end in

1989 was not the Cold War, but in fact, 'the post-cold war order' (M. Cox 1994*a*: 195). The accommodation between the United States and Soviet Union effectively resolved the contested issues within Europe, and it was only the subsequent collapse of the Soviet Union that reopened them. The post-Cold War order had thus already operated during the 1980s but was brought to an end, not initiated, by the events of 1989.

We have here a good illustration of what is at stake in the debate about continuity and change. By employing his own particular version of the Cold War, Lynch is able to argue that its 'fundamentals' had changed by the 1970s, and hence to arrive at a quite different conception of what the post-Cold War order actually was, and when it had started. Cox correctly dismissed Lynch's argument on the grounds that it assumed 'that what had changed in the superpower relationship before 1989 was more significant than what had not. I would suggest the opposite is true' (M. Cox 1994*a*: 199). By redeploying a different conception of the Cold War, we can reach different conclusions about turning points, changes, and continuities. Each brings, in its wake, a different account of the forces shaping the current order. In short, it is perhaps one of the greatest ironies of the end of the Cold War that the debate about the nature of the succeeding order remains very much in thrall to the persisting debate about the nature of the Cold War itself. In that limited sense alone, we are not yet in a post-Cold War world.

How is such an integrated perspective best to be achieved? Here, the suggestion of this book is that it can be accomplished within the framework of peacemaking. If it is the very nature of the Cold War that unifies the debates about beginnings, endings, and aftermath, then the idea of post-Cold War peacemaking comes closest to offering an overarching concept that can likewise straddle these multiple facets of the Cold War. Above all, if the essential nature of the Cold War is the key to all these debates, then it follows also that the kind of peace settlement that has since unfolded is itself fundamentally related to the kind of war that it was called upon to bring to an end. Because the peacemaking also reflects the nature of the Cold War, it provides a way of unifying all these aspects.

The form of the peace tells us something important about the origins and development of the Cold War struggle. It also is sensitive to the evolution of that conflict. The terms and conditions on which wars are brought to an end tend to reflect not only the causes that sparked them in the first place, but also the war aims as they have evolved over time. History is replete with examples of the tendency for these war aims to outgrow the issues that initially gave rise to the war. The mode of prosecution of the war—its casualties, its economic costs, its impact on civilian life, and its duration—can leave a powerful imprint on the final terms of peace. In that sense, the essential nature of the Cold War should be regarded not as static, but as dynamic. The form of the peace settlement required at its ending had to engage with that dynamism, and produce a peace that took note of that evolution. 'The victors naturally assume that their struggle carries deep significance', Kaplan observes more generally, 'of a kind that cannot fail to redeem the world' (2000: xi). The character of this wish for redemption is etched in detail on the face of the peace settlement that resulted from the end of the Cold War.

The nature of the post-Cold War peace is also the best way of comprehending the manner of the Cold War's ending. Peace settlements, for all their ambiguities, are highly illustrative of the precise balance of forces that produced them, and are thus instructive of the manner of the war's ending. Wars can end on a spectrum of notes of decisiveness, reflecting the goals of the participants, as well as their will and ability to prosecute them further. Some peace settlements are imposed with one combatant prostrate and defenceless; others are agreed with both sets of military forces still largely intact. The best measure of this outcome is the resulting peace settlement. Accordingly, if we need to understand how and why the Cold War came to an end, the best place to look is in the ensuing peace. We will find there the most accurate indication of the balance of forces and wills.

We also find, in its terms, good evidence of what was by then thought to be at stake. The Cold War was a complex phenomenon, with multiple dimensions. The author has argued elsewhere (Clark 1997: 125–6) that it had two principal dimensions. The first, and most commonly noted, is that of rivalry between East and West. But the second, if less visible, was the systemic development within the West itself. If the growth of the West—as an economic, security, and normative complex—can be regarded as an intrinsic aspect of the Cold War, then this half of it did not necessarily come to an end in 1989. Peace settlements most obviously reconstruct relations between victors and vanquished, but we should not be blind to the ways in which peace settlements also perform the task of reconstructing relations amongst the victors themselves. The post-Cold War peace thus directs our attention to those areas of change, in which some formal settlement was necessary, but at the same time makes us mindful of those areas where little change took place, and on which the settlement could afford to be relatively silent. The silence, however, does not betoken their irrelevance to the peace settlement as a whole.

Finally, the link between the nature of the Cold War, and the consequences of its ending, is captured also by the idea of peacemaking. A peace settlement prescribes the code of conduct to be followed in the aftermath of war. But this act of prescription is integrally related to the nature of the conflict that it seeks to terminate, and provides an eloquent commentary upon it. A clear measure of the nature of the Cold War is the steps taken to bring it to an end. But peacemaking has never been an infallible process, and it would be naive to imagine that the format of the peace corresponds exactly to those prescriptions. It is intrinsic to the very nature of peace settlements that they are exposed to contingency. The very dynamics of the peacemaking—desires for retribution, bargaining, and compromise amongst both victors and vanquished alike, and the multiplicity of pressing domestic priorities—can distract peacemakers from their goals, and leave the settlement exposed to challenge and overthrow.

It is because the peace is open-ended, and exposed to contingency, that it best captures the essential quality of uncertainty that so much marks the post-Cold War order. To be sure, policy-makers had in mind, in 1990, a set of intended goals and outcomes, reflecting their war aims during the Cold War conflict. There was also a marked asymmetry of power, of the kind that is typical at the ending of a war. But neither of these conditions, together or separately, could guarantee that a particular order would be implemented as envisioned, nor that it would not in due course become vulnerable to other corrosive influences. As such, the idea of peacemaking goes to the heart of the post-Cold War dilemma. The paradox of victory in war is that the material and ideational forces that have resulted in victory in the field cease to be the controlling influences over the ensuing peace as soon as the fighting is brought to a halt. They can only shape the peace insofar as there is a will to resort to them once more. Victory is a depreciating asset, as the course of every peace settlement reveals. This generic quality of all peace settlements captures the ambiguities that abound in the post-Cold War order.

THE ORDER OF CHANGE

The debate about the consequences of the end of the Cold War—as regards the distinctive attributes of the resulting order—will be reviewed in detail in the next chapter. The point to note, however, is the extent to which this, in turn, remains hostage to competing accounts of what it was that had changed, and what had not. It is precisely the issue of continuity and change that lies at its core. This applies above all to the central question of the relationship between the end of the Cold War, and the shifts in the distribution of power. What was so highly ambivalent in the discussions of this relationship was the precise sequence that was being implied. Was it the end of the Cold War that ushered in a structural change in the distribution of power? Or did the structural change precede the end of the Cold War, and serve to bring it about? In short, the manner in which these two developments were sometimes conflated had the effect of blurring the issue of which was cause and which effect. Russett evidently assumed that the end of the Cold War was the independent variable when he puzzled over why the Cold War ended 'before the drastic change in the bipolar distribution of power' (1998: 368–9). However, that the relationship operated in that direction, rather than the converse, was assumed rather than proved. Others began from the alternative assumption that it was the decline of Soviet power (for whatever reason) that eroded its capacity to sustain the Cold War, and that it was therefore a shift in the distribution of power that contributed to the Cold War's end. This latter interpretation came closer to Waltz's account whereby the 'Cold War could not end until the structure that sustained it began to erode' (1993: 49).

Such a posing of the issue also sheds light on the other associated problem, namely why the Cold War ended as peacefully as it did. Gaddis (1992/3: 51–2), amongst many others, had drawn attention to this problematic feature in noting 'how suddenly, how thoroughly, and how *peacefully*, the Soviet Union would relinquish its position as a superpower'. What was so problematic about this occurrence, according to traditional power theories, was that 'hegemons are expected to make every possible effort to retain their principal sphere of influence' (Lebow 1995: 35). Instead, and wholly unpredictably, the Soviet Union 'made concessions that greatly enhanced the relative power of the United States' (Lebow 1995: 36).

Did then the peaceful ending of the Cold War bolster those optimistic accounts that foretold the end of the old rules of realism? Or was the end of the Cold War merely the great exception that would prove the rule of renewed national competition and conflict? Much would depend on the kind of peace settlement that was established, and the effectiveness with which it could be made to hold. In short, what would determine whether the post-Cold War order was to be new or not, and what its principal features were to be, was not the mere passing of the Cold War. Instead, these would be shaped by the content of the peace settlement, and the means by which it would be sustained. In order to explore further this facet of the post-Cold War order, we need to consider the debate sparked off by the end of the Cold War about what it was, precisely, that had changed as a result.

2

FOR BETTER OR FOR WORSE?

The previous chapter considered how the post-Cold War world should be considered to fit into the grand schemes of twentieth-century history. The twentieth century has received a dismal press and, for the most part, deservedly so. It is uniformly seen to have been the most violent in recorded human history, and the one that witnessed the greatest injury to civil life from politically inspired, as opposed to natural, causes. Images of the short twentieth century may actually serve to liberate the post-1990 world from this sullied reputation, by suggesting that a better future beckons from beyond. If, however, we view the post-Cold War era instead as part of a long and continuing twentieth century, with deep roots reaching back into the pre-1945 years, we may still fall under its sinister shadow. So has our entry into the post-Cold War order been for better, or for worse?

Chronological perspectives upon the post-Cold War era are, of course, grounded in substantive interpretations of the kind of order that is emerging. The various continuities and discontinuities that are discernible derive from the real changes that are deemed to have taken place. In turn, these have fed the moods of optimism and pessimism that came to be increasingly ranged against each other at the dawn of the 'new' age. The optimists took great heart because it 'is surely clear that the prospects of major war became far lower after the quiet cataclysm' (Mueller 1995: 9). What struck the pessimists, as former head of the Central Intelligence Agency, Robert Gates, remarked in 1993, was that there was now 'a far more unstable, turbulent, unpredictable and violent world' (Mueller 1995: 14). It is with the substance of these changes, and how they have been regarded since 1990, that this chapter is concerned.

A QUESTION OF PERSPECTIVE

There has been no shortage of reflection on the substantive nature of the post-Cold War order. Ever since 1989, there has been ongoing discussion of its emergent features. However, while there has been a series of mini-debates about the various dimensions of that order, there has been a conspicuous absence of any overarching framework for its conduct. When there has been a more general context, it has been about the validity of entrenched theories of international relations—neorealism, neoliberalism, and constructivism. Those theories have become engaged within this field of battle over their respective rights to claim a continuing or growing relevance (Lebow and Risse-Kappen 1995; Doyle and Ikenberry 1997; Ruggie 1998; Paul and Hall 1999). Nonetheless, after more than a decade's effort, and this theoretical controversy notwithstanding, we seem to be no closer to having an integrated understanding of the constituents of today's order.

The debate about post-Cold War order has been marked by much hesitancy, truly reflected in the title commonly assigned to the period. 'Such a label reveals that people know only where they have been', is one typically wry observation, 'not where they are now, much less where they are heading' (R. Haas 1997: 21). And yet the only fixed bearing in these discussions has been the one left behind, the beacon that reminds us of our point of departure, but gives us no guidance towards our next destination. There may well have been good reason for this. What struck some commentators was the danger of succumbing to the logical fallacy expressed in the Latin tag *post hoc ergo propter hoc*—namely that the qualities of the international system that came *after* the Cold War could be explained *because* of the end of the Cold War. This was the danger of conflating a chronological with a causal relationship. This prompted some, while conceding the 'crucial importance' of the end of the Cold War, to insist also that 'this event alone cannot explain the novel developments in the international system' (Holm and Sorensen 1995b: 4). Others, mindful in particular of the long history of ethnicity and international politics, expressed unease at what seemed to be 'an inadequate understanding of what has made the world turn upside down' (Moynihan 1993: 167). The need was for an account that gave due recognition to the historical stature of the end of the Cold War, without at the same time implying that this event explained everything that took place in its aftermath. A sensible balance had to be struck.

There were, in any case, mixed feelings about undertaking the journey to this brave new world in the first place. The Cold War period had admittedly done little for attainment of a whole range of global values, since many human rights were sacrificed on the altar of success in the Cold War struggle itself. But it had, at least in its later decades, appeared to become a certain and predictable world—tainted but stable. The fairly modest ambition then after the Cold War was to reach a promised land that 'could match the Cold War in durability and stability, while scoring higher on democracy and economic growth' (Freedman 1992: 37). Even so, some remained sceptical of this much-vaunted stability that the 'nostalgists' seemed to remember in the Cold War, by which sleight 'decades of Cold War traumas and fears are casually dismissed out of hand' (Mueller 1995: 19).

Given this loss of certainty and predictability, it was hardly surprising that commentators began to describe the post-Cold War period as one that was characterized, above all, by this very lack of direction. This came to be seen not as an incidental feature, but as part of the very essence, of the Cold War's successor. This central idea is encapsulated in one author's depiction of it as a 'deregulated' world (R. Haas 1997: 27). For Haas, it was an age marked by a 'loosening of international relations', in which the 'nation-state is weaker', albeit that there was a greater number of democratic and market-oriented societies. But what does the notion of deregulation imply for the post-Cold War order? Taken literally, does it mean that there is no order, since order suggests, at the very least, some form of regulation? The suggestion that the present world is deregulated is deeply misleading and, as will be seen later in this study, there are many aspects of regulation embodied in the post-Cold War peace. But certainly the comment captures the predominant mood of the debate about the post-Cold War world.

The wider public debate tended to foster an impression of the end of the Cold War as a moment of world historical transition. In some cases, public officials also adopted this perspective to bolster their policies and political reputations. The declaration by George Bush of a New World Order was the high point of this style of presentation. It drew attention to the apocalyptic nature of the demise of the bipolar struggle, and the great potential for democratic transformation that had been released by its passing. The same spirit was famously captured in Francis Fukuyama's (1989, 1992) more academic justification for viewing 1989 as the new 'year zero'. This culminating victory for liberal capitalism heralded a move beyond the ideological History in which humankind had been entrapped during most of the preceding two centuries. Fukuyama's manifesto perfectly captured, and reinforced, the temper of official policy. Both emphasized the historical magnitude of the transition that had just taken place, but did so from an optimistic perspective.

Other writers were equally to popularize the notion of a fundamental watershed, but in tones that encouraged a more sombre mood. Of those that captured the headlines, two stood out. The first was Samuel Huntington (1996), with his image of an emerging 'clash of civilizations'. It was no part of Huntington's argument to suggest that it was this development that had superseded the Cold War, and brought it to a premature finale. But in pointing towards the new substance of international politics that would follow in the wake of the Cold War, he was directing attention to the importance of this change, and to the new tensions and conflicts that would arise from it. The same can be said of Kaplan (1994, 2000), and his 'coming anarchy'. He described a dystopic vision where segments of the world had moved into a variant form of 'post-history', characterized by insecurity, impoverishment, and collapse. This sounded a quite different refrain from that of Fukuyama. It suggested that the distinctiveness of the post-Cold War settlement lay in its fundamental failure, since it 'did not return us to conditions of peace that we knew at the end of our previous wars' (Kaplan 2000: 171).

Whether inaugurating something better or worse, the end of the Cold War was viewed by both sets of proponents as a significant turning point. International politics, in whichever of its respects, would never be quite the same again. The portentous nature of this shift was dramatized by one author's asking 'is the modern world order cycle broken' altogether (Knutsen 1999: 167), or another's suggestion that it represented a final move towards 'a system without imperialism for the first time in post-medieval history' (Dark 1996: 36). As against these, there was the conservative rebuttal that the 'fundamental rules and institutions underlying international relationships have not changed with the end of the Cold War' (Holsti 1999: 289). On this calculation, we might anticipate regression to a more turbulent era. Apocalyptic transformation for the better was thus starkly set off against intimations of a sharp turn for the worse.

Which was right? There was not, and could not have been, any satisfactory resolution to this disagreement. What separated the various protagonists was not simply old-fashioned optimism versus pessimism, nor idealism versus realism, but fundamentally differing frameworks within which the essential nature of order was to be conceived. 'Since there is no consensus on a conceptual framework upon which to evaluate the multiplicity of ideas about a new order', Holsti (1999: 289) observed by way of clarification, 'it is impossible to say that one is correct and the other incorrect.'

The debate about the character of the post-Cold War order has thus been marked by a multiplicity of fault-lines of this kind. The most fundamental is whether the period should be described as one of order, or as disorder (B. Roberts 1995). Depending upon which perspective is adopted, the change from the Cold War to its aftermath is accordingly depicted as a shift for the better, or for worse. But underlying these judgements, there was also a fluidity of focus that shifted between different aspects of the problem. Some defined change purely in terms of power and its distribution, and assessed the prospects for stability—either enhanced or diminished—as a result. Others were more interested in the potential for management of the international order, and concentrated instead on the prospects—whether brighter or dimmer—for effective international governance. The former adjudged the end of the Cold War in quantitative terms, within an ongoing system of international politics, whereas the latter preferred to see a qualitative watershed in the nature of the very system itself (Holm and Sorensen 1995b: 9).

To make sense of these confusing debates, the following survey will employ the device, crude but helpful, of placing the opposed claims into two categories. The first is about structural adjustments in world politics. It concentrates upon such issues as the following: how relevant remains the idea of the balance of power, and what distribution of world power has resulted from the Soviet Union's collapse; specifically, what is the polarity of the new system; does the power of the United States suggest a fundamental shift in the nature of hegemony, and is there an associated end to 'the rise and fall' of great powers; is the significance of the new world order to be found in the declining viability of the state as the principal structural component of the system?

The second category of claims is about the norms and procedures of the contemporary system. Within this frame of reference, the discussion is principally about such matters as: whether the basis of genuine collective security is now more firmly established; to what extent the system is characterized by a working Concert of the powers; for that matter, whether a new order is now fully in place, or whether we are experiencing an 'interregnum', as we await the new order to develop; to what extent there has been a shift in cognate practices such as sovereignty and non-intervention; whether these foreshadow a new normative order, or simply the unravelling of the old; and whether the prime characteristic of the new era is the prospect for an expanded liberal peace.

This division of labour is artificial, of course, if regarded as rigid. It is employed, nonetheless, because it is resonant of a similar division that will be employed in the subsequent argument to be developed in this book. In sum, we need to explore the existing debates to obtain some feel for the issues that have preoccupied the protagonists to date. By demonstrating the shortcomings of what has been on offer so far, we can appreciate why a more comprehensive framework is required, within which all these issues can be considered afresh. That framework will be presented under the rubric of the making of the post-Cold War peace.

ORDER AND STRUCTURE

The debate about structure, either in its narrowly neorealist version, or in its wider but still substantially realist form, was soon firmly entrenched in the analysis of what the end of the Cold War portended for the balance of power. This came in two parts: first, what it signified for the nature of power itself and, secondly, what it signified for its relative distribution among international actors.

The approach is best conveyed with reference to its counterpoint. Stepping outside realist parameters, some analysts felt confident that 'a new historical epoch' was assuredly in the making. Their argument was based on the sense that 'the permanent features or structural characteristics of the global system, such as superpower rivalry, no longer appear to dominate global political life' (McGrew and Lewis 1992: 312). Such an account that what was so hugely novel about the end of the Cold War was its marking of a new phase in which traditional structures were less salient—flew in the face of the increasingly mainstream argument. This held that it was precisely a shift within traditional structures that marked out what was new about the new world order. This alternative account insisted of the end of the Cold War that 'the structural determinant of international and world order is the distribution of power among the great powers', and that all significant international behaviour after 1989 was 'derivative from this fundamental change in the military-political order' (Fry 1993: 225).

But even if power remained central, did it remain the same? A dialogue about the changing nature of power had been ongoing since at least the 1960s, as the effects of economic interests and interdependence were increasingly included as part of the calculation. Such notions of a trans-formation in the nature of power brought with them suggestions of a reduced capacity on the part of great powers to structure their environ-ment in accordance with their own preferences. Thus, Nye had given a supreme illustration of the emerging paradox in his rebuttal of the case made for American decline. Nye suggested both that the United States remained the leading power—indeed, unassailably so—in the inter-national system, while also staking his claim that there was much less that the United States could do, given the 'diffusion of power' that was taking place (Nye 1990: 175). In short, what was to contribute to the rich uncertainty about the post-Cold War distribution of power was the fact that it was discussed against the background of a collapsed consensus about what power was, and about what great powers could actually do with it. Could power remain as the central prop of a structural theory when there was so much doubt about its continuing capacity to bear the load?

Typically, even those who accepted the evidence for the enormous influ-ence of the United States were equally mindful of the limits to what that superpower could do in the new circumstances. For all its economic resources, the USA was no longer able to act as an economic hegemon. Drawing a sharp contrast with the 1940s, one author remarked that 'America is not strong enough to impose a new economic order', in the sense that 'if America really wanted to restructure the world's financial system, it is not clear that it would be able to do so' (Hobsbawm 2000: 82).

If this were true of the economic realm, traditional concepts were even less relevant beyond it. Scarcely surprisingly, given his long-held views on the matter, Nye himself intervened also on the changed role of power in the international order. He chastised those who sought to force our thinking into 'the procrustean bed of traditional metaphors with their mechanical polarities', rooted in 'traditional military balance of power alone' (Nye 1992: 88).

From a slightly different perspective, but equally disorienting as regards assessments of the post-Cold War order, was the apparent ambivalence felt about the degree of intensity within the global balance of power. In a nutshell, had that balance become more or less integrated, more or less taut, than that which had functioned before? On the one hand, there was the widespread perception that it was looser, because the end of the Cold War 'liberated' regional actors from superpower constraints, and in part because it made them less dependent upon superpowers for protection, at least as regards global adversaries. Some foresaw, as a result, 'the rise of hegemonic Second Tier regional countries', with an aspiration to fill the power vacuums left behind (Snow 1997: 19). To this extent, the period had ushered in a more dispersed balance of power than had been characteristic of the Cold War.

As against this, other dimensions of global activity continued to foster an impression of greater integration and interconnectedness. If economic relations were ever more closely bound up with each other, and also becoming a significant theme within the security calculus, what was the possible justification for thinking of the global balance of power as becoming more diffuse? A period of fixation with a new era of 'geoeconomics' illustrated the contrary viewpoint that the new economic balance of power was more closely knit than ever before. This seemingly contradictory development—on the one hand, the 'weakening of alliance and bloc ties', and on the other 'the rising globalisation of the world economy'—has been presented by some as a fundamental structural paradox at the centre of the contemporary order (Falk 1995b: 4).

If the debate about the post-Cold War structure was about the relevance of the balance of power in general, it was also specifically focused on the nature of the resultant polarity, and the consequences for stability entailed by it. Thinking during the Cold War had generated the widely held view that bipolarity, at least in association with nuclear weapons (Gaddis

1992*b*: 174), had underpinned the stable 'long peace'. The erosion of this structure inevitably led to the suggestion that a more flexible multipolar balance would precipitate new tensions and conflicts, as famously argued by Mearsheimer (1990). Since within this framework stability was regarded as a function of the polarity of the system, a less auspicious polarity spelled doom for international stability. It was thus that a set of interlocking arguments predisposed, in some quarters, a sense of pervasive gloom.

But at least two other questions remained to be addressed before such a confidently dismal conclusion could be reached. What precisely was the polarity of the new system? And was it the case that, as for the prospects of stability, only polarity mattered? Perhaps, on the contrary, other normative and institutional features might have an impact as well, as a host of neoliberals were to suggest (Baldwin 1993). Indeed, one argument in support of a durable form of unipolarity went so far as to claim that the effectiveness of the United States in producing international order would itself be a determinant of whether unipolarity would last or not (Wohlforth 1999: 39). This was not an inherently implausible suggestion except that, unwittingly, it detracted from its own central assumption by making polarity a function of stability, rather than the other way round.

Initially, at least, the preponderant view was that any alternative to bipolarity was likely to be some variation on multipolarity, with all of its depressing implications. Typically, we were warned at an early date that 'neorealists are not sanguine that the Long Peace can endure in the coming era of systemic change'. The reason for this was primarily, we were told, 'the expectation that the world beyond unipolarity will be one of great power rivalry in a multipolar setting' (Layne 1993: 40). Even if less widespread now, that position has certainly not disappeared. It tends to be reformulated, not as something likely to replace the Cold War in the short term, but rather as a trend for the longer-term future. Thus Mastanduno reasserts the likelihood of the multipolar model, not for the 1990s, and not 'in the next decade or two either'. However, 'as time passes', the system will move in this direction (1999: 29). We can thereby see that, for those approaching the end of the Cold War from this perspective, a preoccupation with the implications of multipolarity has in no way diminished; it is only the date of its inception that has tended to be postponed.

Whatever the future might hold, there is a far-reaching consensus that the present system more closely resembles one of unipolarity than anything else. One of the clearest and earliest intimations of this was Krauthammer's famous proclamation: 'The immediate post-Cold War world is not multipolar', he averred, 'It is unipolar' (1991: 23). Set against the background of the late 1980s, this was in many ways a wholly unexpected conclusion to reach. The vogue notion at that time had been, of course, one of American decline, as popularized by Kennedy (1988). This projected for the future a historical trend of rise and fall to which the United States was not immune: 'the United States now runs the risk, so familiar to historians of the rise and fall of previous Great Powers, of what might roughly be called "imperial overstretch"' (1988: 515). In fact, at the Cold War's end, this view did not immediately dissipate, but was instead in certain respects reinforced. The uncertainty about America's future role in the absence of a global protagonist, as well as the diminished dependence of allies upon the United States, persuaded some early post-Cold War commentators that the 'end of the cold war did not put an end to the unease over the future of the American position that the declinists had precipitated'. If anything, it possibly deepened it (Tucker and Hendrickson 1992: 5). Even if there was no atrophying of American means, the end of the Cold War might well diminish American will, in the absence of any plausible and coherent geopolitical account for exercising it.

As the decade of the 1990s wore on, however, this became a minority view, with only the exceptional voice continuing to reiterate it (Dark 1996: 133). Otherwise, the predominant assessment was that unipolarity was indeed the order of the day. So much was this so that the issue tended to shift away from the actuality of American primacy, and towards the subsidiary question of how sustainable it was in the longer term. The challenging question was no longer what the system now was, simply how durable it was for the future. Historically, it was suggested, there were few precedents for unipolarity enjoying any kind of longevity, as it was bound to evoke balancing from second-echelon powers (Carpenter 1991: 27–8).

That consensus is easily documented. Mastanduno set out his view of 'an American-centred international order', an image consolidated by the relative decline of America's geoeconomic rivals, such as Japan, in the second half of the 1990s (1999: 20, 26–7). Thus stated, the residual question was merely how long this was likely to last. The sustainability of a unipolar order had already been questioned, as both relying too much on American power and also on its ability to maintain itself. We were therefore advised that 'America's preponderance and its will to underwrite international order will not last indefinitely'. Indeed, in this implicit foreshortening of it, we were told that 'America's unipolar moment will not last long' (Kupchan 1998: 40–1). This view was tacitly supported by earlier remarks that America's strategy of preponderance 'could prolong unipolarity somewhat', but even this was something less than a ringing endorsement of its future (Layne 1993: 33–4).

The principal rebuttal of these claims was to come from Wohlforth (1999). His intervention set out a variety of grounds for believing that unipolarity enjoyed a much longer life expectancy than it had been credited with so far. More importantly, he challenged one of the assumptions that had infected much writing about unipolarity. This was the closet belief that unipolarity was itself an unstable condition. According to Wohlforth, the presumption should be the very opposite. What the critics had conflated was the belief that, on the one hand, unipolarity would not endure, with, on the other, the claim that unipolarity by itself encouraged international instability (1999: 24). Instead, his own contention was that unipolarity defused the normal pressures for power competition and, accordingly, the system's stability would be proportional to the extent of the preponderance embodied in the unipolar situation: the more the better (1999: 23).

There remains to be considered one final structural component that has featured in the post-Cold War debate. This concerns the fundamental constituent of the international order, namely the state itself. It is this structure which, of course, is the foundation of any distribution of power built upon it. No one has suggested that the viability of the state had been suddenly called into question simply because of the end of the Cold War. There had, on the contrary, been concerns of this kind expressed for quite some time beforehand. However, there was a widespread sentiment that the eclipse of the Cold War had removed key supports that had hitherto helped to hold together internally divided states. These states were now fully exposed to apparently novel forces of disintegration that impacted upon them both from the outside and the inside. This became a prominent *motif* of the commentaries of the 1990s. Typically, the key threat to international order was diagnosed as being, not 'wars among states' as such, but rather 'the very nature of the state', and the fact that we faced a world of increasingly 'disintegrating states' (Hoffmann 1995: 167–9). This, in turn, might come at a high human cost. Speaking a decade into the post-Cold War order, Hobsbawm warned that the 'less armed conflicts are structured and state-governed, the more dangerous they become for the civilian populations' (2000: 15).

As suggested, this disintegration was argued to have two interrelated aspects. The first was described as external, whereby the capacity of the state was diminished by new forces of globalization. Principal amongst these was the claimed supremacy of the global economy itself. The viability of the state was being called into question by the seeming erosion of its autonomy in a world where economic forces operated over and above, but also through, the institutions of the state. What credibility could state structures command when they were seen manifestly to be beholden to a more powerful and universal capitalist order? 'The principal world order danger is no longer the absolute security claims of the sovereign state', argued Falk (1999: 144–5), 'but rather the inability of the state to protect its own citizenry, especially those who are most vulnerable, in relation to the workings of the world economy.'

This external erosion of the state is related to, and aggravates, its internal loss of control. Part of the 'social contract' of recent times had been a greater penetration of the state into the civil sphere domestically, in return for the various forms of provision and protection supplied by the state. The less competent it appeared to have become in that provision, the greater the pressure for domestic compacts to unravel as well, and hence the 'return' of divisive tendencies based on regionalism and (sub-) nationalism. The weakening of the state in its external functions damages its internal cohesion: in return, that loss of unity internally further diminishes the ability of the state to act coherently and effectively in support of 'national' interests. One observer has noted this circularity, as well as its potential for viciousness. 'I think that both this reversal in the process of strengthening nation-states over several centuries and the disintegration and effective disappearance of some states', Hobsbawm conjectured, 'are linked to the sovereign state's loss of its virtual monopoly over coercive force' (2000: 36).

There are objections and qualifications that can be raised against all such claims and analyses (Clark 1999). Nonetheless, there is no denying that this has been a powerful characteristic of the debate after the Cold War. In question, as regards the structural features of the new order, was not merely such matters as distributions of power, and the polarity of the system, but the sustainability of the state as the underpinning of this kind of structure at all. These analyses explicitly raised the possibility that the key watershed represented by 1990 was the passing from a system of inter-national order to one that was much more complex, and less state-centric, than that of the previous several centuries. In the favoured terminology of the day, the demise of the Cold War either revealed more clearly, or itself did much to usher in, a post-Westphalian order. In this emergent order, structures were themselves being reshaped in a more fundamental sense than that covered by the debate about polarity. The ground rules of the state system, such as sovereignty and the code of non-intervention, were being reformulated in proportion to the reduced role of the state within the order as a whole.

This part of the debate has been inconclusive in two senses. First, although there developed a greater consensus about the leading role of the United States in the post-Cold War system, there remained many who were unconvinced about how long this would last. Secondly, and more funda-mentally, it was inconclusive because many participants either felt that there was more to international life than these structural features in any case, or that these structural debates were a distraction from the real issues. For that combination of reasons, we now have a measure of agreement about the leading role of American power, less agreement about how hard or soft that power is, and even less still about how significant this might be in explaining the behavioural traits of the post-Cold War world as a whole.

ORDER AND PROCEDURE

The focus of this second aspect of the debate has been, not upon the constituent elements as such of the post-Cold War order, but upon how they relate to each other, the norms that prevail in those relations, and the characteristic procedures of the international system. Central to it is again the query as to whether there is something novel that has emerged and, if so, how best it might be depicted.

There is a neutral view of this. The essential core of this perspective is that the post-Cold War order has not yet been able to develop its own

distinctive regulatory procedures. Without doubt, some of those that operated during the Cold War have passed away, and it is for this reason that it
has been dubbed, however mistakenly, the age of deregulation (R. Haas
1997: 1). But while the old order may be dead, the new is still struggling to
be born. This is best captured in the imagery of the 1990s as an 'interregnum' (Cox, Booth, and Dunne 1999a). What this implies is that the
decade or so after the end of the Cold War should be thought of as a hiatus
in the regulative order. We do not yet know what form this new order will
take when it is finally formed. The suggestion is similar to the pessimistic
interpretation, as summarized by Skidelsky (1995: xii): 'there was no ready-
made world order into which the post-Communist societies could slot, but
a set of transnational Western institutions bound to unravel with the end
of the Cold war which had created them'. The clear assumption of this
argument is, not only that the old Second World order dissolved, but also
that the old First World order would dissolve with it. For that reason, the
new order as yet should be defined in terms only of its transience: we know
what has passed away, but not what will emerge to take its place.

Otherwise, the narrowest view within the procedural debate is that
expressed by neorealism: its logic is that procedure is essentially shaped by
structure. Accordingly, neorealists are dismissive of the neo-institutionalist
view that institutions, independently, shape international outcomes
(Mearsheimer 1994/5: 26): it is the structure, in power distributional terms,
that does all of that. There has thus been a debate, within these narrow
parameters, about the kind of balancing behaviour that typifies the
post-Cold War order. There has also been a somewhat wider debate,
incorporating the neo-institutionalist agenda, and extending to the
elements of collective security and concert that have been fostered since
1990. Finally, there is an even wider debate still, characteristic of some
constructivist analyses, that is concerned not simply with what states do,
but also with what they have become: procedures reflect not just structures, nor institutions and norms, but the changing self-perceptions of the
states themselves.

These are at once distinct, but frequently overlapping, areas of concern.
They range across the behavioural impacts of intensifying degrees of interdependence and internationalization. They include the potential shifts
towards more peaceful behaviour, as a result of 'second image' influences
from the spread of democratic institutions and norms. They also extend to

the entire gamut of theoretical claims entailed by the concept of globalization in its many, and contested, variations. At stake is the nature of the
forces that shape our present destiny.

The portrayals of the post-Cold War procedural order have admittedly
suffered from large measures of uncertainty. For all the dogmatism that is a
feature of this debate, it is hard to find a convincing account to persuade us
that today's order is governed, respectively, by balancing, concert, or a full
return to principles of collective security. At the edges, these are all fuzzy
positions, and it is difficult to determine where one breaks off, and the
others begin. The varying claims have also been hostage to changing circumstances: projections of concerts and collective security seemed more
convincing in the early 1990s than by the middle years of the decade while,
at the same time, the worst excesses of a return to multiple power
balancing also failed to materialize. In short, no consensus has emerged,
and no position has captured anything like the high ground.

The Cold War was scarcely dead when champions of collective security
presented it as the favoured, indeed as the only, basis for post-Cold War
order. They made it the central issue in the debate (Kupchan and Kupchan
1991: 115), in the same way that the concrete example of the Gulf War could
be construed as a vindication of collective security's new potential. Thus
was collective security to be described as a 'relevant, plausible, and useful
regulator for conflict', in a world marked by 'high levels of interdependence and growing zones of peace' (Starr 1999: 147). Of the many grounds
advanced for its being the favoured option, two in particular were singled
out, both deriving from classical components of the original Wilsonian
position. The first was its advantage as a form of deterrence, since the
community of all would always be more than a match for any one; the
other was its ideological attraction in appealing to cooperation, unlike
balance strategies which appealed to, and possibly intensified, conflict
(Kupchan and Kupchan 1991: 118).

The experience with peacekeeping in the early years of the post-Cold
War order confounded much of the optimism of these supporters. The
reasons for this were essentially threefold. The first was the precarious
consensus amongst the great powers within the Security Council: what had
been more or less possible in 1990–1 against Iraq proved unsustainable in
the longer term, as the crises in former Yugoslavia unfolded. The second
was the growing awareness that the indivisibility of peace placed high costs

on the relatively few potential peacekeepers, and encouraged a trend to selective security as a result: there would be an international community response in some situations, but not in others. And finally, the early gloss was removed by the inability of the existing United Nations machinery to bear the sudden expansion of missions imposed upon it. Disenchantment with the United Nations bred disenchantment with the very idea of collective security, or at the very least encouraged the quest for means of implementing it that fell outside the strict confines of that organization.

It was for basically the same set of reasons that the appeal of a concert-based system was also to decrease. Reviewing several years of the post-Cold War order, one analyst felt confident in pronouncing that 'the notion of a standing concert of powers that would regulate post-Cold War international relations is far-fetched' (R. Haas 1997: 44). At the same time, albeit in a much more attenuated form, some kind of concert behaviour seemed to have become more prominent as an actual feature of post-Cold War order maintenance. Certainly, elements of the Security Council concert collapsed, as both Russia (over Kosovo), and China (over intervention and human rights), protested Western actions. Thus early hopes of a viable concert system, based on the UN, have indeed been eroded. At the same time, the actual workings of the peacekeeping system more broadly have come more closely to resemble a concert, albeit one that is limited and exclusive. The second half of the 1990s witnessed the pragmatic development of a rudimentary collective security system, directed by a small handful of powers, acting in concert as 'coalitions of the willing'. This had been foreseen, and already condemned many years ago, as a kind of 'pseudo-multilateralism' in which a dominant great power, 'still worshipping at the shrine of collective security', sought enough tokens of support from other states to lend 'its unilateral actions a multilateral sheen' (Krauthammer 1991: 25). The principal vehicle of this—in Bosnia and Kosovo—was to be NATO. In the continuing, if sporadic, air campaign against Iraq, the operational concert has been little more than a duumvirate, the United States and Britain. One critic, accordingly, has dismissed Operation Desert Fox because it has undermined international order, rather than contributing to it. It was the unacceptable face of unilateral military action and, as such, corrosive of international law (Weller 1999/2000: 96).

Early support for a concert-based system had been fully cognizant of its realist advantages. It was deemed cheaper than balance of power and deterrence, and reflected a brief post-war opportunity: since post-war concerts tended to dissolve in a matter of years, the emerging post-1989 concert had to be made to work quickly (Rosecrance 1992: 82, 65). The problem with a fully developed system of collective security is that it is virtually impossible to get all states to agree, and hence there is a need for a small group of great powers to take the lead. The advantages of a concert are that its 'small membership facilitates timely joint decision making', and consensus is more likely to be found, the smaller is the number of key players (Kupchan and Kupchan 1991: 140). Certainly, in originally setting up the Security Council, the architects of the United Nations had themselves followed this logic. Self-appointed coalitions may then be thought the next best thing, when agreement is unattainable through formal institutions like the Security Council. One supporter adjudged that 'coalitions bring with them some of the advantages that derive from collective effort . . . without the need for consensus or prearranged authority' (R. Haas 1997: 98).

However, the forms of concert that actually developed after the Cold War suffered from two acute problems. The first was intrinsic to the very 'virtues' specified above. If key decisions are confined to a small concert, then there is a high risk of their consensual decisions not enjoying any widespread legitimacy amongst other members of the international community: cabals may be cosy, but they are not representative. This is compounded when, as actually transpired in the 1990s, there has been an informal concert (NATO and friends) usurping the role of the formally accepted concert, namely the UN Security Council. It was these forms of activity that came to be dubbed 'foreign policy by posse' (R. Haas 1997: 93). Beyond a certain point, the pragmatic argument—that a small powerful group can act as the sponsors and catalysts of collective security—becomes self-defeating. This point is reached when there can be no pretence that they are acting as the legitimate guardians of a genuine community of interests, but simply as the self-appointed representatives of particular interests. E. H. Carr (1939) had warned that it would ever be thus.

We can see then that there have been some secular trends in the analysis of the post-Cold War procedural order. The short-lived optimism associated with the New World Order drew attention to the re-emergence of a real potential for a fully institutionalized system of collective security. As the stresses and strains of the first half of the 1990s took their toll, and a heavy one, on that prospect, it came increasingly to be replaced by visions of a more modest concert-based system, the so-called coalitions of the willing. This would fall short of collective security, but would not fall so short as to require abandonment of the aspiration altogether. In any case, convenient scapegoats and pretexts were at hand. Just as the defenders of collective security attempted to exonerate its failure in the 1930s by pointing to the 'abnormal' conditions in which it was called upon to operate, so the case could be made that collective security was asked to do too much, too quickly, in the 1990s. Moreover, collective security had been developed within the framework of a clearly defined inter-state order enshrining principles of sovereignty and non-intervention. The world after the Cold War was, instead, one in which the wars were largely civil and internal, and the purview of the international community was being stretched, away from aggression and self-defence and to encompass wider notions of humanitarian intervention. We should not be disappointed, in these daunting circumstances, by the seemingly paltry record of achievement. Instead of abandoning multilateralism, the record seemed to demonstrate, we should build on the areas of consensus that did exist, albeit that these were to be found only amongst the near allies of the United States. Concerts would perform what the UN could not; and no matter that the concerts might be composed of ever diminishing numbers. To read the unfolding of this debate over a decade is to bear close witness to a tale of disillusionment, but not one of despair.

CONCLUSION

This is about as far as we have been able to come in reaching assessments of the general qualities of the post-Cold War order. As such, it leaves the debate in an inconclusive condition, and falls far short of any clear resolution of differences. Is it possible to do better? The remainder of this book explores the notion that what is missing from the above is a serious engagement with the notion of the post-Cold War order as the negotiation and implementation of a post-Cold War settlement. This peacemaking might be 'virtual', but, for all that, shares fundamental characteristics with the real thing. At the very least, such a frame of reference offers a key insight into the contemporary order and one that remains largely underdeveloped in the existing examinations of it.

Why should this hold out any promise of sharper insight? What can peacemaking reveal that other approaches have failed to do? For the moment, and by way of bringing together the themes that have dominated this chapter, three arguments will be advanced. Collectively, they demonstrate that peacemaking is sensitive to the very qualities that are manifest in the post-Cold War order, while seeking to move beyond the divisive and fragmented condition of the present approaches to it. It does not minimize the difficulties of interpretation, but offers a way in which existing approaches can be combined into a more effective synthesis.

The first is the capacity of peacemaking to offer an integrated perspective. As can be seen in the discussion above, commentators have debated various facets of the post-Cold War world from a variety of distinct perspectives. While this was perhaps inevitable, given the theoretical diversity within which the problem was addressed, it finally disappointed by its failure to provide any cumulative insight. This fragmentation is revealed in the above attempt to review these debates as 'structural' and 'procedural'. The problem in the existing accounts is that it is difficult to see how those two dimensions relate to each other, unless one subscribes *a priori* to a neorealist belief that the former commands the latter. In contrast, the attraction of a peacemaking approach is that it has the potential to combine and integrate these two facets in a more subtle, and balanced, way. When we turn to the central features of the post-Cold War peace settlement, we will discover that it had to deal with two sets of issues that are similar to the structural and procedural. The first, as with any post-war peace settlement, is the need to dispose of the spoils. In other words, a peace settlement, by its very nature, makes 'structural' adjustments in the aftermath of war. It most certainly sanctifies the new distribution of power, and the spoils are divided to further entrench this in the post-war period. But peace settlements do more than that. They seek to set in place those elements that will, at the very least, give some prospect of sustaining the peace in the longer term. Without any such assurance, victory in war is necessarily hollow. It is the common rhetoric in the aftermath of wars that, with the war once won, the peace must not then be lost. What does this mean, if not the construction of a regulatory system that is favourable to the durability of the new structure? This leads into an analysis of some of the wide-ranging procedural aspects of the post-Cold War order. Thus conceived, peacemaking offers us a framework within which the two contested realms of the post-Cold War order can be brought together, rather than being analysed in splendid isolation from each other.

Secondly, peacemaking captures the essential condition of uncertainty that has been such a feature of the post-Cold War period. Participants may know what their preferences are, but there can be no assurance that the peace can deliver them in practice. Although peacemaking allows a greater interventionism and activism in the construction of international order than at other historical periods, the results of these endeavours remain uncertain. There is a plethora of accounts of the post-Cold War order that highlights this indeterminacy and fluidity: it is not already an order, but only an order in the making. There is much force to these perspectives, and the concept of peacemaking captures them well. It describes a dynamic, not static, situation. If we think of peacemaking as occupying an extended period of time, then this fits well with the sense of protracted uncertainty that has endured over the past decade. It responds well to the sense of an 'absence of order', because the settlement may establish the bases of order, while the order remains inchoate for the time being. It resonates with the sense of transience, because peacemaking, however protracted an affair, does come eventually to an end. It is not a permanent condition of international politics and, by definition, is one that must yield to something else.

Finally, the model of peacemaking does full justice to the historical significance of the events of 1989–90. It is with good reason that historians have been drawn to equate it with the great settlements of yore. During that period 'the world underwent a cataclysm that was something like the functional equivalent of World War III' (Mueller 1995: 1), and this has issued in a peace settlement. But we must be careful to judge precisely the grounds for such attribution. Peace settlements are historically charged because they embody the potential for more radical change than is normally possible in routine international intercourse. They are the great opportunities to speed up history, or to catch up with the changes that have already occurred. But that is not to say that their significance lies solely in bringing about these changes. Many peace settlements are as noteworthy for what they have 'conserved' (as in 1815), or allowed to 'continue' (as in 1919), as for what they have changed.

If what characterizes the great historical periods of peacemaking is that sense of opportunity, and of a meeting with destiny, then the end of the Cold War certainly meets that particular test. This also helps explain the complex, and shifting, responses to it. Judged by those standards, peacemaking at the end of epochal wars is almost always doomed to disappoint. It is beyond normal human political artifice to deliver the full hopes that people invest in it. Thus viewed, the parallels between peacemaking, on the one hand, and the steady onset of disillusion from the high hopes of 1989, on the other, are very striking indeed. Much is to be gained if we view the period as an instance of this kind. 'Following World Wars I and II it took a few years for the basic political order to be settled', it has been noted, and a 'similar process of shaking-out seems to be going on now' (Mueller 1995: 2). It is to a fuller elaboration of the essential features of this perspective—post-Cold War order as post-Cold War peacemaking—that the next chapter will turn.

3

PEACEMAKING AND ORDER

The scene has been set for what follows by the preceding review of the debates to date about the nature of the post-Cold War order. It has been suggested that much of the uncertainty running through these reflections can be traced to a lack of clear historical guidelines as to where we now stand. We remain puzzled as to whether the end of the Cold War marks a new departure from the depressing themes of the twentieth century, or whether instead it means a more direct re-engagement with them, after the seeming diversions of the Cold War. Following from this, the analysis of the post-Cold War order has been further clouded by its lack of any agreed focus. Were the changes wrought by the end of the Cold War to be found in the new structures, or new procedures, of international politics? If in both, how were we to understand the interaction between the two?

This book offers an alternative to these existing frameworks of discussion. The best way to think about the post-Cold War order is in terms of traditional notions of warmaking and peacemaking. The classical statement of this perspective has been offered by Gilpin (1981: 197): 'Throughout history the primary means of resolving the disequilibrium between the structure of the international system and the redistribution of power has been war, more particularly, what we shall call a hegemonic war'. He elaborates:

The great turning points in world history have been provided by these hegemonic struggles among political rivals; these periodic conflicts have reordered the international system and propelled history in new and uncharted directions. They resolve the question of which state will govern the system, as well as what ideas and values will predominate, thereby determining the ethos of succeeding ages. The outcomes of these wars affect the economic, social, and ideological structures of individual societies as well as the structure of the larger international system (Gilpin 1981: 203)

What happens to our thinking about the post-Cold War period if we conceive of it, by way of analogy, as the outcome of a war of that kind? More particularly, we should think of it not as the direct outcome of war, but as having been mediated through a process of post-war peacemaking. The distinction is important, as Kissinger pointed out long ago. War-making and peacemaking do not operate to the same logic. 'Although every war is fought in the name of peace', he commented incisively (1977: 138), 'there is a tendency to define peace as the absence of war and to confuse it with military victory'.

The suggestion that we think of the post-Cold War order in this light is far from new. Knutsen, for example, speculates that 'the final phase of the cold war . . . was the functional equivalent of a great war'. He then rejects his own suggestion. Since the Cold War never became actually hot, 'it can hardly compare with any of the waves of great wars of modern inter-national history' (1999: 262). Crockatt (1995), in his choice of title, more explicitly invites the comparison to be made when he directly refers to a *Fifty Years War*, even if he does not follow this through into an analysis of that war's aftermath. But if we allow the possibility, by analogy, of the end of the Cold *War*, this opens up the novel opportunity to think about the post-Cold War era to date as an exercise in *peacemaking*.

The most comprehensive attempt to date to follow through on this logic is that by Ikenberry (2000). He identifies a historical trend within peace-making whereby states have sought to distance themselves from the full opportunities presented by their victories, in order to sustain them in the longer term. He argues that short-term gains have been traded for stability:

Beginning with the 1815 settlement and increasingly after 1919 and 1945, the leading state has resorted to institutional strategies as mechanisms to establish restraints on indiscriminate and arbitrary state power and 'lock in' a favorable and durable postwar order. (2000: 4)

The 1990 settlement can accordingly be explored in the light of this historical pattern. However, the instance of peacemaking after the Cold War is less straightforward than are the others. The core of our puzzlement about the present order is that we think we have fixed landmarks when we do not. The uncertainties of the post-Cold War order are a function of earlier uncertainties about what it was that shifted in 1990–1. These, in turn, reflect the uncertainties of what had been put in place in 1945, and subsequently. To sum up the problem: we had in 1945 a war without a formal peace at the end of it. Now we have experienced a period of peace-making without a formal war to precede it. This is what makes it so difficult to think clearly about the post-Cold War peace.

THE NATURE OF PEACEMAKING

If the Cold War was a kind of a war then its end marks a kind of peace. The problem, of course, with presenting the end of the Cold War in these terms is that not only was the Cold War cold, but so was the peace. The absence of global hot war has its counterpoint in the absence of a definitive global peace. It is at this point that the imagery of post-war peacemaking becomes most helpful. This perspective allows us to focus on both the elements of continuity and discontinuity embodied in the post-Cold War order. The former points to continuities between the 1945–90 period, and what was to come after. The latter draws our attention to what changed after 1990, but allows the possibility of longer-term continuities that stretch back to the period before 1945 as well.

The function of this chapter is to establish some conceptual tools that can then be employed to dissect the post-Cold War peace. What, then, is the general nature of peacemaking? When, at the end of war, peace is made, what is it that is *made*? Does all of this happen immediately at war's end, or can we think of peacemaking as an extended process, and lasting over a lengthy period of time? Historically, taking the recent examples from international history, can we discern any notable trends in the forms of peacemaking, and what might these signify for our understanding of the world after 1990?

In the most basic sense, peacemaking can be thought of as the resolution of the problems that gave rise to the war in the first place. From this perspective, peacemaking is the implementation of the war aims of the victorious party, and at the expense of the defeated: the peace enshrines the goals of the war. This, however, is superficial as virtually all wars in history have revealed a tendency for the war aims to change, and usually to expand, once the war is under way. The very effort of fighting, and the consequent losses incurred, can change the objectives of the participants, so that what is sought at the war's end might be quite different from that sought at the outset. By its end, the First World War had transformed itself into 'a war to end all wars'. Is the peace required to achieve all the aims developed in the course of the war? In any case, most modern wars have been fought by coalitions, and the cost and sacrifice has not been shared equally amongst the allies and their associates. For this reason, war aims do not simply evolve, but are subject to intense, and often acrimonious, negotiation within the coalition. Unsurprisingly, these tensions manifest themselves in sharply contrasting perspectives on the appropriate content of the peace.

Furthermore, it is conventional to assume that the nature of the peace is related to the *decisiveness* of the military victory. Those victors who have won well, and possibly retain the capacity to inflict further damage upon a defeated foe, are in a stronger position to impose their own terms. But as has been often pointed out, there are few defeated foes who do not retain some residual bargaining power since, with victory assured, the will to sustain a further war effort might dissipate on the winning side as well. Peace spares the vanquished from further punishment, but also spares the victor from the costs of inflicting it. Does the post-Cold War peace embody the decisiveness of the victory achieved in the Cold War? Or has the peacemaking been a distinct process, responding to its separate logic, and yielding a settlement unrelated to the extent of that victory?

Beyond this, a key issue of historical interest has been the relationship between a particular peace and the longevity of the order that has followed upon it. Do decisive victories produce lasting peace, whereas inconclusive military results lead to speedy revisionism, as the defeated seek again to overturn the verdict? Or is it less the decisiveness of the victory, and more the wisdom of the peace terms, that determines the future viability of the international order? Such a conclusion might seem to follow from the differing logics of the two domains, since 'the success of war is victory; the success of peace is stability' (Kissinger 1977: 138), and the latter results from a sense of proportion that is difficult to attain in war. Is a harsh peace a recipe for future resentment and challenge, and is it the far-sightedness of restraint and generosity that is best designed to rebuild the order and restore stability? This last perspective is certainly Kissinger's (1995: 81) reflective judgement, when he insists that in 'dealing with the defeated enemy, the victors designing a peace settlement must navigate the transition from the intransigence vital to victory to the conciliation needed to achieve a lasting peace'. If this is not accomplished, the risk is that 'a punitive peace mortgages the international order'.

How, then, should we begin to construct the tools for understanding peacemaking? At minimum, it can be suggested that there is a distinction to be made between the substance of the peace, and the means for keeping it in place—between the *making* of the peace, and the *keeping* of it. It is not, however, clear that that distinction has always been observed historically. In its simplest terms, the substance of a peace embodies a new balance of power that is favourable to the victor. It is precisely that new balance of power that underlies and perpetuates the substance of the peace. Accordingly, once the substance is imposed, there may be no need for any *additional* instruments of enforcement, since the peace is its own guarantor. This might be most easily demonstrated in a peace of despoliation. Despoliation was often regarded as the obvious, and legitimate, entitlement of victory. Seizure of the lands and animals, butchering of the men, and enslavement of the women and children, was an all too common substantive peace. Thus implemented, it required no other form of enforcement.

Times, however, have changed and the nature of war and peace with them. In the discussion below, the chapter will review the salient episodes of peacemaking since 1815. One of the reasons for this selection is that, at least from 1815, there has been an obvious trend towards thinking about the enforcement of the peace as an issue, over and beyond the determination of the substantive division of the spoils themselves. Prior to this, the common belief was that a peace was self-implementing. The historical evidence for this claim lies in the fact that, in the peacemaking of 1648 and 1713, 'the big powers had little sense of special rights and responsibilities' (Osiander 1994: 323). Without any such concept, there could be but dim awareness of the need for 'underwriting' a peace settlement, because only the great powers could perform such a task. It might then be argued that, within the European state system, the self-conscious awareness of great powers as a class with certain responsibilities developed as an adjunct of their thinking about the relationship between a specific peace settlement, and the preservation of a wider international order predicated upon it. This analytical distinction—between peace settlement and the preservation of it—becomes critical in thinking about the nature of the post-Cold War peace.

The core of the issue, and the centre of this argument, is that the concept of peacemaking embraces two dimensions that are analytically distinct, although historically profoundly interrelated. The first concerns the new division of the spoils that emerges from the preceding conflict. This extends to a variety of tangible goods—territory, populations, rule, military assets, indemnity, reparations, and the like. The second embraces the wider set of instruments whereby that settlement is justified, defended, and possibly modified. This operates at a deeper level. It is akin to what Kissinger (1977: 145) referred to as the 'legitimizing principle', in the name of which the equilibrium is constructed. While these legitimizing principles may be formally ordained in the peace treaty, it is worth noting that they often 'triumph by being taken for granted' (Kissinger 1977: 145). Historically, when we speak of distinct international orders, both of these aspects have been present, even if related in highly complex ways. They will be called, respectively, the distributive and the regulative aspects of peacemaking.

This echoes other ideas already present in the literature, but will form the basis of a different argument about the relationship between them. Ikenberry (2000: 57–8) operates with the twin categories of 'substantive' and 'institutional' agreements. These, in turn, are similar, though not identical, to the distinction made in another important study of historical instances of peacemaking. Osiander (1994) has surveyed the cases of peacemaking from Westphalia to Versailles. He distinguishes in that study between 'structural principles' and 'procedural rules'. The former he specifies as the basic assumptions of the system about 'the identity of the international actors, their relative status, and the distribution of territories and populations between them'. The latter he sees as influencing 'the way that relations between the actors are conducted'. He is of the opinion that the former is more important to the stability of the system than the latter (1994: 5). This book suggests, to the contrary, that the stability of the post-Cold War order is very much dependent upon its regulative provisions, and that these represent a powerful force for continuity rather than change. This is what is so unusual about the post-Cold War peace.

How is a settlement to be sustained, and stability guaranteed? There would seem to be two broad alternatives in theory, even if they are certainly far from always being distinct in practice. The first is enshrined in the notion that the peace will be preserved by the favourable balance of power that has already emerged from the war. On this basis, the distributive peace is itself an important manifestation of its regulative counterpart. The second follows from the acceptability of the conditions of peace: a settlement can be made durable if it finds little cause for rejection by any of the main parties. At this point, we move beyond power, narrowly conceived, and enter the wider realm of consent. 'Any world order', it has been observed, 'must . . . if it is to become durable, eventually be seen to be legitimate' (Chubin 1995: 434). Part of the strategy for rendering it so is, in Ikenberry's terms, the establishment of an order which allows 'the leading state to engage in very little direct management' (2000: 259).

There are venerable precedents why this should be so. As early as the renaissance, one historian of the peacemaking of that time informs us, it was common that a 'treaty which had been imposed under duress . . . could . . . be repudiated as invalid' (Russell 1986: 82). Even then, treaties required more to sustain them than the mere ability of the victor to exert his will. This is why peace settlements provide powerful historical evidence of what is acceptable in the international order, because 'a general peace congress, faced with the task of reconstructing . . . the international system, is likely to be a particularly rich source of consensus notions' (Osiander 1994: 14). On the other hand, since the settlement will be so crucial to the future of the international order, it is likely also to reveal the fundamental clash of interests and preferences. By extension of this same logic, regarding the post-Cold War order as an exercise in peacemaking will help reveal the elements of consensus and legitimacy that underpinned it, as well as drawing our attention to those areas in which these were wanting.

With respect to which aspects of the peace is the attainment of legitimacy a desirable goal? This must extend both to the physical distribution, as well as to the norms and procedures that will help sustain this distribution in the longer term. Far from there being a rigid separation between the two—the distributive peace being the realm of power, and the regulative peace being the realm of legitimacy—there is a much more subtle interplay between them. Issues of legitimacy do manifestly arise within the distributive peace, just as the regulative order is far from immune to the application of power.

However, a third dimension has become equally conspicuous during the last two centuries. Certainly since 1815, peace settlements have had a third objective that seems to straddle the other two. Its purpose is not simply the physical distribution, nor just the general regulation of the status quo, but both. This dimension specifically addresses the character or identity of the defeated power which, in all peacemaking exercises since 1815, has been required to undergo transformation as a basic condition of the peace. In this way, peace settlements have become increasingly interventionist into the social and political forms of the vanquished (Ikenberry 1998: 151). Moreover, this has a dual bearing both on the division of the spoils, and on the prospects for ensuring the peace in the longer term. The political transformation of the defeated power (or, at least, of its governing regime) can either be regarded as the third dimension of recent peace settlements, or as a means of securing the other two. Change in the character of the defeated may be regarded as a way of dividing the spoils, as it can align the former enemy with those victor states with which it is now ideologically compatible. Alternatively, it may be thought of as a mechanism for legitimizing and sustaining the peace because the 'reformed' state, thereafter, internalizes and supports the peace that it has had to accept. It was on this basis that a distinction has been made between a 'retrospective' peace that seeks to ensure that the enemy 'is *unable* to fight again', and one that deals with the enemy 'so that he does not *wish* to attack again' (Kissinger 1977: 138). Traditional interpretations, now often challenged, depicted Stresemann's policy of 'fulfilment' of the terms of Versailles, on the part of German policy in the 1920s, in this way. The peace was regulated, and thereby preserved, by the altered political complexion of Germany. But it has to be appreciated that this was also a consequence of transposing German power to the side of the liberal states: regulation and distribution frequently operate in tandem in this way.

To repeat, the wider context within which these ideas are presented is that, historically, wars have been the initiators of successive phases of international order. As a recent survey has attested, 'the rise and fall of world orders is tightly related to waves of global warfare' (Knutsen 1999: 8–9). The outcome of war both reflects, and accentuates, the new distribution of power on which an order is based until it is progressively unsettled by further changes in the balance of power. Peacemaking, both as theory and in actual practice, is therefore the gateway to the post-Cold War order. This peacemaking has two important dimensions to it. The first is the physical redistribution at the end of the war. The second is the attempt to preserve the elements of that peace by constructing norms and procedures for the regulation of the status quo, or for permitting agreed changes to it. Both are critical elements in any post-war order. The point of this exercise is then to apply this framework to the 1990s, and beyond. Part of the perplexity we feel about the post-Cold War period results from a failure to give weight to the significance of these two distinct elements.

PEACEMAKING IN HISTORY

Historically, we have witnessed a complex interaction between these two aspects at the end of successive wars since 1815. In this section, there will be a short review of the main peace settlements since then, in order to provide some illustrative examples of this framework in practice, and to assist our understanding of the nature of peacemaking.

At the Congress of Vienna, there was simultaneously, but separately, a distributive and a regulative peace. The first concerned the traditional agenda of territorial distribution, military occupation, and financial provisions. The second concerned the assertion of the role of the great powers, and the development of the principles of a concert. The settlement as a whole thereby issued in a subtle combination of 'the old European logic of balance', along with 'new legal-institutional arrangements meant to manage and restrain power' (Ikenberry 2000: 114).

In the most obvious sense, the peace at the end of the Napoleonic Wars was 'about' France, and the terms that should be imposed upon it. But it was also 'about' a number of other, more general, issues. These included the post-war balance of power as a whole, although this was in part directed against any recurrence of French aggression. It was also concerned with various other political movements and pressures, such as revolution, legitimacy, liberalism, and nationalism, even if the latter two were more honoured in the breach than in the observance. The settlement has been the subject of rich historical discussion and, in general, has been much praised for its success in establishing a durable and stable peace. This has been attributed, implicitly, to the nature of both the distributive and the regulative peace set in place by it. As to the former, it is acknowledged to be 'a paradigm of a lenient treaty toward the vanquished', even if this was driven 'less by sentiments of compassion than by *realpolitik* thinking about the *balance of power*' (Kegley and Raymond 1999: 99). The celebrated champion of Vienna has, of course, been Henry Kissinger (1977), and he has pointed to the success of its regulative apparatus in creating a sense of legitimacy. 'Paradoxically', he remarks, 'this international order, which was created more explicitly in the name of the balance of power than any other before or since, relied the least on power to maintain itself . . . There was not only a physical equilibrium but a moral one' (1995: 79).

In any event, the settlement came in stages. We tend to think of the Congress of Vienna as being the forum at which the fate of France was determined but, in fact, this came sandwiched between the two Treaties of Paris, where the main terms of the peace with France were actually set. Vienna was concerned with the wider territorial settlement, since the outline agreement of conditions for France was already in place (Dakin 1979). This sequence, as Gulick remarked of the first Treaty of Paris, served to enhance the role of France. 'By immediately determining what terms France was to get', he notes, 'the treaty gave France a certain freedom of action later on; this freedom came before the allies had been able to agree on the European settlement, and it enabled Talleyrand to influence their later agreements' (Gulick 1967: 177).

Notably, the first distributive treaty was lenient towards France. It set France's borders at those of 1792, thus allowing it some actual gains relative to the pre-war situation (Dakin 1979: 25). There was to be no indemnity, nor occupation. This was then notable 'for its resuscitative policy toward the defeated power' (Kegley and Raymond 1999: 112–13).

There was an additional consideration that pushed the settlement towards leniency, and that was the relationship of the 'transformation' of France to the distributive provisions. Since there was to be a Bourbon restoration, there was an implicit distinction made between the regime (Napoleon), and the people on whom the peace was to be imposed. This had certain implications for the nature of the settlement itself. First, in the words of Gulick, 'the allies logically did not make their chosen rulers of France the heirs of their understandable hostility toward Napoleon' (1967: 178), and this encouraged a policy of moderation. Secondly, the very logic of a restoration of the previous monarchy tied the hands of the victors to some degree. 'Louis XVIII could hardly be restored to his "legitimate" inheritance', it has been neatly pointed out, 'if he were at the same time deprived of any part of it' (Albrecht-Carrie 1965: 12). Legitimacy thus impacted on the moderation of the distributive settlement while, at the same time, providing a principle that would help sustain the treaty in the longer term: in this way, restoration was also a key element in the regulative order put in place.

As noted, the Congress of Vienna itself did not much concern itself with France: 'there was no French problem since peace had been restored with France' (Albrecht-Carrie 1965: 11). The Congress cast its net more widely to effect a more general equilibrium. As it turned out, in the quest for a balance of power, and with due regard for the principle of mutual compensation, its energies were largely devoted to the fates of Poland and Saxony, and how much these should be sacrificed to the expansion of Russia and Prussia respectively. Before the Congress could publish its Final Act, Napoleon made his escape from Elba and embarked on his hundred days' campaign. The final defeat at Waterloo necessitated a further distributive peace with France, reached at the second Treaty of Paris. This imposed marginally more severe terms (Dakin 1979: 29–30). France's borders were less generously withdrawn to those of 1790, there was to be an army of occupation for up to five (actually three) years, and an indemnity of 700 million francs was to be exacted by way compensation.

What is so striking about the post-Napoleonic settlement as a whole was the self-consciousness with which the peacemakers distinguished the two tasks that they were required to perform. Not only was a peace to be put in place, but it was necessary for it to be kept there. Leniency in the distributive settlement was itself part of this wider regulative design, the expectation being that it would inspire a legitimate and consensual order. But measures for keeping the peace went beyond this distributive process alone, as a number of historians have readily testified.

Hinsley captures the essence of the same distinction when he points to the twin set of hopes that the peacemakers had for the post-war order. These hopes, he noted, 'found expression at Vienna in the spirit in which the assembled victor states agreed among themselves about the detailed resettlement of Europe'. But there was also another dimension to their deliberations, and this revealed itself even 'more prominently still in the measures adopted or advocated for upholding that resettlement' (Hinsley 1967: 194). Gulick makes a similar claim. For him, what was noteworthy was the quest for 'a formula of enforcement in order to give some structural strength to the new territorial equilibrium'. This was needed, he adds, since the 'enforcing of a territorial balance of power is by no means automatic' (1967: 280). Although an explicit great power guarantee of the entire settlement could not be achieved, what was finally restated in the famous Article VI of the reaffirmed Quadruple Alliance of November 1815 was the intention to manage the existing settlement through regular meetings of the powers. In that article, they agreed

To renew at fixed intervals . . . meetings for the purpose of consulting upon their common interests, and for the examination of the measures which at each of these epochs shall be considered most salutary for the repose and prosperity of the Nations and for the maintenance of the peace of Europe. (Hinsley 1967: 194–5)

Thus was set in place the concert, as the capstone of the regulatory order that was to replace the laissez-faire of the pre-Napoleonic international system.

The peace reached at Versailles in 1919, in addition to the other associated settlements, offers us similar insights. There are many contrasts between the Vienna and Versailles settlements, not least in terms of their apparent consequences. The former is credited with inaugurating the best part of a century of peace, whereas the latter is attributed with responsibility for bringing about a second catastrophic World War within barely twenty years. There also was a difference in scale, and in the scope, of the respective settlements. Historians are broadly agreed of Versailles, if about little else, that 'the world had seen no postwar settlement conference like it before and has seen nothing like it since' (Keylor 1998b: 472). A. J. Williams (1998: 41) attests that neither Vienna, nor the end of the Second World War, nor the emerging settlement since 1989, 'were as ambitious as Versailles'.

Versailles has struggled to lose its rapidly acquired reputation as a flawed and failed peace. It is widely regarded as part of an unsuccessful phase of peacemaking, stretching from 1919 to 1925, within the wider context of an ongoing Thirty Years War in Europe (Bell 1986). Even so, it has in recent decades received some more favourable notices. An authoritative collection of studies, compiled to mark its seventy-fifth anniversary, notes with modest approbation that nowadays scholars 'view the treaty as the best compromise that the negotiators could have reached in the existing circumstances' (Boemeke, Feldman, and Glaser 1998: 3).

It is possible, of course, that some of the problems faced by the peace-makers in Paris resulted from the oddities, and perhaps from the incompleteness, of the war's termination. What was so unusual about the armistice in November 1918 is that it was signed without any allied occupation of German territory. This had a direct impact upon the issue of reparations insofar as it produced a situation in which, atypically, 'four years of ruinous combat on all fronts had paradoxically been confined to the territory of the eventual victors' (Keylor 1998b: 497). A related consequence of this asymmetrical ending of the war—and one which stands in such stark contrast to either 1815 or 1945—was 'the lack of the peacemakers' effective control over many of the areas whose future was being considered' (Sharp 1991: 128). These points, in turn, relate to the broader issue of whether the problems of the peace derived from the precipitate ending of hostilities, and before the scale of the defeat of Germany had been fully driven home. It is not uncommon to assign the difficulties of the peacemaking to the premature ending of the warmaking.

The 1919 distributive treaties dealt with such matters as the military status of Germany, its territorial losses, the dispersal of its colonies, economic reparations, and the like. Superficially, it might appear that Versailles consisted of a distributive peace alone. This might reasonably be inferred from the observation by one of its principal historians that 'for all its 440 articles there were remarkably few provisions to ensure its enforcement' (Sharp 1991: 188–9). But a regulative peace there most assuredly was, and it was within its broad principles that the specific distributions were to be legitimated. That settlement inaugurated new procedural rules of international relations enshrined in the League, designed to 'lock European states into a new type of order' (Ikenberry 2000: 139). These extended beyond the League alone to more general doctrines of national self-determination. Ironically, many of the paradoxes and inconsistencies of the peace, as well as the compromises to which the victors were driven, arose from these very 'higher standards' that the victors had set for themselves, including the disparagement of the 'time-honoured formula of "winner takes all"' (Sharp 1991: 100).

Notoriously, the hindsight wisdom is that Versailles made the mistake of running the two together, in the sense that the regulative order of the League was actually a formal part of the Versailles distributive treaty. Hence revisionist disenchantment with the distributive settlement infected and damaged the wider regulative peace as well, since the latter was identified specifically as the means of preserving the claimed injustices of the former.

There are two other dimensions that should be examined with respect to the post-First World War peace settlement. The first was the attempt to reshape Germany politically, and the second was the duration of the peacemaking process. Both touch on important aspects of the past practice of peacemaking, and help us clarify the functions that it can perform.

By the end of the war, Woodrow Wilson hoped for a liberal revolution in Germany, whereas the Bolsheviks anticipated a socialist revolution. The actual overthrow of the Kaiser meant that a change of regime was imposed internally. Had it not been, it would most certainly have been imposed externally as part of the peace settlement in any event. Because Wilson's view drew such a close connection between the nature of the German autocracy, and its reputed responsibility for war, it was evident that a reconstructed German polity was a major war aim as far as Wilson was concerned. Thus the Versailles Treaty was not simply about what was to be done to Germany, but also about what Germany was to become. The point this raises, as mentioned generally above, is whether the reconstruction of the defeated enemy should be understood, in this case, as part of the distributive or regulative peace—or as an aspect of both.

Historians such as Arno Mayer had long claimed that the New Diplomacy was the West's counter-manifesto to Bolshevism, and that containment of communism was a principal concern of the peacemakers at Versailles (Mayer 1959, 1968). If this is allowed, then the quest for a democratic Germany can be construed as a gambit within the balance of power, and hence as an important dimension of the distributive settlement: the balance would be affected not only by Germany's size, but by its political complexion. A strong and liberal-leaning Germany at the heart of the continent would form an effective containment of Bolshevism. At the same time, however, it is also possible to see German transformation as integral to the regulative settlement. This is true in the general sense that the New Diplomacy assumed liberal states would steadfastly support the League, and hence a democratic Germany would contribute to preservation of the existing order. But it is also true in the more specific sense that Germany would become its own enforcer of the Versailles peace. Hence, it has been said of the regulative order of 1919, that the Big Three 'thought they had created new rules, new techniques, new mechanisms that would uphold the integrity of the system that they had designed'. Fundamentally, they expected 'once the Germans had been disciplined and democratized that they would become a part of the system' (Martel 1998: 615). From this perspective, the forging of the Weimar Republic is better understood, not just as a move in the distribution of power, but also as a major contribution to the preservation of Versailles settlement as a whole.

The other matter is that of the duration of the peacemaking. The common tendency is to think of Versailles as possibly the last of the old-style peace conferences (in the absence of one in 1945), whereby a peace is made at a single set of negotiations. Even so, it is worth recalling that a 'single' peace conference may be a deceptively protracted affair. The peace negotiations at Westphalia extended over a five-year period (Croxton 1999). As we have already seen, the notion that peace was made, instantly and at a single congress, had not quite been the case in 1815 either. However, as regards 1919, although there was to be a cluster of treaties relating to the other defeated states, it is commonly assumed that the main business of peacemaking with respect to Germany was completed at Versailles, and embodied in its treaty. Anything thereafter is best understood as implementation, enforcement, or revision of the treaty, but the peace had already been made.

This may, however, be misleading. Obviously there were important aspects of the settlement still to be worked out after 1919. Conspicuously, there was no agreement at Versailles on the absolute level of the reparations to be paid, even if the general principle of paying reparations had been established. The figures were left to the work of the subsequent Reparations Commission to determine. Whether that body was then merely to implement the policy of reparations, or actually to decide what that policy should be, is a moot point. Moreover, if we allow that enforcement of the peace should be understood as an integral aspect of the peacemaking itself—in the regulative sense above—then arguably there was much unfinished business after 1919. The occupation of the Ruhr by French forces in 1923 can be seen as the clear assertion of the French concept of regulation, but one that was to be challenged and replaced thereafter. The Dawes financial arrangements in 1924, and then the Locarno Treaty of 1925, established the primacy of an Anglo-American system of regulation in its stead. These are commonly viewed as adaptations and revisions of the original Versailles design, but the argument that post-First World War peacemaking extended into the mid-1920s—as a single, if sporadic and disjointed, process—deserves at least a respectful hearing.

If this argument is allowed, then the protracted peacemaking after 1945 becomes less exceptional than traditionally claimed: the precedent for it had already been partially set in 1919. As noted in the Introduction, historians appear uncertain as to whether or not there had been a peace settlement in 1945 at all. Ikenberry reaches the positive conclusion that 'there was also—eventually—a successful agreement' (1998: 151). Maier concurs: not only did one exist, but it was also successful. 'The post-1945 principles of settlement', he avers, 'proved a more robust structure than those of 1919' (1996: 13). Others see its distinctive trait as being its self-consciously piecemeal nature. Mindful of the gloomy precedent of Versailles, there was no wish to replicate the single historic meeting. Instead, statesmen 'sought to create a workable set of temporary expedients at a series of meetings and separate conferences rather than a comprehensive and final settlement' (Sharp 1997: 5).

If we adopt the framework of distributive and regulative settlements, how can it be applied to the problematic case of 1945? There appears initially to be some overlap between this scheme, and Ikenberry's notion of the two distinct settlements that issued after 1945. Ikenberry has repeatedly, and cogently, set out the main lines of his argument:

World War II produced two postwar settlements. One was a reaction to deteriorating relations with the Soviet Union, and it culminated in the containment order . . . The other settlement was a reaction to the economic rivalry and political turmoil of the 1930s . . . and it culminated in a wide range of new institutions and relations among the Western industrial democracies—a Western liberal order. (1999: 125)

This helpfully reminds us that, when war came to an end in 1945, there were, retrospectively, two types of explanation in circulation as to what had caused it in the first place. The one was specific to Germany and to Hitler's aggression: the war, thus understood, was a product of this latest manifestation of the 'German problem'. The other was wider in inspiration, and regarded the war as the result of the economic and social breakdown of the 1930s. Each of these required its own element of peacemaking, and the quest for a settlement in 1945 was driven accordingly: there was need for a peace with Germany, and, additionally, a wider peace that would prevent the conditions that Germany had been able to exploit for its own ends. Given these manifold objectives, it was natural that peace should come in stages, and that the 1945 settlement would be 'fragmented', being put together by a 'protracted and multidimensional process' (Ikenberry 2000: 163, 263)

Mindful of the mistakes made in 1919, Roosevelt planned to have the regulative order in place before the specifics of the distributive peace (Knutsen 1999: 203). Moreover, this order was to be more broadly conceived. Its purview extended widely into the fields of economic management, since this had been a principal source of collapse in the 1930s. It also embraced a universal organization that would have a range of functional responsibilities, over and above core tasks for preserving peace and security. Bretton Woods and Dumbarton Oaks were to be the twin pillars, establishing the economic and security orders respectively. Bretton Woods encapsulated the liberal belief 'that economic forces can be used in the service of a better, more orderly world', and symbolized the realization by 1939 that 'no NWO was possible without a more open global economic system' (A. J. Williams 1998: 212).

It was just as well that these principles preceded the substantive peace because that other dimension of the settlement was to be a long time in coming. Much of the Cold War period can be understood as a phase of protracted peacemaking subsequent upon 1945. This is the compelling thesis that Trachtenberg has set out. In the absence of a formal peace treaty at war's end, there was a long period of 'construction' during which a quasi-settlement emerged. But this was not finally set in place until 1963 (Trachtenberg 1999: vii). The Cold War was in part about the terms of the post-Second World War peace, and these centred upon the fate of Germany. Resolution might have come sooner, as Byrnes and Stalin had reached the semblance of an agreement at Potsdam, and this gave each side a *de facto* free hand within its own occupation zone. But the settlement failed at that point because the US government retreated from this policy (Trachtenberg 1999: 32–4).

The problem was not simply a failure to reach agreement between victor and vanquished, but principally amongst the victors themselves. Germany was the object of the protracted peacemaking after 1945, not its subject.

This, in turn, reflected the nature of the victory in 1945, resulting from the policy of unconditional surrender, and from the determination to learn the lessons of 1918. But in so doing, the victors ensured that the axis of conflict in the peacemaking would run between them. Nowhere was this more conspicuous than in their attitudes towards German reparations. While the post-1945 settlement is normally hailed for its policy of resuscitation towards Germany, this was by no means a foregone conclusion. There were constituencies in both the USA and in Britain that sought recompense from Germany, both as a form of just reparation, but also for the distributive bonus that would come from its weakening of Germany. The two ideas were certainly powerfully present in Soviet thinking in 1945. Paradoxically, the regulative ambition of a lenient peace to encourage Germany into good behaviour was itself an outcome of distributive calculations, not least amongst which were the financial costs that would otherwise be borne in the Western sectors in support of the German population. Regulative leniency was encouraged, in part, by this distributive concern to avoid paying reparations in reverse to Germany (Reynolds 2000: 25).

Beyond this, there is an intriguing contrast between the types of orders that were to be promulgated in 1945 and 1919. At the end of the First World War, Wilson's New Diplomacy led him to espouse a wholly new form of military-security order in the shape of the collective security machinery of the League. This was intended to supplant the rival alliances and balance of power that had precipitated conflict in 1914. But whilst radical in the form of the military-security order to be initiated, the peacemakers in 1919 wanted to turn the clock backwards when they turned their attention to the economic settlement. The pre-1914 economic order was recalled as the 'golden age' to which all aspired to return: order was defined in terms of resurrecting, not supplanting, what had gone before.

Arguably these verdicts can be reversed in relation to 1945. As to the military-security order, the essentials of the peace revolved around the second great experiment in collective security. For all its seeming failures in the 1930s, the 'old' security order was to be dusted down, given some new features, but then essentially tried again. The universalism of 1919 was to be repeated in the context of 1945. As to the economic order, there was to be no going back, and no second chances. While the United Nations order was based on resurrection, the Bretton Woods economic order looked to a fundamental rejection of the policies that had brought disaster in the

1930s. Something new—an economic great experiment—was required to take its place. Indeed, it was only in this context of the creation of more favourable social and economic conditions that collective security could be given another chance. What had failed in the 1930s was not the rationale of collective security, but its falling victim to the pernicious effects of economic depression, and the aggressive pursuit of national salvation. If a repetition of these conditions could be prevented, collective security could deal with 'normal' international instabilities. These two sets of beliefs—political universalism and economic multilateralism—formed the core of the regulative peace that was already in place by 1945.

The experience of 1945 also reminds us that the eventual form of a peace settlement may not be as originally envisaged at the outset of the peace-making process. Nowhere is this better illustrated than with regard to Germany. If the final peace took the form of a division of Germany, this had not been the original goal. On this, most historians are in firm agreement. Gaddis says of this 'striking anomaly' of the Cold War solution that 'no one in Washington, Moscow, or anywhere else had sought such an arrangement' (1997: 115). His view is echoed in the identical judgement that 'the Big Three were all genuinely committed to preserving the unity of the country' (Mazower 1998: 232). Such a solution—the partition of Germany—emerged then by accident as much as by design. The reason for this, after 1945, was not entirely due to conflict between East and West, but also to indecision and confusion, to what has been called 'disarray within as much as among the victors' (Gaddis 1997: 115).

The fact that Germany was administered through separate zones, and that those in due course congealed into two halves, makes problematic any single assessment of whether the distributive peace against Germany was punitive or not: it was both punitive and lenient, depending upon which zone is under discussion. The Soviet Union vigorously extracted reparations from its zone, as well as additional payments from the others, until such time as the British and Americans changed tack and prevented further economic punishment against (their zones of) Germany. Henceforward, a policy of resuscitation was pursued towards Germany, just as it was also to be towards Japan.

Finally, comment must be made upon the political transformation of Germany and Japan as part of the peace settlement. It has been observed of the Treaty of San Francisco with Japan in 1951, that it 'signalled the forceful conversion of Japan to a liberal democracy dedicated to peace' (Kegley and Raymond 1999: 192). A similar strategy was already under way with regard to Germany. Again, we face the conundrum as to whether this should be seen as part of the distributive or regulative peace, and again the most appropriate answer would appear to be that it displays elements of both. The point can be illustrated with reference to a telling observation of one historian about perceptions in 1945:

It was this convergence of concerns—how to avoid the danger of a resurgent Germany itself, on the one hand, *and* the threat of a Germany on the wrong side in the Cold War, on the other—that made its future so central an issue. (Gaddis 1997: 116)

The latter dimension brings out the role of Germany in the distributive peace, since a conversion of Germany to either liberalism or socialism would profoundly affect the balance of power. From this point of view, the enforced conversion of Germany in the image of either of the victors can be regarded as the division of the territorial spoils by other means. Imposition of one's own system, as Stalin freely admitted in his familiar dictum, was the new game for dividing the spoils of war. Hence, political reconstruction of the vanquished can be understood as a strategy for a distributive peace.

Alternatively, but with equal validity, Gaddis's former point indicates Germany's centrality to the regulation of the peace, since liberalization would be its own instrument of pacification, and would avoid the need for the peace to be enforced in perpetuity against Germany from the outside. Once 'socialized', Germany would become the instrument of its own regulation.

PEACEMAKING AND THE END OF THE COLD WAR

If the *form* of the post-1945 peace settlement had not been anticipated, then even more strikingly no one had predicted that any peace settlement would be required at all in 1990. The incidental, but not inconsequential effect of this was that, unlike the cases of the two World Wars, there was to be no opportunity to plan the peace that would ensue after the Cold War. There was no comparable post-war planning while the Cold War was still under way (Gaddis 1992a: 135).

Once the unexpected happened, profound questions were left unanswered about the shape of the peace settlement that was required. Pointedly expressed, the question was, 'to what is this to be the settlement'. This may appear to be a perplexing and obscure formulation of the issue. Surely the settlement that was required was to the issues of the preceding Cold War? That war was over, and what was now needed was a peace to draw a line beneath it. However, as the earlier discussions of the issue of continuity and discontinuity have already suggested, the matter could not be so straightforward. To the extent that the Cold War was about a failed, or partial, or temporary, settlement to the issues left over from the war in 1945, it could plausibly be suggested that what was now needed was a peace settlement to the Second World War, rather than to the Cold War as such. It was not so much that a peace settlement had brought an end to the Cold War, as that the demise of the Cold War had, belatedly, paved the way for a 1945 peace settlement. Even this perspective may be unduly limiting, and suffer from a short-term perspective. It has been suggested that we need to go all the way back to 1919, to make sense of the meaning of the end of the Cold War: 'It may be a mistake to refer to Versailles and the other treaties made in Paris in 1919 as a "peace settlement". The real legacy of Versailles was neither peace nor settlement, but rather "a seventy-year crisis" . . . ending only in 1989' (Jacobson 1998: 451). By this reckoning, we are fully justified in approaching the post-Cold War order as an exercise in peace-making, but the moot point is which war was being laid to rest by it: the Cold War, or the Second World War, or the First World War?

In turn, the long duration of the peacemaking process suggests a pos-sibly interesting parallel between the 1990s and the years after 1945. The manner in which the end of the Second World War merged with the Cold War gives an already existing example of the trend in the twentieth century for peacemaking to become an extended process, rather than something that could be neatly performed at a single congress, or embodied in a single treaty. Peace settlements have become increasingly protracted affairs. As noted elsewhere of the events of 1990–1, the 'sudden collapse of the Soviet Union was not followed by any general peace treaty' (Hall 1996: 164). Indeed, the relationship of the post-Cold War peace to the Cold War itself may be the mirror image of the relationship between the Second World War, and the peace that ensued upon it. It has been said of the latter that there was 'in reality, no Year Zero, no clean break between hot and cold war' (Mazower 1998: 216). In the same way, there has been no Year Zero in the formation of the post-Cold War peace.

How is all this relevant to an understanding of the 1990s? Our confusion about the meaning of the period is compounded by our inability to distinguish the distributive aspects of post-Cold War peacemaking, from the process for establishing a wider regulative order. Once we think of the quest for peace in the 1990s as containing these discrete elements, two arguments begin to emerge. The first is that the peace treaty with Russia, while now substantially in place, may not yet be fully complete. Secondly, what also becomes clearer once these aspects are separated out, is that the novelty of the post-Cold War order is less striking: the continuities impress us as much as do the discontinuities. The fact that the distributive settlement was substantially new does not entail that the regulative peace had to be so also. Much of the discussion that purports to be about the post-Cold War order is, narrowly and mistakenly, actually about the post-Cold War distributive peace alone. Since the wider constellation of interests that 'won' the Cold War was still substantially in place after its end, it would in any case have been surprising had it been seen fit to devise a wholly new set of instruments for regulation of its victory. That happens with a changing of the guard in the aftermath of hegemonic wars, but, in this case, the guard had not changed. Any wholesale revision of the regulative order would therefore have been superfluous, and possibly damaging to the durability of the peace.

It is for this reason that the imagery of the 1990s as an interregnum is somewhat misleading. The image implies a hiatus in the system of rule and thus, at the very least, a discontinuity in that regard. But it is precisely in its regulative aspect that the continuities with the Cold War period are most striking. There has been no hiatus in the regulative system, albeit that there has been a distributional change in balances and resources. The point again shares a family resemblance with Ikenberry's analysis. 'Although the Cold War reinforced this liberal order', he comments, 'it was not triggered by or ultimately dependent on the Cold War for its functioning and stability. The "containment order" ended along with the Cold War, but the much more deeply rooted liberal order lives on' (1999: 124). *Mutatis mutandis*, this echoes the present claim that there is now a new distributive peace largely in place, whereas the regulative order has survived the transition largely intact.

What are the core elements of this post-Cold War peace settlement? Its provisions cover the areas that would broadly have been anticipated, had the Cold War actually been fought and won/lost. They mark the changes consequent upon the new distribution of power, and the material/ territorial embodiments of that new situation. This is the distributive aspect of the post-Cold War order. In summary, the following are its principal provisions: unification of Germany within NATO; the dismantling of the Warsaw Pact; the disintegration of the Soviet Union; NATO and European Union enlargement; and a diminished role for Russia as a broker of the world's principal affairs.

If that is the distributive settlement, what are the characteristics of the post-Cold War regulative peace? Again, in summary form, these can be seen as: the salience of norms attached to the working of the global economy; the continuing dominance of Western-controlled multilateralism; a reformulated style of collectivization of security; and the continued assertion of a liberal rights order. In short, whatever discontinuity there might be in the distributive settlement, there is a marked continuity in the regulative sphere.

That there has been a peace settlement at the end of the Cold War is not doubted by those who have already pronounced it a failure. There are, we are told, 'baleful lessons' to be learned from what has gone wrong. 'A settlement that was supposed to correct the injustices suffered in Europe in 1945', fell short of that objective because it 'instead reverted to the illusions and well-meaning failures of 1919' (Steel 1998: 34). The reason that 1990 warrants comparison with 1919 and 1945 is precisely that, along with them, it failed to deliver us to the promised New Jerusalem. In order to assess the appropriateness of this verdict, the remainder of the book will now attempt to describe the provisions of that post-Cold War peace settlement.

II

THE DISTRIBUTIVE PEACE

4

THE EUROPEAN SETTLEMENT

If the idea of the post-Cold War order as a phase of peacemaking is to hold, it must be thought applicable above all to the course of events in Europe. Since this constituted the heart of the Cold War, it was demonstrably there that a peace was most required to bring hostilities to a halt. As President George Bush stated in a speech in Mainz, in May 1989, 'the Cold War began with the division of Europe. It can only end when Europe is whole' (Rotfeld and Stutzle 1991: 93). Accordingly, this chapter explores the nature of the European settlement. What were its terms and how were they implemented? Was the peace negotiated immediately at the end of the Cold War, or have its terms unfolded progressively over the ensuing years? How are we to judge this peace in comparison with historical precedents: has it been a harsh or lenient peace?

The epicentre of the end of the Cold War lay in Europe, and the territorial map of that continent was substantially transfigured as a result. Historians note, amongst these seismic movements, the unification of Germany, the restructuring of NATO, a new phase of European integration, and the dissolution of the Soviet Union (Reynolds 2000: 568). How are we to think of these events? At the very least, they enjoin us to regard the post-Cold War settlement in the broadest terms. We cannot make judgements about the nature of the peace imposed upon the Soviet Union—say, its territorial provisions—in isolation from the other powerful forces that lashed across that country.

What is unique about the post-Soviet experience, we are reminded, is that 'the building of state structures, emergence of societal institutions, proliferation of market relations, and exposure to all the effects of global interdependence are happening simultaneously' (Zubok 1995: 103). The distributive peace, in this way, was only a part of the total post-Cold War settlement. Similarly, part of the package that was to make German unification acceptable included the transformation of NATO (Risse 1997: 173). It also required new programmes for European integration, resulting in the Maastricht Treaty in December 1991 (Rotfeld and Stutzle 1991: 5; Reynolds 2000: 565). So powerfully interlocking were all these developments that measures undertaken as part of the settlement with the Soviet Union alone also had pronounced knock-on effects on arrangements elsewhere.

There are several potential obstacles to construing the end of the Cold War in Europe as tantamount to post-war peacemaking. The main objection is that, while there was a decisive shift in the balance of power and a profoundly important redistribution of territory and of political control, this was brought about by an inadvertent concomitance of events, rather than by any Western calculation. In effect, the problem with the idea of peacemaking is that it implies a degree of deliberation and intent on the part of the West, neither of which was actually present in sufficient degree. Does this objection not damage the framework of this study?

At the most basic level, this criticism derives from a fundamentally different assessment of the nature of the dynamic that brought the Cold War to an end in the first place. As against the triumphalism of some of the accounts of the end of the Cold War, and their privileging of the role of the West in bringing it about, this view shifts the focus to a home-grown Soviet and eastern European product, developed without any Western assistance. In the words of one analyst, 'it was more an acquiescence by the Soviets than a defeat' (D. Cox 1996: 124). With the emphasis thus shifted, the imagery of peacemaking at the end of the Cold War becomes unsettled, and perhaps seems less appropriate. This, in turn, links in with a further argument: 'Its defeat finally came not on the battlefield but as the result of a change of heart, and then of character, and then ultimately of system' (Gaddis 1998: 146). Gaddis makes this part of his plea for a more generous treatment of Russia, on account of the costs spared to the West by this transition. Again, however, the central point is that the redistribution resulted from Soviet choice, rather than from American exaction.

Secondly, there is the claim that much of this redistribution was too fortuitous to be thought of as an exercise in peacemaking. This was not a peace that was carefully determined and then implemented: it developed spontaneously, with no premeditation or conscious planning. These issues will be examined in detail below; for the moment, they can be illustrated by the following examples. At the heart of the redistribution was the disappearance of the German Democratic Republic into a reunited German state. Of this, and not atypically, one German historian has observed:

The Federal Republic simply watched in amazement; hardly anyone there still wanted unification ... They were consequently unprepared for unity, and the problems to which it gave rise; there were no plans; suddenly unity was upon them. (Geiss 1997: 106)

Thus understood, German unification was thrust upon Germany, and the West as a whole, much more than it was a conscious decision thrust upon the Soviet Union. In the same way, the loss of the Soviet Union's empire in eastern Europe was the wider framework within which the great redistribution of power in Europe took place at the end of the Cold War. Once more, this is better conceived as an unintended outcome, rather than as a conscious choice, as has been variously testified. Garthoff (1994: 622) insists of the liberation of eastern Europe that the 'United States had encouraged and greatly welcomed these developments, but rather than attempting to push the process, it wisely stood aside and let Gorbachev bring them about'. Even at Gorbachev's hands, the changes were much more radical than intended, and best understood as 'unplanned byproducts of change in the USSR' (Dean 1994: 35). As the provisions of a peace settlement, this all looks rather odd, being a process initiated by the vanquished rather than imposed by the victor.

There are two provisional responses that might be made to these comments. The first is that the idea of a peace settlement should not be discounted merely on the basis that much of it was not planned nor intended. Such a sequence is not uncommon in historical instances of peacemaking. Most notably, what became the settlement of the Second World War, namely the division of Germany, was by most accounts not the intended resolution of that particular conflict. It was a solution that evolved over time, but no less crucial to the post-war peace for that.

Secondly, this in turn directs our attention to important aspects of chronology. If we return to Trachtenberg's notion of a 'constructed peace', and hence to the associated idea of 'protracted' peacemaking, we circumvent the issue of original intentions, and replace it with a view of the peace settlement as an adjustment to changing circumstances. A peace is not necessarily made at one moment in time, but can progressively evolve.

After 1945, the division of Germany became the *de facto* peace, however little foreseen or intended at the outset. In the same way, the elements of the post-Cold War distributive peace can be regarded as part of the settlement, regardless of initial premeditation or forward planning.

There seems a *prima facie* case for regarding the events in Europe that marked the end of the Cold War as a kind of European settlement. Collectively, as all commentators would readily acknowledge, this marked the greatest transformation in the European order since 1945, or possibly since 1919 (Reynolds 2000: 561). The principal reason for viewing the events of 1989–91 as a European settlement is that since the Cold War had been brought about by the division of Europe, it was only its 'undividing' that could bring about its end. Since the Cold War had been about the failed settlement in Europe in 1945, it was only the final settlement of the unresolved issues of the Second World War that allowed it to be put aside. As Gorbachev himself pointed out in an interview in early 1990, 'there is still no peace treaty with Germany' (Rotfeld and Stutzle 1991: 102).

It was also manifestly a distributive peace. Sovereignty over territory was redistributed; existing spheres of influence and tutelage were abrogated; deployments of military power were fundamentally shifted; and the economic and political complexion of many states was radically transformed. Whereas the Cold War had been characterized by an equilibrium that had largely ossified over recent decades, its end issued in a dynamic series of shifts that led to a marked disequilibrium of power. From superpower with its own European empire, Russia was relegated to fringe player with only vestigial influence in the remnants of its near abroad. There can be scarcely any better example of a 'hegemonic war' that has so decisively redistributed the spoils, and so fundamentally redrawn the international balance of power. If this is not a distributive peace, then it is difficult to think of one that merits the name.

In order to acquire a clear perspective upon the post-Cold War order, we must penetrate to its heart. Since the Cold War was itself defined in terms of the relationship between the two superpowers, of which the Soviet Union was one, then it follows assuredly that the essential quality of the order that has succeeded it must be found in the nature of the post-1989 relationship between the West and the Soviet Union, and its Russian successor. This relationship played itself out in a redrawing of the map of central and eastern Europe which both reflected, and contributed to, the shifting balance of power between the parties. If the Soviet loss of its empire in eastern Europe was symptomatic of its diminished power, this in turn reinforced the relative weakness of the post-Soviet state. But has this loss of hegemony been a punishment imposed by the West on Russia, or is it an outcome of Russia's own making? Has the West subjected Russia to its own post-Cold War 'diktat', or has it paradoxically moderated the consequences for Russia of its own precipitate actions? Unless we can answer some of these teasing questions, we will continue to be mystified by the fundamental nature of the contemporary order.

HOW HARSH A PEACE?

This leaves us with a puzzle to resolve. In comparative historical perspective, just how punitive has the post-Cold War peace actually been? More problematically, has the dissipation of Soviet power been an enactment by the West, or simply the result of a process of domestic transformation within the USSR itself? We are then confronted with the issue of finding the appropriate historical analogy, and the earlier experience of 1917–18 might illustrate the point. Was the fatal weakening of Russia on that occasion brought about by the harsh terms of the Treaty of Brest-Litovsk imposed, from the outside, by Germany? Or was the weakening already a reality brought about by domestic revolution, of which Brest-Litovsk was merely a symptom? Likewise, in thinking about the end of the Cold War, it is essential to disentangle those elements of the redistribution of power that were consequent upon a domestic revolution within the Soviet Union, and those that were self-consciously wrought by the Soviet Union's opponents in the Cold War. But as that earlier example reminds us, it is hard to disentangle the effects of revolution from the effects of war.

How punitive a peace was it? There has been a chorus of voices raised in protest against its overly vindictive nature. Many have pointed to the potential parallel with 1919, presenting Russia as falling into 'the same category of a loser nation as Germany did in 1919–1933' (Zubok 1995: 107). This viewpoint has been eloquently expressed by the historian John Gaddis. His lament was that, instead of following the enlightened precedents of 1815 and 1945, the United States in the 1990s seems to have succumbed to the attractions of the model of 1919, and to be bent on a punitive peace. He criticizes this because it 'preserves, and even expands, a security structure left over from a conflict that has now ended, while excluding the former adversary from it' (Gaddis 1998: 146). He also chastises the Clinton Administration for behaving towards Russia in a manner in which the latter has been left 'to gulp and swallow yet again. We, the victors, are free to impose upon them whatever settlement we choose' (1998: 146). Gaddis dismisses this approach as 'arrogant' and 'short-sighted'.

Much of the following discussion will lend weight to that judgement. However, at the outset, it is best to acknowledge the opposite point of view. According to this interpretation, the standing and esteem of Russia would have been even more adversely affected, had it not been for considerate and protective intervention on the part of the United States. Thus construed, Russia was saved from the worst consequences of its own actions by the active support of the USA. This, in turn, is hard to reconcile with the view of a harsh peace imposed by the West. How are two such diametrically opposing interpretations both to be advanced with any credibility?

It is worth noting that the post-Cold War peace is not alone in attracting such diverse verdicts. Even Versailles has divided the historians into those that felt it was too harsh, and those who considered it too lenient. The two assessments are often combined, as in the famous judgement it was 'trop doux pour ce qu'il avait de dur' ('too soft for the hardness it contained'). While much of the historiography has concentrated upon the 'unjust' treatment of Germany, the other side of the coin was that territorial redistributions in eastern Europe arguably, in the longer term, left Germany stronger rather than weaker. Thus combined, it was the harsh peace that made future German revisionism likely, while it was its lenience that made it possible. Hence we can see the basis of the two alternative verdicts.

There is, in this respect, an instructive parallel with the post-Cold War peace. While it will be shown that the settlement in Europe was certainly a decisive one, it is possible that it could have been harsher still. This, at least, was the implicit conclusion reached by one seasoned and well-placed observer:

Bush and Baker, as they had promised, did not seek to use the opportunities that were there to exploit the collapse of Soviet hegemony in Eastern Europe either by moving to extend NATO forward to the Soviet borders or by trying to exploit the widening fissures within the Soviet Union. (Garthoff 1994: 608)

If anything, the principal criticism that has been directed against the Bush Administration's handling of the end of the Cold War is precisely that it was too conservative in trying to preserve the existing Soviet Union, and too solicitous of the interests of successive leaders, Gorbachev and Yeltsin. Because Bush linked Western interests to the maintenance in power of those with whom he could do business, it became a fundamental objective of American policy to preserve those leaders. It was a consequence of such a strategy that there were limits to the concessions that could be wrung from the defeated Soviet state. Moreover, in continuing to accord priority to the relationship with the former superpower, the United States offered a salve to damaged Russian *amour propre*. Indeed, one can go further. The United States did not only moderate its own demands, but also was seen by the Soviet/Russian leadership as a potentially protective force against other revisionist Western claims. 'The United States also provided a means of managing other powers in the Western coalition that had their own claims on Russia', notes Buszynski (1996: 53). 'In its weakened state, Russia would be vulnerable to Japanese pressure over the territorial dispute or to German demands over a host of outstanding issues'. Any such assessment, if valid, takes us some way from the contrary appreciation of the end of the Cold War—as an imposed and vindictive peace—and it will be necessary to find some means of dealing with, and possibly reconciling, these conflicting views.

This forces us to address once again the chronological parameters of the post-Cold War peace. What is being suggested here is that if we widen these, then the framework of peacemaking becomes less problematic. This is also the best means of reconciling those conflicting judgements about the severity of this peace. How might this argument run?

Part of the difficulty in assessing how the USSR/Russia has been treated since the end of the Cold War lies in the variability of those relations over time. There has been much more harmony in Russian–United States relations at some periods than at others, and it is possible to discern a secular trend towards gradual deterioration since 1990. In terms of making a judgement about the content, and severity, of the post-Cold War peace, this leaves the problem of deciding what is the appropriate chronology for the peacemaking. Was the peace made in 1989–91? Or has the peace been under progressive evolution across the whole period since then? Different assessments might be made of its content, depending upon which framework is the one adopted.

For purposes of the ongoing argument, a particular scheme will be presented in this chapter. It proposes that we regard the making of the post-Cold War peace in Europe as occurring in three stages. The first, covering the period until the end of 1991, might most appropriately be regarded as the armistice: this is when the fighting was brought to a halt, and provisional arrangements were made about the shape of the post-bellum order. The armistice, of course, was subject to subsequent ratification in the more formal period of peacemaking. This next period, the peacemaking as properly understood, has taken place in two phases. The first of these demonstrated a substantial degree of cooperation with Russia, and extended from 1991 through to 1993. During much of this period, there was also a high level of Russian compliance with Western preferences. This was the phase during which a relatively moderate peace seemed to be in the making. In the next phase, which extended from 1994 onwards, the relationship with the West became more testing, and the terms exacted of Russia correspondingly more demanding. In short, we are not in a position to make a single judgement about the post-Cold War peace because it has come in different stages, and with varying degrees of Russian compliance or resistance.

This, in turn, reinforces the earlier comments about the 'unintended' quality of much of the final settlement. The entire peace was not put in place in 1989–91, because it would have been precipitous to do so. It might also have been highly dangerous. To the extent that Western demands of the USSR were relatively moderate during the armistice phase, the reason for this can be understood in terms of the continuing dangers of the situation. Had the terms demanded of the Soviet Union been unduly draconian, the West would have run the risk of the USSR choosing to 'fight on', or, at the very least, of weakening those very forces of liberalization in the USSR that they sought to foster. Thus the course of peacemaking with Russia across the past decade has been influenced by a number of cross-currents and concerns: the degree of residual danger to Western interests; the degree to which the West has felt uninhibited about ignoring Russian preferences; and the development of the domestic politico-economic situation within Russia itself. As will be seen, the distributive peace overlaps with the regulative peace at that point where the process of determining

Russia's place in the new balance of power came down to a struggle over the nature of Russia's political and economic soul.

In order to develop this argument further, we now need to review the elements of the European settlement, and how they have unfolded over the years since 1989.

THE REUNIFICATION OF GERMANY

What is the problem and what the question, is notoriously dependent upon the historical perspective from which it is viewed. For much of the late nineteenth and early twentieth centuries, the German 'problem' was thought to reside in the country's unification. In contrast, it has been observed that 'after 1945, it was the division of Germany, and how to overcome it, which was thought to constitute the German Question' (Geiss 1997: 83). In a nutshell, the division of Germany was the historical anomaly that epitomized the affect the Cold War had on Europe. It was the standing embodiment of the failure to settle the continent in the aftermath of the collapse of the Nazi state. But that failure, as already suggested, became itself the basis of a settlement of a kind that would endure as long as the Cold War: it was the non-peace that became the best peace that was attainable.

Of all the distributive challenges to Soviet interests that could have been envisaged, German unification was the second most dangerous. Worst of all, and representing the truly nightmare scenario, was the unification of Germany within continuing membership of NATO. And yet this is precisely the principal provision of the peace that was demanded of the Soviet Union in the course of 1990. To the extent that the post-Cold War peace warrants description as a 'diktat', then surely this is the substantial basis of that claim?

The reality is more subtle and complex than this would suggest. Once more, the evidence is ambiguous and interpretations have become polarized. On the dissenting side, there is a clear perception that, while the Soviet Union was reluctant to accept German unification in NATO, it was finally won round to acquiescence: the reassurances extended to it created a negotiated outcome, rather than a 'diktat'. This is Garthoff's (1994: 608) assessment:

On the most critical issue, the reunification of Germany, though the positions of the two countries initially differed significantly (above all on the question of a united Germany remaining in NATO), they worked cooperatively to resolve the problem by working out a series of provisions to reassure the Soviet leadership and public that their security would not be jeopardized.

On the other side, reporting unsubstantiated rumours, there is the view that the Soviet leadership remained profoundly unhappy with that final outcome, so much so that desperate forms of resistance were contemplated. Thus, we are told, 'the Soviets viewed a unified Germany in NATO to be such a threat to the stability of the European balance that they apparently considered a pre-emptive military strike' (D. Cox 1996: 89). This was apparently twice contemplated, in autumn 1989 and winter 1990. Such an account, whatever credibility can be attached to it, is obviously much more in keeping with the 'diktat' version of events. However, the chronology referred to in this version is revealing, and needs to be placed in the context of a basic narrative of the unfolding dialogue over the issue.

Pressures for unification generated their own momentum in the early part of 1990. They arose 'from below', and from a quarter—East Germany itself—where they had been least expected of all (Garton Ash 2000: 16, 56). While Chancellor Kohl seized the political opportunity to swim with this tide, there is nothing to suggest that rapid unification had been planned or envisaged when the wall first crumbled. Nonetheless, given the sensitivity of the issue, means had to be found of dealing with the influx of refugees from the east with the minimum destabilization possible. Kohl's quest for immediate unification found complete backing from President Bush who regarded such an outcome as the just fruits of victory, as 'the positive fulfillment of forty years of resolute and farsighted containment policy by the United States and its allies' (Dean 1994: 40). The British and French were by no means so enthusiastic, but were reassured by the American President (Zelikow and Rice 1995; Risse 1997: 160).

There is some suggestion that Gorbachev was coming round to accepting the inevitability of unification by the beginning of 1990 (IISS 1989–90: 56). By February 1990, in a meeting in Ottawa, the basic 'two-plus-four' formula had been settled, allowing for parallel agreements between the two Germanys on the one hand, and the four external powers on the other. This was in spite of British preferences, expressed by Foreign Secretary Douglas Hurd, that the formula should instead be 'four-plus-zero', leaving the Germans out of it altogether (Beschloss and Talbott 1993: 185).

Even if the Soviet leadership had been opposed to unification in the autumn and early winter, that opposition seemed to be crumbling by February, although clearly the issue of NATO membership was still to be resolved. On this, there remained substantial Soviet dissent during the spring. Gorbachev's own public stance on the matter, in an interview in March 1990, was that 'we cannot agree to that. It is out of the question' (Rotfeld and Stutzle 1991: 104). Apparently, Politburo instructions prepared for talks to be held with Secretary of State Baker in May continued to take this stance. Indeed, Garthoff regards the wording of them ('unacceptable to us'), as a toughening of instructions compared to those for the previous month's Schevardnadze visit to Washington ('we cannot agree') (Garthoff 1994: 417). According to this account, the real turning point did not emerge until the Washington summit of 31 May–3 June 1990. On this occasion, Bush consolidated a set of nine points of reassurance to the Soviet Union to persuade it that unification in NATO would not be detrimental to Soviet security. Although Gorbachev did not assent at this stage, he 'was unexpectedly responsive to the argument that every country should have the right to make such decisions for itself' (Garthoff 1994: 426–7).

Thereafter, events moved quickly. In early July, the NATO summit in London sought to reinvent the alliance in ways that would be more broadly acceptable to the Soviet Union. This paved the way for the famous meeting in mid-July between Gorbachev and Kohl. This issued in agreement that a united Germany could make its own choice of future alliance, coupled with a complex package of German economic assistance, limitations on the overall size of the German armed forces, and limitations on future NATO deployments to former East German territory. In return, the Soviet Union undertook to withdraw all its forces from East Germany by 1994 (IISS 1990–1: 174–5). The full package was contained in the final Two-plus-Four Treaty signed in Moscow in September.

Other details are important to this history of the distributive peace. First of all, it should be noted that German unification self-consciously took place without the formality of a final—that is to say post-1945—peace treaty with Germany. Chancellor Kohl's rush to unification would have been stymied by any such lengthy procedure, and his wish carried the day with American support (Dean 1994: 40). Secondly, and paradoxically, elements that would have been part of a post-Second World War treaty were, in fact, dealt with as part of German unification. The United States and others insisted that Germany's existing border with Poland had to be accepted by the new Germany, as a precondition of unification (Risse 1997: 171). Also, by a Declaration of 1 October 1990, the authority of the Four Powers in relation to Berlin and Germany as a whole was rescinded. The Powers declared that 'the operation of their rights and responsibilities . . . shall be suspended upon the unification of Germany' (Rotfeld and Stutzle 1991: 187). In that sense, the post-Cold War settlement did tidy up one of the last pieces of business hanging over from the Second World War. Germany lost its 'singularity', and could be regarded as now fully normalized.

Clearly, there are elements of this story that do not sit comfortably with a simple notion of a dictated peace. One oddity, at the very least, is striking indeed. As mention of the date 1994 reveals, it was part of the agreement that the USSR could retain forces in the former East Germany, but now within the unified Federal Republic, until that year. In effect, this allowed Soviet forces to be stationed on NATO territory for the duration of that period. In addition, Germany agreed to pay the USSR towards the costs of stationing these forces, and then towards the costs of their final removal (D. Cox 1996: 2). It is a commonplace feature of peace treaties to include provisions for periods of military occupation, and to exact financial indemnity for costs, but normally these are provisions imposed by the victor upon the vanquished. No other examples come to mind where, as in this case, the occupation and indemnity were imposed by the vanquished on the victor.

There is an irreducible ambivalence in the outcome of the negotiation over NATO membership. No matter how it is looked at, there is no doubt that the USSR made a concession that, in any other set of circumstances, it would have been exceedingly reluctant to yield. To be sure, there was some potential benefit to the Soviet Union in avoiding German neutrality, and having Germany tied into NATO structures, as American negotiators reportedly pointed out (Beschloss and Talbott 1993: 189). Also, other Warsaw Pact states had their own deep misgivings about German neutrality as well (Dean 1994: 47). That said, the USSR conceded on a matter that it had previously claimed to be non-negotiable. That it did so must presumably be attributed to a combination of its own sense of weakness, the priority attached to domestic change and economic management, and to the wider set of foreign policy goals that Gorbachev was committed to achieving.

It is hard to imagine that the Soviet Union could have done much to prevent German unification, once the momentum towards it was under way. However, there is a widely held view that Gorbachev could have blocked German membership of NATO, had he been resolute in wishing to do so. 'Moscow could have forced the German people', we are told on good authority, 'to choose between unification and NATO membership' (Risse 1997: 164). The Soviet leader opted not to force that decision upon the German people. His reasoning must have been that to do so would be counter-productive to the wider ambitions of his policy. What would be the point of letting East Germany go in the first place, if only to result in a clash with the West over the NATO issue? In short, the costs of a policy of obstruction would have outweighed its likely benefits. That this was so had been intimated to the Soviet President at the time, as Secretary of State James Baker was happy to divulge to the North Atlantic Council in June 1990:

President Bush also assured President Gorbachev that no one wanted to isolate the Soviets. But the Soviets' own policies on Germany could well have this effect if the Soviets were to take negative stands on the external aspects of unification. In this event, their approach would put them in conflict with most European govern-ments, East and West. The very logic of new thinking would be contradicted. (Rotfeld and Stutzle 1991: 99)

What this suggests is that Gorbachev's strategic objectives allowed him far less room for manœuvre than he would otherwise have wished, and com-pelled him to make fundamental concessions. As a consequence, the linger-ing sense that he had been responsible for a 'sell-out' was to have lasting effects on Russian policy throughout the 1990s (Reynolds 2000: 565).

On the other side, and given that very same set of circumstances, it can be argued that Gorbachev secured a deal that was better than some he might have been given. Certainly, Chancellor Kohl was willing to pay a high financial price in order to speed the process of unification through, and while the benign figure of Gorbachev was still in control. Kohl was pressed to double the German contribution to the costs of Soviet troop withdrawals (Reynolds 2000: 564), in what has been described as an instance of the Soviet leadership playing 'hardball' (Risse 1997: 167). Para-doxically, the notion that Gorbachev's long-term future was not secure became, for the Soviet leader, one of the strengths of his bargaining hand. As a result, while the USSR made concessions that were very real and significant, it emerged less humiliated than it might otherwise have been.

This is a fair reflection of the ambivalent outcome. It is symptomatic of the balance of interests at the time, which pressed for a moderate rather than a punitive settlement with the USSR. On the side of the West, and particularly the Federal Republic, there was the incentive to make as much hay as possible while the Gorbachev sun still shone. There was the need to make the settlement as reassuring as possible, in order not fatally to weaken the power base of the liberals in the Kremlin. And there was the incentive to persuade Gorbachev to accept the armistice, in the expectation that a not unreasonable deal over Germany might portend acceptable terms elsewhere. On the side of the USSR, the options were limited. The only sensible strategy on offer was to negotiate the best terms available, and this is what was done. A policy of serious dissent to German unification, including military resistance, would have contradicted all the domestic and foreign policy objectives that Gorbachev had pursued during the 1980s.

In sum, the settlement over Germany reflected the balance of interests and strengths. It represented a trade-off between Soviet fears of an even worse deal, given its weakness, set against Western fears that the situation, if not handled with some sensitivity, might become even less stable than it already was. A punitive peace might turn out to be no peace at all. In those circumstances, the West secured its principal objective, but made the concessions necessary to make this palatable to the Soviet Union. But this was the first stage in the process, not the last. It remained to be seen whether, in the years that followed, the two subsequent phases of actual peacemaking would be in keeping with the spirit that had informed the signing of the original armistice.

DISSOLUTION OF THE WARSAW PACT

The next element in the European settlement was the dissolution of the Warsaw Pact. As that other embodiment of the Cold War, in addition to NATO, it was inevitable that a final settlement of the abnormal division of

Europe, and a return to full sovereignty for the states of eastern Europe, would require the elimination of this security structure. Again, however, the anomaly in trying to present this as part of the post-Cold War peace is that the dissolution was wrought entirely from the inside, rather than being imposed from without. Gorbachev did much more to dismantle the Warsaw Pact than did George Bush. The Warsaw Pact had disappeared before the West had the opportunity to insist it should, and possibly before it was thought even desirable.

The disappearance of the Warsaw Pact was not an additional event, over and above the other processes that brought the Cold War to an end. It was merely an expression of these processes and, above all, of the political developments within eastern Europe. In that sense, it was the foreordained, albeit unintended, consequence of two policy decisions taken by Gorbachev. The first was to persist with reform and liberalization, even beyond the point when it was reasonable to expect these regimes to retain their broadly communist character. The second was not to intervene militarily to check the tide of liberalization, once it began to get out of control. Gorbachev had, in any case, given assurances to the United States that the Soviet Union would not resort to military suppression of this kind (Garthoff 1994: 607).

Thereafter, it became unavoidable that the emerging political groupings, especially in central Europe, would come out vocally against the old systems of Soviet control, of which the Warsaw Pact was the epitome. It therefore came as no surprise that, by early 1990, Czechoslovakia and Hungary—both of which had suffered from the fraternal assistance of Warsaw Pact forces in the past—were already demanding that the Soviet Union withdraw its forces from their countries (IISS 1989–90: 31). This was followed, but more slowly, by Poland which remained warily attentive to its own security concerns about Germany, as well as to those about the Soviet Union. The Pact was formally wound up in March 1991 (Reynolds 2000: 566).

On the face of it, the Warsaw Pact was NATO's great military rival during the Cold War, and it would be natural to assume that, with the end of the Cold War, the West would seek to dismantle its challenger. In fact, this is a misconception of the true situation. NATO had been in existence for some six years before, in 1955, the Soviet Union saw fit to invent the Warsaw Pact. Whatever military functions it fulfilled thereafter (and there certainly were some), it is important to realize that these were secondary. The principal reason for the existence of the Warsaw Pact was as an expression of, and instrument for, Soviet political control of eastern Europe. Once Gorbachev was determined no longer to exercise that control, the Warsaw Pact became an affront to the new popular regimes of eastern Europe, and surplus to Soviet political requirements. It was dissolved because the east Europeans would no longer tolerate it, and the Soviet Union no longer wished to pay the political price of maintaining it.

In that sense, the West was largely irrelevant to the dissolution of the Warsaw Pact. Nonetheless, whatever the real causes of its demise, there was obviously an immense symbolic significance attached to the event. Even if it was not the peace settlement that brought about a great shift in the balance of power, but a shift in the balance of power that brought about the peace, the disappearance of the Warsaw Pact did much to symbolize the new power realities. No longer would there be some kind of equilibrium between the two opposed halves of Europe. In its place would be a dynamic West, looking to the Soviet Union across an eastern Europe that was now in some kind of economic and strategic limbo. But unlike the episodes of decolonization earlier in the twentieth century, when many newly independent states had, at least formally, sought some kind of nonaligned status, the newly decolonized states of eastern Europe showed alarming indications of wishing instead to defect to the West.

Again, however, the moment of the Warsaw Pact's disappearance is best understood as an element within the armistice at the end of the Cold War. What had been agreed at that point was that eastern Europe was no longer to be the Soviet Union's political and military preserve. Beyond that, the armistice was silent. What would become of the eastern half of the continent—in terms of its future economic links, political development, and military alignments—remained yet to be addressed, let alone determined. If the scrapping of the former Soviet sphere in eastern Europe was the minimum requirement needed to make the armistice acceptable, it remained to be seen what the maximum extent of Western demands would yet turn out to be. The European armistice had been struck: the full settlement was still pending.

THE DISSOLUTION OF THE USSR

The next ingredient of the European peace was another not imposed by the West, and indeed a development about which the West was seriously unenthusiastic when it took place. The dissolution of the USSR was propelled almost exclusively by internal dynamics, and not by external intervention. What sealed its fate was the failed August coup of 1991 in Moscow. The plotters 'had intended to save the party and the Union. Instead, they hastened the demise of both' (Reynolds 2000: 575).

The Cold War in this sense finally ended with the implosion of one of the former protagonists, the USSR, first behind the fig-leaf of the CIS, and finally into the successor states. As with previous peace settlements, this might be regarded as either the infliction of a loss of territory (as on Germany at Versailles), or as a kind of partition (as with Germany at the end of the Second World War). But the situation is more complex than these superficial analogies might suggest.

There were two separate, but interconnected, issues at stake in this matter, both concerning the 'identity' of the party defeated in the Cold War. As noted above, it is at this point that the relationship between the distributive and regulative dimensions of the post-Cold War peace becomes difficult to disentangle, and recalcitrant to satisfactory analysis. At one level, the West certainly sought and welcomed a visible transformation in the political identity of the USSR: this was a fitting price to exact for its defeat in the Cold War. Hence, economic restructuring on market principles and political liberalization were necessary components of the new identity that was to be created for the former Soviet Union. Just as Germany and Japan had been reinvented after 1945, so would be Russia after 1991.

Whether or not this would, or should, entail a territorial dismemberment was another, but not independent, matter. Hobsbawm (1994) assessed that the Russian empire would have dissolved with the other empires in 1919, had it not been for the Bolshevik Revolution. If this was correct, then the problem was that the dissolution of the *Soviet* state would most likely bring in its wake a host of territorial issues related to nationalities, and independence for the constituent republics. While the West clearly welcomed the former, it was much more guarded about the latter, as it neither wished an unstable region on the Russian periphery, nor the attendant dangers of nuclear proliferation that would follow from any such dissolution. The dilemma then was whether it would be possible to change the political system at the heart of the Union, without the risk of such negative consequences as well.

The problem of inducing Soviet/Russian transformation has, for the West, been one of finding means that would not obstruct the ends, when at the same time the means also had a tendency to become the ends. It was hardly conceivable that there could be a proper ending of the Cold War, nor a stable peace in its aftermath, without some public acknowledgement of the demise of the ideological and political system that had sustained it for the preceding four decades. Such a transformation could be the only valid symbol of the end of the Cold War, and the exaction of such a price is one that has come to be accepted practice in the aftermath of great global wars. At that level, the emergence of a Russia committed to Western economic and political values was sought as an end in itself.

But this was also a means to an end. There could be no long-term confidence in the stability of the post-Cold War peace, without palpable faith in the conversion of the old Soviet system. As long as the *ancien regime* remained in existence, there could be no assurance against a recrudescence of the Cold War because, in the Hobbesian sense, there would remain a 'known disposition thereto'. At this level, the reshaping of Soviet politics and society was a means to the creation of a genuine post-Cold War order. But Soviet transformation as end, and Soviet transformation as means, did not necessarily sit comfortably with each other. There was the rub.

This central tension can be explored in a number of related respects. It was evidently the pre-existing shift in the distribution of power that allowed the West to encourage Soviet transformation, and increasingly to take a leading role in prescribing the directions in which it should develop. At this point, the analogy with, say, America's treatment of post-1945 Japan might be thought instructive. Such was America's unconditional victory over Japan that it found itself in a position to set about a root and branch reform of the very institutional bases of the Japanese economy, society, and polity. In due course, and certainly by 1947, the onset of the Cold War had led to subtle changes in the American conversion of Japan and, of course, the peace settlement was not finally reached until this phase was substantially in place. In the same way, there have been fluctuations in what the

West has thought it possible, and sensible, to aim to do with Soviet society, and these ambitions have been influenced by wider political and strategic calculations. To that extent, Soviet transformation could never be regarded as an end in itself, regardless of context. Perceptions of the balance of power, and the residual dangers in pressing Soviet reform too far and too fast, have continued to shape the agenda of a reconstruction of Russian identity.

At the same time, assessments of the degree of change possible within Russia have been instrumental in setting the security agenda, and in adjusting perceptions of the balance of power. The more Russia was seen to be responding to Western preferences, and the more stable its reform projects appeared to be, the greater has been the Western inclination to cooperate with it. Unhappily, viewed from Moscow, this has issued in a relationship more neglectful of Russian national interests. Conversely, the more obdurate Russian policy has appeared, and the more faltering and recidivist its economic performance, the more inclined has been the West to punish its disciple, by holding back on economic assistance, or by sheer indifference. When doing so, it has undercut the basis of political support for the very policies preferred by the West. In these various ways, the West has been grappling with an insoluble conundrum. How was it to exploit its indisputable preponderance to reshape the Soviet system—in ways that would contribute to a stable post-Cold War order—without at the same time exacting concessions from Russia that could come only at a cost to the reformers' position domestically, and to Russia's relations with the West internationally? Another way of making the same point is to say that the West has been unclear whether the weakness of Russia has been a situation to be exploited, or a dangerous prospect to be treated with caution and concession.

The second illustration is a specific case of the above general propositions. It relates to the matter of NATO enlargement that will be discussed in greater detail below. In the present context, however, this demonstrated the same tension between Western means and ends. For some, the rationale for NATO enlargement was to serve as a form of social pressure to induce good behaviour on the part of Russia. There was, in this appraisal, no intention on the part of the West to isolate or ostracize Russia. Implicit in this, once NATO had embarked on its expansion eastwards, was that the question of Russia's future relationship with NATO lay squarely in Russian hands. If it was able to sustain its economic restructuring, and consolidate a liberal political system, then all things were possible in that relationship; if not, not. This is the scarcely veiled language of Brzezinski (1995: 31):

Prudence therefore dictates that the issues of Russia's association be kept open, depending on how fast, deep, and wide the expansion of the European Union will be and whether the Euro-Atlantic security system matches that expansion. The question of Russia's participation will have to be faced only when a wider NATO has actually reached the frontiers of Russia—and only if by then Russia satisfies the basic criteria for membership.

The logic of the argument is that, if Russia is excluded, then this will be down to the failures of the reform in Russia. The two issues are not, however, independent of each other. The problem with this argument is, of course, that bringing NATO up to Russia's frontier is unlikely to do much to enhance the political standing of those in Russia seeking to build a good working relationship with the West. As has been documented on the basis of studies of Russian opinion, and stated categorically, 'it was the issue of NATO expansion, above all, that undermined the influence of liberal westernizers in Russian foreign policy' (Light, White, and Lowenhardt 2000: 79).

The third version of this same basic tension is that which brings us back to the relationship between the distributive and the regulative dimensions of the settlement. Those critics of Versailles who believe that peace failed because it was too lenient are firmly of the distributive school. Their position is that if the distributive peace had been sufficiently effective, nothing else would have mattered. Provided that the balance of power had been sufficiently robust, it mattered little how resentful, wounded, and revisionist was the resulting sentiment in the vanquished state. This becomes irrelevant because compliance is unimportant: the peace is maintained by active enforcement, not by passive consent. The problem with Versailles, on this reckoning, was that it was not sufficiently severe to be reliant upon the distributive settlement alone. At the same time, it was too punitive in its distributive dimension to hold out any real prospect of regulative compliance being able to do the job for it.

As previously argued, transformation of a defeated enemy can often be regarded as part of a distributive settlement. This was palpably so in Germany after 1945 when both its halves were reshaped, not simply as ideological statements, but as means to the consolidation of the balance of power. But it can be part of a regulative strategy also, the expectation being that a defeated power, once reformed, will become an active participant in the maintenance of the peace settlement imposed upon it. Both Japan and the Federal Republic provide perfect illustrations of this outcome.

In this sense, the West has also faced a choice as to whether its strategy for the transformation of the Soviet Union was to be understood as part of a distributive, or as part of a regulative, peace. At the extremes, both may end up being mutually exclusive; in the middle, there is the danger of falling between the two stools. The West has been sufficiently distributive to wish for an open conversion of the Soviet Union to its own political and economic system. The question is whether, in doing so, it has eroded the basis on which Russian compliance with the Western order might otherwise have been built. If so, it may well have weakened that order, but also have contributed to self-destructive tendencies within Russia itself. This is one such gloomy prognosis:

Russia is still continuing to disintegrate as a state . . . We can no longer say that, whatever else occurs in the future, Russia will be one of the principal players on the international stage . . . Its tragedy is so great that even its future existence is in question. The true magnitude of this catastrophe has been seriously underestimated. (Hobsbawm 2000: 45)

Such a scenario is perhaps unduly apocalyptic. But even a more moderate statement of it would underline just how fateful for the Soviet and the Russian states has been the end of the Cold War, and the settlement resulting from it.

THE RUSSIAN–AMERICAN BILATERAL RELATIONSHIP

The Soviet–American relationship constituted much of the Cold War. Accordingly, the redefinition of that relationship had to find its place as a major element within the post-Cold War peace. Although, as will be seen in the next chapter, the implications of these changes have extended far beyond Europe, it was also through the instrumentality of the evolving

Russian–American relationship that the settlement in Europe has been progressively defined. Nowhere can we see more clearly the formative stages of the European peace than in the shifting basis of that relationship. It lends weight to the suggestion that the peace has so far developed in three stages: the armistice; the co-operative phase of peacemaking; and the more antagonistic phase in which the distributive peace has been finally marked out.

There is a reasonably solid consensus in the literature about these phases of the relationship. The armistice phase was underpinned by the rapidity of the changes that took place, the consequent surprise that it induced, and the residual fear that if the United States did not tread warily, major unrest might result. During the armistice, the terms of the peace were conditioned by these influences, as much as by the habitual regard still retained for the Soviet Union as the other remaining superpower, with its formidable nuclear arsenal. The second, and cooperative phase, was characterized by prospects for Western economic aid, a continuing strategic partnership between Russia and America, and solicitous American concern not to weaken the position of its favoured Russian leaders. As for Russia, its behaviour was dominated by a compliant regard for Western policies. Subsequently, Russian commentators have dismissed this as the phase of 'romanticism' (Nikitin 1997: 149), during which 'Russia merely followed the Western lead', and failed to formulate 'the new Russian national interests' (Arbatov 1997: 17–18). By 1993–4, a new and more realist phase had set in, the atmosphere of which described a new turn in the relationship. On the side of the United States, this was captured by a downgrading of the relationship with Russia, increasing scepticism about the viability of the reform programme, and by attaching greater priority to wider aspects of its European strategy. It was consistent with the faltering of Clinton's determined efforts to forge a 'strategic alliance' or a 'new democratic partnership' with Russia, and a widespread sense in the United States that 'an alliance with a reforming Russia had run its course' (M. Cox 1994b: 643, 646). As regards Russia, the hallmarks of this phase were a more robust assertion of its own national interests, a heightened disillusionment with the returns from its cooperative policy with the West, and a greater appreciation of the remaining conflicts of interest between the two former enemies and now would-be partners.

It would, of course, be possible to argue that the peace was established in

1989–91, and that what has evolved since then is merely a departure from that new status quo. However, given the enormity of the shocks of 1989, and the need for a period of time to adjust to them, we are more likely to capture the provisional nature of these first reactions to the end of the Cold War by referring to them as a kind of armistice. During this phase, the agreements on Germany were put in place, the USSR cooperated with the West over the Gulf crisis and war, the Conventional Forces in Europe (CFE) Treaty was completed, and all the major initial adjustments to the end of the Cold War were laid down.

During the next phase, and while there remained great potential threats to Western interests from nuclear proliferation, there was considerable incentive to hold out a moderate peace in which Russian interests would be properly safeguarded. Russia, for its part, had at that time every reason to reciprocate to these terms. Presentation of its amenable face to Washington and to Bonn seemed the best way of securing financial support, retaining some residual status as a semi-superpower with which the West felt it incumbent to continue to deal, and regaining its place as part of Europe.

Arguably, it was only after 1994 that the final terms of the end of the Cold War were clearly set out to Russia. These have become more assertive, and shown a more marked disregard for Russian sensitivities, in proportion with the assessment that Russia was now much less in a position to damage Western interests. Just as Germany in 1919 complained that the final terms of Versailles contravened the assurances of the armistice, so Russians in the 1990s have been confronted with a peace settlement that has departed noticeably from the terms indicated in the armistice phase of 1989–91.

The shift occurred on both sides of the relationship. 'The change in Russian foreign policy from 1992–93 to 1993–94', Garthoff (1994: 781) informs us, 'can most succinctly be described as a turn from a more self-effacing and passive role . . . to a more assertive pursuit of national interests'. This was expressed through a refocusing of foreign policy concerns. In particular, much greater emphasis was placed upon Russia's relations with its 'near abroad' (Marantz 1997: 87; Shearman 1995b: 131). It was in the context of this reorientation that the Chechen issue took on a new prominence (Arbatov 1997: 19).

At the same time, the United States downgraded its preoccupations with Russia, Yeltsin, and reform in order to pursue a more broadly based set of interests. 'Sensitive to the charge that it had tilted too far towards Moscow and Yeltsin', M. Cox (2000: 270) suggests, 'Washington now began to make a much greater effort in building stronger relations with countries other than Russia'. In sum, by early 1994, we are told that 'influential figures in Russia and the West were warning of deteriorating relations' (Marantz 1997: 78).

It might be tempting then to think that it was this simultaneous parting of the ways that contributed to the distancing in the Russian–American relationship. But another, and perhaps more revealing, interpretation of the same development is as the imposition of this more severe peace settlement, during the final phase, and one that revealed the full price Washington now felt able to exact from the end of the Cold War. This, in turn, explains why Russia had to be more self-regarding of its own perceived interests. To be precise, it was not a worsening of the Russian–American relationship that led to a new phase of the post-Cold War order; rather was it the move to lay down the definitive terms of the post-Cold war peace settlement that led to a worsening of the relationship.

Why then had this phase come about? Most accounts seem to imply that the deterioration was little more than the unintended consequence of mutual disillusionment, and the onset of a greater realism on the part of both sides. Westernizers in Russia found it increasingly difficult to justify to sceptical domestic constituencies what benefits had been gained from compliance with Western strategies. And the argument that such a foreign policy course was essential as a means to the end of domestic reform itself—which had been Gorbachev's line—became much less persuasive, the more domestic disenchantment with these reforms developed anyway. The disillusionment was intensified when the West's rhetoric was not matched by its actions. 'NATO–Russian relations from 1993–99', complains Antonenko (1999/2000: 126), 'produced more political declarations and myths than practical joint action or decision-making'. This seemed only to confirm those lingering suspicions in Russia that the Cold-War NATO leopard was incapable, in any case, of changing its spots (Dannreuther 1999/2000: 153). On the domestic front, Russians were to be further disappointed by the failure to emerge from the West of anything like the levels of financial support anticipated by the early rhetoric. 'Having encouraged . . . Russia down the path of painful economic restructuring', M. Cox (2000: 263) reminds us, 'neither Congress nor the American people were prepared to extend very much material aid'. For its part, according to this perspective, Washington drifted away from Russia as it too became disappointed with the achievements of its Russian policy to date. This had contributed to a disregard for other European interests, and had been naively based on woefully optimistic assessments about the prospects for change in Russia. The new realism in Washington about the scale of the problems still to be overcome in Russia just happened to coincide with the new realism in Moscow about the disappointed hopes of the West.

Persuasive up to a point as this is, it is by no means clear that this account gets fully to the heart of the matter. It relies too much upon drift and inadvertence, and does not take seriously enough the extent to which the evolution of Russian–American relations up to 1994 had still not fully come to terms with the issues left unresolved by the end of the Cold War. Matters had been left in limbo that now had to be addressed definitively. It was this exercise in peacemaking that brought to the surface the disparity in Russian and American interests, rather than simply the fading of a set of unrealistic illusions. One author comes close to such an assessment when he points to the *temporary* nature of the earlier phase of accommodation:

The idea of strategic partnership with the United States was a response to a particular set of circumstances that arose after the collapse of the Soviet Union, which cannot be expected to endure . . . The notion of a partnership with the United States tended to gloss over the very real foreign policy differences that were subsequently revealed, most serious of which was the clash of geopolitical interests that emerged within Europe. (Buszynski 1996: 70)

This argument is revealing, but does not go quite far enough in defining the true nature of this incompatibility. What gave rise to it were the peace terms that Washington now chose to set out for the end of the Cold War. These, as will be seen shortly, amounted to a very substantial marginalization of Russia. Again, however, the critical point to note is that this was not the incidental outcome of a failure to establish a more productive relationship; it was instead an intrinsic part of the final and definitive post-Cold War peace. This mapped out the full extent of the redistribution of power that was to be entailed by the end of the Cold War.

That such a marginalization of Russia has been a trend of the years since 1994 is scarcely in doubt, and certainly goes beyond any mere Russian paranoia. Its principal instantiation, to be discussed below, is the enlargement of NATO, but it is a process that extends beyond that issue alone. 'The plain fact is', Haslam (1998: 119) asserts, 'that both the enlargement of NATO and the expansion of the EU relegate Russia to the margins of Europe'. If this is indeed the case, is it simply the outcome of policy drift, and of inauspicious combinations of circumstance? Or should it more properly be viewed as the real manifestation of the distributive peace that has been progressively put in place since the mid-1990s?

Some Russian commentators are in no doubt. 'The tension in US–Russian relations today', is one expression of the point, 'stems largely from the inability, or refusal, of American policy-makers to respect the proper limits of US power' (Mikoyan 1998: 112). The demarcation of 'the proper limits of US power' may be read as a transcription of the post-Cold War terms of peace. During the last several years, these have been inscribed in a number of Western, and specifically American, policies. The most salient demonstration was to be provided, in 1999, by the NATO war with Serbia over Kosovo which, within Russia, 'had clearly been seen as a watershed' (Light, White, and Lowenhardt 2000: 80). The NATO decisions to proceed with its intervention, and to mount a bombing campaign against Serbia, in the face of Russian protests, did more than anything else to underline Moscow's new impotence. Cynically, but perceptively, Russian observers saw this as the reality of the 'new world order': 'Russia's political elites faced the strongest evidence yet of their own isolation and inability to influence NATO policies, even on matters close to Russian territory' (Antonenko 1999/2000: 131, 124).

This is a point that Ikenberry himself has conceded, even if it places some strain on his own account of the institutionalized restraint that was Washington's own preferred strategy. Writing about the end of the 1980s, he maintained that the United States was prevented from pursuing 'a hard-line and aggressive foreign policy' by its own complex of institutions, and that this 'made Gorbachev's reforms and accommodations less risky' (2000: 255). However, in his analysis of the NATO bombing of Serbia in 1999, he notes 'a new path of military intervention outside alliance territory', and worries that it may have a long-term impact on views of American power (2000: 273). Evidently, on Ikenberry's own admission, the institutional restraints had not been sufficient to prevent Washington from this course of action.

This was a strategic reality that had nowhere been intimated during the armistice of 1989–91. It revealed the extent to which the new freedom to assert a distributive peace had taken priority in Western policy over any lingering quest for a regulative order, in which Russia would be encouraged to comply because it was in its interests to do so. The search for a moderate peace was now all but over. Even those token institutions that had been put in place to create the appearance of negotiation and consultation with Russia proved ineffective. Those sweeteners for the bitter pill of NATO enlargement, such as the Russia–NATO Founding Act of Mutual Relations (1997) 'failed not only to ensure joint decision-making, but even a working mechanism for crisis-management' during the Kosovo War (Antonenko 1999/2000: 125).

What the second half of the 1990s revealed was the artificial basis of the original terms of the armistice. These had been set out, and were for some time to be honoured, largely because of Washington's fears about the fallout from the domestic Soviet/Russian crisis. Once it was thought increasingly safe to ignore this concern, a harsher peace could be—and so was—imposed. Liberated from its anxieties about Russian implosion, 'the United States had no need for a global partner in Russia' (Buszynski 1996: 88), and the more exacting terms of the post-Cold War peace could be safely unveiled.

This makes a hollow mockery of one manifesto: 'it is easy to forget that, in the nineteenth century, Russia was very much an integral part of the European state system and a leading figure in the Concert of Europe . . . After a long interlude, a democratizing and liberalizing Russia is gradually reclaiming its rightful place within Europe' (Danilov and De Spiegeleire 1998: 50). Such a role is no longer Russia's to claim, and it is the post-Cold War peace that determines what its 'rightful place' will be. For the time being, the peace inscribed in Europe reflects a more hostile vision, in which the suggestion that Russia 'should be readmitted and reincorporated into the twenty-first century's equivalent of the Concert of Europe naturally seems not only an affront but dangerously naïve' (Haslam 1998: 120).

THE ENLARGEMENT OF NATO

Such a perception is reinforced by the final element of the European settlement, namely the decision to enlarge NATO eastwards. This new policy was encouraged by the central European powers, and responded to warmly by President Clinton. By late 1993, 'Russian opposition to NATO's expansion was loud and clear' (Marantz 1997: 93), and this symbolized the new turn that had been taken in Russian–American relations. Without doubt, it seemed to embody a degree of punitive intent. 'The West appears to be punishing Russia, most notably through the process of NATO enlargement, for its failure to conform to the norms and values of the democratic and anti-imperialist standards of the modern self-contained national state' (Dannreuther 1999/2000: 154). But more significantly, it denoted a marked shift in the post-Cold War balance of power. Former members of the Warsaw Pact have not simply defected from that alliance, but have joined what was once its opposition.

We must then be careful to distinguish between some of the motivations for the NATO enlargement, and what might instead be termed its historically objective meaning. Haslam, himself a harsh critic of enlargement, enumerates various reasons for this policy initiative: eastern European desires; German policy objectives; institutional interests within NATO; and American electoral politics (Haslam 1998: 120). Equally, some have supported enlargement with 'a potentially dangerous Russia in mind', whereas others have opposed it 'not to antagonize Russia' (Bertram 1995: 31). No doubt these calculations, in varying degrees, all played their part. But to view NATO enlargement as no more than the sum of these parts is to miss the larger point. NATO enlargement finally took place because it could, and a peace was instituted on that basis, because the end of the Cold War had resulted in precisely such a new distribution of power.

For all the reasons already considered, this logic did not immediately manifest itself in full-blown form. The march eastwards of NATO represented not just a triumphal progress, but the undertaking of significant new responsibilities and liabilities by the West, and by the United States in particular. These were not to be undertaken lightly, and were not. There were various pauses at way stations en route. In 1994, Russia had accepted, but not without considerable heel dragging, its own package for admission in the Partnership for Peace with NATO (Marantz 1997: 95) In 1997, and to mollify opposition to proposed enlargement, the Founding Act established a Permanent Joint Council between NATO and Russia (Reynolds 2000: 626), however inoperative it was to be during the ensuing Kosovo affair. But the course of enlargement itself has proved largely irresistible.

Interestingly, Western supporters of this course were prone to justify it as being in Russia's best interests, whatever the Russians might mistakenly think. 'It is not in the interests of Russia', one team of analysts proclaimed, ' . . . to have a zone of instability, renewed nationalism and potential conflict on its western flank' (Asmus, Kueler, and Larrabee 1993: 37). But others advanced the cause in a more forthright way: enlargement could now proceed because Russia was in no position to resist. Some appealed to the wisdom of what had already been done with regard to the adhesion of a reunified Germany to NATO, and drew the appropriate lesson that Western policy must be as steadfast on enlargement as it had been on that earlier occasion. Brzezinski (1995: 35) warned that the 'Kremlin must be made to understand that bluster and threats will be neither productive nor effective and may even accelerate the process of expansion'. In short, Moscow would lose if it acquiesced, but lose also if it chose to demur. What Brzezinski failed to point out was the dissimilarity in the conduct of the two episodes: German unification was pursued with due regard for Soviet concerns whereas, as Brzezinski's own words amply reveal, NATO enlargement was to proceed regardless. It should happen because it could, and this amply confirmed the different stage that the peace settlement had by then reached.

One former US diplomat has spoken of the current European security architecture as representing a blend of collective security, and spheres of interest (Goodby 1998: 199–200). He thought that 'for a long time to come, a hybrid system of security will prevail' (1998: 179). The justification was that, rhetorically, there still remains the cloak of a continuing aspiration towards a Europe-wide security system. At the same time, NATO enlargement, as long as it is open-ended and does not preclude even the very remote possibility of eventual incorporation of Russia, can itself be presented as in conformity with that ideal. In practice, however, it must be realized that the latest phase of European post-Cold War peacemaking has resulted in a distributive settlement that further entrenches an enlarged sphere of interest, and gives a clear priority to collective defence over collective security. Paradoxically, this same trend may also have reinforced the legitimacy of Russia's own quest for a residual sphere of influence within its near-abroad (Zagorski 1994: 78). This outcome may be hybrid in name and appearance, but its governing logic is strikingly one-dimensional. It is a distributive settlement that has left Russia at the margins because of a belief that this is where it can now safely be left.

What drove this process was a growing confidence that Russia was less important, because less potentially damaging to Western interests. This calculation fed off, and reinforced, a sense of the progressive marginalization of that country. The trend is captured in the sharp contrast between the handling of the process of German unification in 1990, and the enlargement of NATO in the second half of the 1990s. On the former, the USSR was pressed and cajoled to accept Germany's continuing membership of NATO. While this was an exaction of power, and in the face of an almost irresistible momentum, Gorbachev was also persuaded that opposition to it was inconsistent with the Soviet Union's own goals. Hence his obstruction of it desisted quickly, and surprisingly meekly. The same cannot be said of the latter case. Russia's leaders have not been persuaded that NATO enlargement corresponds with their interests in any respect. Their objections have not been answered, but simply ignored. This is the measure of the distance travelled in the consolidation of the European settlement between 1990 and the latter part of the decade. The Soviet Union may once have surrendered conditionally to a relatively benign armistice; Russia has now capitulated to the harsher terms of the final peace.

5

THE GLOBAL TERMS
OF PEACE

Historians of former peace settlements have told us how important, especially in the case of the Vienna settlement of 1815, was a carefully wrought
and judicious distributive settlement. The demands of the international
society, in that instance, required that the impositions upon France be
moderate. 'The statesmen of Vienna understood', we are instructed by one
eminent historian, 'that a European balance required at least as much
assurance as deterrence, that a *sage repartition des forces* was needed for
moral, political, and psychological equilibrium rather than merely for balance of power' (Schroeder 1992: 697). It is this *repartition des forces*, or the
distributive settlement after the Cold War in its global aspect, that is the
burden of this chapter. What has been its content and how sagacious its
terms?

That the post-Cold War order should indeed be thought analogous to
such a peace settlement is, once again, not a radical thought. It emerged
clearly in the commentary of one noted former practitioner. Content to
regard the Cold War as being, indeed, a form of war, Brzezinski (1992: 31)
was drawn by the analogy to suggest that we think of its aftermath 'in
terminology derived from the usual outcomes of wars, that is, in terms of
victory and defeat, capitulation and postwar settlement'. Thus conceived,
what was his judgement about the nature of the peace exacted at war's
end? Brzezinski speculated about the various ways in which the Cold War
might have been resolved earlier, and about the concessions that might
have been made by either side. He came to the conclusion that the actual
terms of peace would have been unimaginable at any earlier stage of the
Cold War: 'the most likely conventional Western scenario of victory has

been exceeded to a degree that is truly staggering'. This is but another way of saying that the result of the Cold War has been dramatically asymmetrical. Does this mean that, in global terms, a draconian peace has been exacted? If so, how much sagacity is there in this distributive peace?

Seductive as is this imagery of a post-Cold War peace settlement, it is necessary first of all to dispose of certain difficulties in its application. There are at least four of these that need to be addressed. When this has been accomplished, we can then review the terms of the global settlement. This will be done by means of illustration, rather than by attempting the impossible task of presenting a comprehensive account of all areas of international life that have been reshaped by the end of the Cold War. These illustrations will be divided into two categories. The first is geographic or regional, and will explore the terms of peace as they have applied to Pacific Asia and the Middle East. The second is functional, and will consider the peace settlement as it applied to the principal area traditionally governed by peace settlements, namely the distribution of military power.

A PROBLEMATIC PEACE

There are a number of reasons why the conception of the post-Cold War order as a peace settlement in its global aspect is problematic. These do not undermine the utility of this framework; indeed, they actually reinforce it. However, in order to see the full complexity of the analytical points at stake, it is necessary immediately to confront these issues.

The first concerns the relationship between the European settlement, as previously discussed, and the wider global settlement. It derives from fundamental appraisals of the nature of the Cold War confrontation. How extensive was the Cold War and where was its centre of gravity? Was it a European phenomenon, and were its global manifestations simply symptoms of this central clash? If this was indeed the case, then the European settlement should be regarded as the core peace settlement of the Cold War. There was no need for a settlement as such elsewhere, as the Cold War would have disappeared in any case with its resolution at its epicentre in Europe. Regional transformations in other parts of the world should not, from this point of view, be regarded as part of the post-Cold War peace settlement, but rather as consequences of the one and only peace settlement that emerged in Europe. There is no *global* peace settlement to review because none was put in place, however momentous and universal the consequences of the European settlement that were to be experienced elsewhere.

This objection has some superficial appeal. It corresponds with the widespread perception that it was, after all, the course of events in Europe that represented the end of the Cold War. If any single event marked the passing of the Cold War, it was probably the large gathering of leaders in Paris at the end of 1990. And yet at that point, there had been little fundamental change in other areas of the world, apart from Europe. Accordingly, it is difficult to see why any settlement was required beyond the one that had already emerged there.

Appealing as this objection is, it misses one central point. This was seized upon very early by Robert Tucker (1990: 94):

The end of Europe's division signals as well the end of the great conflict that has dominated world politics since World War II. It does so not because, as the conventional view has it, the Cold War arose out of the division of Europe and will therefore end when this division is ended, but because the abandonment by the Soviet Union of its core external interest marks the onset of the long-term decline of Soviet global power and influence ... It is not so much, then, the end of Europe's division that signals the end of the Cold War as it is the circumstance that above all led to this end: the decline of Soviet power.

The point is an astute one and clarifies the general issue under consideration. Given that the Soviet Union was a global superpower, then the terms of the peace settlement consequent upon the end of the Cold War could not be other than global in scope. If what needed to be distributed were the spheres of Soviet power and tutelage, the reallocation of these could not be confined to Europe alone. A global peace settlement was thus required, and one was duly forthcoming, even if it was to fall short of comprehensiveness.

This very formulation, however, moves us closer to a second type of objection. This concerns the relationship between the balance of power and the distributive peace. In essence, it enquires which is the cause and which the effect. While it may not be important to make any such distinction simply to understand what the new distribution was, it remains vital to separate these out if we wish to understand the post-Cold War peace as a fundamental element of the post-Cold War order. Succinctly expressed, what is doing the order-producing work here—the new balance of power, or the peace settlement which enshrines it?

The point can be clarified by historical example. In a controversial piece of revisionist writing, Paul Schroeder once challenged the conventional wisdom that the Vienna settlement of 1815 was underwritten by a balance of power. In its stead, Schroeder maintained that there was nothing balanced about the post-1815 distribution of power. In fact, it was based on a kind of bi-hegemonial distribution, dominated by Britain and Russia, on the two flanks of the continent. These imbalances of power 'were no accident', but instead represented 'the goals Britain and Russia had pursued throughout the Napoleonic wars and were the fruits of their victory' (Schroeder 1992: 689). What is so pertinent about Schroeder's argument is that, despite its denial of *balance* of power as a constitutive element of the Vienna order, it certainly gives pride of place to the *distribution* of power in maintaining that order. This is explicitly acknowledged in his claim that its 'essential power relations were hegemonic, not balanced', and that 'a hegemonic distribution of power . . . made the system work' (1992: 684).

The more general issue to which this relates is whether it is the peace settlement that is productive of the ensuing order, or is merely reflective of its prior existence. This can be seen in another facet of traditional peace settlements, namely their military provisions, which will be explored further below. A telling history of post-war 'enforced disarmament' reveals the strenuous efforts that were made in 1815 to diminish French fortifications, as it was believed that recent French aggression had been encouraged by its unduly favourable military position. And yet it was not these disarmament provisions of the Peace of Paris that were to contain French power during the remainder of the nineteenth century. The peace was made at the 'cusp' of a historical trend that had already turned away from French preponderance. Accordingly, the judgement has been expressed that it was not the efforts of the peacemakers, 'but the changing economic and demographic balance . . . which preserved the Peace of Paris for four decades' (Towle 1997: 89). This can be contrasted with the efforts of the peacemakers in 1919, when the underlying measures of power remained still favourable to Germany, and the peacemakers were working against the tide rather than with it.

In short, the analytical dilemma is whether peace settlements issue in new distributions of power, or whether it is the new distributions of power that underlie the peace settlements: they can either reinforce, or erode, stability but do not themselves create it. Where this matters critically is in the third potential objection to the idea of a global post-Cold War settlement. This relates back to the problematic relationship between the European settlement and events elsewhere. Indeed, it has implications for events within Europe as well. At base, the issue is how, and how meaningfully, we can make any demarcation between the actual settlement at the end of the Cold War, and the ensuing train of events that was consequent upon it. This becomes all the more problematic, given that the framework of this study employs the notion of a constructed peace that is protracted in time. If almost everything is considered as peacemaking, when does that stop? How do we distinguish the peacemaking from its later effects and revisions?

The point can initially be demonstrated within the European context. There is a considerable division of opinions about the core dynamics that led to the disintegration of the former Yugoslavia. Despite this, analysts are agreed at least that this was related to the end of the Cold War, if only in the minimal sense that it would not have happened as it did while the Cold War remained in place. But what are we then to conclude about this relationship? Should we regard the dismemberment of Yugoslavia as part of the European settlement, an aspect of the terms of peace by which the Cold War was drawn to a close? Or do we distance the relationship somewhat, and claim merely that the peace settlement in Europe created a new distribution of power which made possible, in turn, various chains of events: the collapse of Yugoslavia was one of those, but only contingently. It was most certainly not a part of the peace settlement as such.

If anything, this dilemma is even more acute in the case of the relationship between the global terms of peace, and the whole series of developments that took place around the world in the aftermath of the Cold War. Was this *the* peace? Or were these only related developments, consequent upon the peace already in place? The key to resolving this dilemma must once again be a focus upon those aspects that engaged with the demise of Soviet power. These, in turn, cannot be understood in separation from

American power and interests. 'The change from worldwide bipolarity to *unipolarity*', Betts (1993/4: 43) intimated, '*makes the global dimension of strategic competition irrelevant*'. The consequence of this, in terms of regional commitments, has been that if 'the United States intervenes somewhere now, it cannot be because of a derivative interest in the place as it affects the worldwide balance . . . but because of an intrinsic interest in the place itself'. Succinctly expressed, the function of the post-Cold War global settlement was precisely to bring about such a reordering of affairs in which the regional distributions that had become integrated into the Cold War would now be progressively extricated from it. A global settlement would be necessary to disassemble the hitherto existing structure created by the 'global dimension of strategic competition' during the Cold War.

This does not fully resolve all the problems of demarcation. Without doubt, the end of the Cold War was accompanied by a sequence of developments that indicated some progress towards the resolution of regional conflicts: there were 'peace processes' in the Gulf, Afghanistan, southern Africa, Cambodia, the Middle East, and elsewhere. Some of these preceded the 'official' ending of the Cold War, and some developed apace in its aftermath. There have also been 'internal' peace processes, such as that in Northern Ireland, which some commentators (M. Cox 1997) have linked directly to the wider contextual shifts associated with the end of the Cold War. The issue then is whether these peace processes should be seen as part of the global terms of post-Cold War peace, or merely as new initiatives that have resulted from the altered configuration of power put in place by the end of the Cold War. This third point then touches upon, and restates, the issues already addressed above—the relationship between the European and global settlements, and the relationship between peace settlements and distributions of power.

It also touches upon a fourth issue about the chronology of the peace settlement. As noted, peace processes in some regions gained momentum before 1989, and before the Cold War had properly been brought to an end. Are they to be considered part of the peace settlement or not? Otherwise expressed, to what extent was it the peace settlement that allowed the end of the Cold War to take place, rather than the end of the Cold War creating the necessary conditions for a peace settlement to be effected?

It was argued above that the 1815 settlement was in the happy position of enshrining the new distribution of power; it did not itself have to create it. Many of the problems associated with the 1919 settlement are accountable to exactly the opposite situation. Viewed in these terms, what assessment should be made of the settlement at the end of the Cold War?

This raises the question of when the Cold War should be thought to have ended. We tend to think of peace settlements as being negotiated once the war is ended. But peace settlements, or at least those provisional aspects of them embodied in armistices, may also be preconditions that allow the fighting to come to a halt. The prospective terms of peace can therefore be inducements for hostilities to end. In that sense, peace settlements serve a dual function—prospectively in encouraging an end to the fighting, and retrospectively in institutionalizing it when the fighting has actually stopped. This makes sense of the seeming puzzle that what might otherwise be regarded as aspects of the post-Cold War peace actually preceded 1989, whilst others came in its aftermath. Collectively, all were part of the global settlement, even though some preceded the final termination of hostilities, and were actually instrumental in bringing it about.

In short, it must be insisted that the core provisions of the global peace centred upon the redistribution in the wake of the collapse of Soviet power. Brzezinski places this in wider historical perspective when he observes that 'the collapse of the Soviet Union, which endured for some seventy years, is more than overshadowed by the disintegration of the great Russian empire, which lasted for more than three hundred years' (1992: 34). The global settlement had to deal with the historical consequences of both events—the demise of the Soviet Union and the disintegration of the Russian empire. It can now be traced in its regional and functional aspects.

THE SETTLEMENT IN PACIFIC ASIA

Superficially, there seemed to be a strong similarity between the ending of the Cold War in Pacific Asia, and in Europe, with respect to its asymmetrical impact on the Cold War alliances. In Europe, the Warsaw Pact disappeared whereas NATO endured. In Pacific Asia, the Soviet alliances—with Mongolia, North Korea, and Vietnam—likewise came to an end (Malik 1998: 147), whilst the USA's bilateral treaties were to persist. But the contrasts are more striking than this similarity. In the years immediately after the end of the Cold War, evidence for its end in East Asia was almost wholly absent. The contrast with Europe was frequently drawn. 'In Europe, the balance of power that dominated the continent since the late 1940s has been destroyed', noted one commentary, whereas, 'in Asia, the balance that has existed since the 1960s . . . has only been altered, and with effects that are not yet apparent' (Tucker 1990: 100–1). Others stressed that awareness of change had been much slower to develop in Asia than in Europe (Buzan and Segal 1994: 3). Others again claimed that the effects of globalization were more important in shaping the region than were the consequences of the end of the Cold War (Inoguchi 1995: 135). This scarcely sounds like the stuff of which global peace settlements are made.

It has been claimed that East Asia lacks the key structures and shared norms that define a working regional security system. In particular, it has been asserted, 'the region lacks a framework for regulating great-power relations . . . there is no developed security system embraced by Asia Pacific's leading powers' (Acharya 1999: 84). In that sense, if we accept the judgement, whatever has been put in place at the end of the Cold War does not amount to a regulative settlement. If there is a post-Cold War peace in Asia, it has been solely distributive in form.

What indeed had changed with the putative end of the Cold War? The surviving communist regimes of the world were still predominantly to be found there, China foremost amongst them. Virtually all the other strategic appurtenances of the Cold War remained stubbornly in place in the early 1990s—a divided Korean peninsula, a separate Taiwanese state, and US alliances with, and military presence in, both South Korea and Japan. As far as Pacific Asia was concerned, not only did there seem to be no post-Cold War peace settlement, but even the case that the Cold War was over at all was fairly hard to sustain.

However, the fact that black had not become white was not to deny change into various shades of grey. Communist political systems like China and Vietnam now ran increasingly 'open' and 'marketized' economies. There have been subtle shifts in relations among various great powers in the region. An increasingly economically beleaguered North Korea has become, at once, more dangerous and more responsive to gestures from the South. Things in East Asia moved more slowly after 1989 than they did in Europe, but that is not to say that they did not move at all.

In any case, the situation in Asia during the Cold War was not the same as it had been in Europe, and so both regions were changing from different starting places. Superficially, their Cold War roles might seem to have been remarkably similar. Both defeated powers, Germany and Japan, had been co-opted into Cold War blocs as integral elements of Cold War containment. These served the dual purpose of bolstering the constraints upon the Soviet Union, while simultaneously encouraging a radical transformation in the polity and society of the two defeated powers. Beyond this, the similarities begin to fade. Most of western Europe was incorporated into a single defensive structure under US auspices, and this worked in tandem with powerful institutions of economic and political integration. Such regional institutions were never replicated in Asia (Friedberg 1993/4: 22; Kupchan 1998: 44). To be sure, the United States established a series of bilateral Cold War alliances, and found it unnecessary to share the devising of the peace with Japan with any of its other allies (unlike the four powers that had functioned in Germany). But the Cold War in Asia was played out against a backdrop that diverged in critical respects from its European counterpart. In short, the fact that a post-Cold War settlement for Asia should differ from that in Europe is scarcely surprising, since each performed a different task. Above all, the settlements differ in consequence of the fact that Soviet power had never been as fundamental to the Asian Cold War structure as to that in Europe (Inoguchi 1995: 124). The effects of the peace settlement have, proportionately, been lighter.

The evidence that things have nonetheless changed, if not necessarily for the better, emerges most clearly from assessments of present and future security in East Asia. For all the diffidence about admitting to any radical transformation, it became increasingly apparent by the early 1990s that things in Asia were not standing still. At the very least, the generic logic that regional security systems would be increasingly set free from their former Cold War ties gave rise to an emerging note of pessimism about the future in this area (Friedberg 1993/4: 5). The regional impact seemed to be negative because the end of the Cold War had 'generated new and sometimes potentially very disturbing security issues' (Ball 1996b: 1). In standard format, the argument was simply that the elimination of the Cold War nuclear overlay would heighten the risk of local wars as, once again, it might be felt safe to fight conventional wars, or because regional states had become less reliant upon superpower protection (Mak 1998: 88). There was soon a chorus asserting that 'the ending of the Cold War has resulted in a more unpredictable Asia-Pacific' (Mak 1998: 92–3). In an adaptation of a slogan originally applied to Europe, two seasoned commentators concluded that 'Asia is in danger of heading back to the future' (Buzan and Segal 1994: 7). The problem with this diagnosis, as the same two authors conceded, was that in the Asian case, there was no future to go back to. Because Asia had been dominated by external powers since the intrusion of European colonialism in the nineteenth century, there was no indigenous tradition of conducting a regional international system. The danger was, in that sense, that removal of the Cold War would leave a vacuum, rather than a return to any kind of effective regional system (Acharya 1999: 84).

The tangible evidence for this instability and unpredictability—and the reason that some commentators were reluctant to concede the ending of the Cold War at all—was to be found in Pacific Asian patterns of arms imports and defence expenditure after 1989. While Europeans and North Americans were initially impatient for the promised post-Cold War peace dividends to materialize, secular trends towards reduced military expenditures did eventually begin to assert themselves. This was not to be the East Asian experience (Wattanayagorn and Ball 1996). In sharp contrast, we are informed, 'the region's military spending and arms procurement have grown rapidly' (Huxley and Willett 1999: 9), increasing by some 40 per cent during the very period that the European Cold War was markedly decelerating (Huxley and Willett 1999: 15). This was perhaps as much in response to a 'supply push' as to a 'demand pull', as Western and then Russian defence manufacturers sought for new markets to take the place of those that had collapsed closer to home (Huxley and Willett 1999: 23).

Such pessimistic assessments were given further leverage by events in the region later in the 1990s. By decade's end, well-placed observers felt that where once there had been bright prospects for a future 'Asian century', these were now giving way to dominant images of 'Asian insecurity'. What had prompted these fears was the further nuclearization of the region (including India and Pakistan, along with North Korea), the hard-hitting economic crisis in 1997–8, and the growing instability in states such as Indonesia (Dibb, Hale, and Prince 1999: 5). These negative developments, however, again pose the question: is this enhanced insecurity to be regarded as part of the post-Cold War settlement for the region, or simply the consequence of the dynamic and unpredictable forces unleashed by it?

If we examine the putative elements of the East Asian settlement, they revolve around two principal, and interlinked, themes. The first of these, of necessity, was the fate of Soviet power, and how its demise was to be configured into the new regional balance of power. This, in turn, was to lead to subsidiary effects, such as on aspects of Russia's relations with Japan and, more especially, on its relations with China. The second element that has been enshrined in that settlement, and serves as a point of continuity between the Cold War and post-Cold War security arrangements in the region, is the role of the United States. Not surprisingly, many of the expressed fears of instability were themselves associated with doubts about the future tenability of that role. In the remainder of this section, the interplay between Soviet decline and America's continuing role will be explored in the emerging regional context.

As already noted, Soviet power was certainly an important element in the Cold War balance of power in East Asia. From the time of the Sino-Soviet split in the 1960s, and the Nixon administration's playing of the 'China card' in the early 1970s, the USSR had become part of a loose quadruple balance of power. Japan, albeit tied to its American alliance, developed distinctive if limited links with its two communist neighbours. However, for a host of reasons, Soviet power was never to be as important in the Asian context as in the European, as its own centre of political and demographic gravity lay firmly in the west facing Europe, rather than on its Pacific maritime frontier. Moreover, in East Asia, the Soviet Union confronted historical rivals, over and above its Cold War competitor, the United States. Both China and Japan nursed territorial claims against the USSR and the tacit combination of an unfriendly China, Japan, and United States served to dilute, if not to neutralize, the efficacy of Soviet policy in the region.

The end of the Cold War has not changed this essential picture, but has if anything drawn it more sharply. If part of the European settlement in the 1990s was a progressive marginalization of Russia, and a growing indifference to its ruffled sensibilities, then much the same was to occur in East Asia. The only real difference was that, in Pacific Asia, Soviet power had less distance to fall. The best illustration of this is offered by American responses to the North Korean nuclear programmes, in which Washington seized the initiative without any reference to Russia's former links with that state: 'To Russia, it was therefore natural that, as a major power, it should be involved in negotiations on the North Korean nuclear issue. However, once bilateral negotiations began between Washington and Pyongyang, Russia was completely left out of the process' (Harada 1997: 63).

This marginalization was not something that had to be imposed by the West, as it simply reflected the new realities of the situation. However, Russia's exclusion was highly symbolic. It was a clear demonstration that, in post-Cold War Asia, Russia had lost its entitlement to be consulted on an issue that related to nuclear weapons and proliferation, and just as significantly, that concerned a former member of the Soviet sphere of interest. 'The real reason for Russia's marginalisation', be it noted, 'is its weakened political, military and economic power' (Harada 1997: 69), not because the West had decided that this should be so. Russia had been ignored because it could be.

The recession of Russian power from the region has, of course, had knock-on effects on other aspects of the regional balance of power. In particular, it has drawn attention to the potential role of China. The effects of the end of the Cold War on China were complex and ambivalent. On the one hand, the collapse of Soviet power, both globally and within the Pacific region specifically, was troublesome for China as it removed one significant counterweight to the United States, and held out the grim prospect of an even more assertive and interventionist US policy. At the same time, the eclipse of the Soviet Union raised China's own status in the region: it could claim to have discovered the magic formula that had so completely eluded the Soviet regime—namely that which allowed the perpetuation of a centralist political system with economic liberalization and reform. Close observers thus began to speak of a 'new strategic architecture' in the region, and of the worrisome prospect that the 'country cited as being most likely to upset the power equilibrium is China' (Dibb 1995: 70). Others spoke explicitly of China as the chief beneficiary of the withdrawal of Soviet power. 'Wherever there had been Soviet influence in a third country', it was suggested, 'China filled the vacuum' (Ross 1999: 83–4).

This was scarcely the redistribution that the West sought consciously to effect and, as such, highlights the double-sided nature of the peace settlement at the end of the Cold War. The emphasis on the West's victory draws our attention to Western interests, and to the terms that the West has seen fit to exact from its former Cold War enemy. This is only a partial, and distorting, perspective. Part of the process of the ending of the Cold War, and one that was expected to influence the subsequent settlement, was the policy of accommodation pursued by the Soviet Union during the Gorbachev period. This had implications, not simply for Soviet relations with the West, but also for its relations with China. From the Soviet point of view, the USSR had been engaged in a Cold War not only with the West, but also with China. From that perspective, the period 1989–91 was as potentially momentous in Asia as were the events in Europe, precisely on account of developments in Sino-Soviet relations. This is an aspect often lost to sight by the overly Eurocentric accounts of the ending of the Cold War:

In May 1989, Gorbachev visited Beijing, re-establishing ties and advancing border and demilitarisation negotiations. Then Soviet Foreign Minister Eduard Shevard-nadze announced that 250,000 troops would be removed from the Far East, includ-ing 120,000 directly facing China. Gorbachev proposed complete demilitarisation along the Sino-Soviet border, opening the way for a meeting later in 1989 which began to negotiate a demilitarised zone. In 1991, the two powers signed an agree-ment outlining democratic principles for their disputed eastern border. A final 1991 Sino-Soviet Joint Communique included an 'anti-hegemony' provision which, in the view of most analysts, marked the end of the Cold War struggle to dominate the regional balance of power. (Anderson 1997: 14)

This is a powerful reminder that the end of the Cold War occurred not just in Berlin, but was widespread and multilateral. The West was not in a position to control the entire diversity of that process, nor was the distribu-tive settlement for East Asia exclusively in its gift. To the extent that there was an end to the Sino-Soviet Cold War in Asia, and that China has been a beneficiary of it, the resultant distributive settlement has produced con-sequences not sought by the West, and certainly not thought desirable as an outcome.

No more appealing was the further intensification of Sino-Russian rela-tions in the mid-1990s. Although most commentators did not take this too seriously, there remained some disquiet about the possibility of a re-emergence of the communist alliance that had originally been a feature of the early years of the Cold War. When Yeltsin's disillusionment with his cooperative policy with the West, pursued in the early 1990s, gave way to a set of more rounded policies, it found expression in a further development of Russia's relations with China. An important material dimension of that shift was the sale of Russian armaments to China, at a time when hard-pressed Russian defence industries welcomed any potential market of this kind. But when the language of Russia's 'strategic partnership' with the West began to be deployed to describe Russia's developing relationship with China instead, there was understandable concern in the West (Anderson 1997: 10).

The other aspect of the Pacific Asian settlement has been the quest for a legitimate basis to America's continuing role. In that sense, the settlement is not yet fully in place, even though America's security guarantees remain critical to stability in the region. Just as the Cold War role of the United States in Europe was legitimized by the containment of Soviet power, so had the US presence in East Asia been justified by the same need. However, in Europe the US role had become part of a more ambitious regional project to construct a 'security community', and hence the transition to post-Soviet realities has been managed reasonably well within the NATO framework. In contrast, the demise of the containment role in Pacific Asia has left the US presence bereft of any commanding rationale, and hostage to shifting political attitudes as a result. Moreover, in the absence of these wider regional security arrangements, there is much less to fall back upon, and it is in that sense that the 'settlement' of American power is seen to be provisional in the Asian context.

Once again, the differences between the European and Pacific Asian scenarios are as instructive as are the parallels. To be sure, the United States had been a major part of the solution to the 'German problem' in Europe. But there were also other supporting features of that solution, most notably the dense fabric of European integration and institutionalization. There has been no counterpart to these in Asia, and hence the future role of Japan is if anything seen to be more problematic, since the USA–Japan security treaty is the single solution to that problem, and all the more exposed for being so. It is frequently pointed out that whereas regional integration was an adjunct of American containment policy in Europe, in the case of East Asia the US security role has tended, if anything, to inhibit any such development. Typically, the point is conceded in one analysis:

Although America's presence in East Asia is indispensable, the particular nature of US engagement also has high costs: it impedes the intraregional integration essential to long-term stability. American might and diplomacy prevent conflict, but they do so by keeping apart the parties that must ultimately learn to live comfortably alongside each other if regional stability is to endure. (Kupchan 1998: 62–3)

This is but another way of saying that, in one sense, the European settlement was more straightforward. When the post-Cold War settlement for that region had been set in place, it automatically dealt with the residual legacy of the Second World War as well. If the Soviet Union could accept a militarized and united Germany as part of a potentially hostile alliance, then that ghost had been finally laid to rest. The same, however, could not be said for East Asia. The provisional distributive settlement at the end of the Cold War did not fully dispose of the agenda left over from 1945. If anything, that agenda stood out more starkly. It has certainly not resolved the territorial issues that continue to endure from the Second World War, notably as between Japan and Russia. Neither has the regional unease with Japan, nor other historical forms of regional suspicion, finally been addressed. All that now stands between the present status quo and its full exposure to this unresolved agenda is American power, and the settlement that will provide a long-term rationale for that presence is yet to be completed. Hence, there is prevalent throughout the region a 'widespread apprehension' about the 'future strength of the US presence' (Ball 1996b: 4). In the meantime, the devices that have so far been resorted to can be seen as little more than a crypto-settlement, not the real thing. This certainly is the implicit critique offered by perceptive commentaries on regional structures, such as Asian Pacific Economic Cooperation (APEC):

Indeed, APEC can be viewed as an attempt to avoid confronting the consequences of the ending of the Cold War. Its objective is to keep the US as guarantor of Asian security, which both flatters waning American power and keeps the Asians from having to come to terms with each other. (Buzan and Segal 1994: 15)

Thus understood, the Pacific Asian settlement has not advanced much beyond the armistice phase. What we have now is little more than a set of transitional arrangements, and we must expect that the peacemaking will extend for a further protracted period into the future. The principal reason for this is that it was possible for the West to deal with Soviet power in Europe, and with the immediate implications of its collapse. This did not mean, however, that it could arrive at an overarching settlement for East Asia as well. The West could make its demands of the USSR in Europe but, unlike in the case of eastern Europe, East Asia was not the Soviet Union's to give in the first place.

THE MIDDLE EAST

In this respect, there is an immediate similarity to the analysis that can be afforded of the Middle East. Some specialists on the region have decried the use of the Cold War as a suitable framework for explaining developments in the Middle East, and insisted instead that the impetus came all along from local actors, not from the great powers (Karsh 1997: 271). For the same reason, the end of the Cold War has done comparatively little to reshape the region.

Others dissent. While no single set of arrangements has been set in place that deserves to be called a post-Cold War settlement for the Middle East, nonetheless the end of the Cold War has been factored into the calculations of the various parties as to how things will develop in future. Major consequences of the ending of the Cold War were felt by the Arab states, Israel, and the Palestine Liberation Organization (PLO). Above all, it 'left the United States free to pursue its own preferred strategy in Arab–Israeli matters' (Niblock 1994: 4). It has thus demonstrably changed the context of regional politics, even where this has not issued in a final endgame.

The extreme version of the argument against any notion of a post-Cold War settlement in the Middle East takes the form that profound changes have been in train there since at least 1973. More pointedly, the claim could be made that, as far as the Middle East was concerned, the Cold War had already effectively come to an end in that year. The logic for saying so is that, with regard to the central dynamics of the Arab–Israeli dispute, the Soviet Union had been largely marginalized since that date. The dynamic that drove closer US–Egyptian relations during the 1970s, culminating in the Camp David agreements towards the end of the decade, was that peace could be brokered only under the auspices of American power. The Soviet Union was largely superfluous to this process. In that sense, those key features of Soviet and Russian marginalization that have occurred in Europe and Pacific Asia in the 1990s were already very much a part of the

Middle East landscape, fully a decade and a half before the Cold War came to an end.

This is, of course, something of an overstatement. Whatever the reality of the Middle East peace process, insofar as there had been one to speak of, the Soviet Union remained a player within it, even if at one remove. Its very existence, and its continued links with clients in the region, allowed it to have an impact indirectly by bolstering those who were opposed to it. 'It therefore suited Moscow for the rejectionist Arab states to maintain their hardline stance regarding a negotiated solution of the Arab–Israeli conflict', it has been pointed out, since any such solution was one from which 'Moscow was almost certain to be excluded' (Ahrari 1996b: 21). Moscow possessed no veto on a settlement, but links with it gave tacit allowance to others to obstruct.

This much at least has been changed by the end of the Cold War, and it is important to acknowledge the extent to which a new context was created by this development. On the face of it, the new situation was much more conducive to an Arab–Israeli peace process. Thus it was widely held, as one report maintained, that such a process 'emerged from the Gulf War' in 1991, and that the war 'provided the necessary impetus for the peace talks to get under way' (IISS 1991/2: 84). Others have pointed to the combination of reassurance given to Israel by that war, and to the disarray in the Arab world in its aftermath, as favourable preconditions for talks (Ahrari 1996b: 28).

The Gulf War was both symptom, and further cause, of the changes under way. At one level, it seems reasonable to regard the war as evidence, and further confirmation, of Washington's unrivalled dominance as external power. 'The New World Order', it has been claimed, 'was essentially the extension of mono-polar US influence over the region' (Murphy 1994: 82). Indeed, paradoxically, it may have been this very condition that had tempted the Iraqi leader to embark on his Kuwaiti adventure in the first place. His calculation was that a United States no longer beset by Soviet power would be that much less inclined to exercise itself robustly in the region (Starkey 1996: 148). On the other hand, and in his transparent efforts to garner legitimacy for his own expansionist designs, Saddam warned of the dangers for Arab security created by the 'void' left in the wake of the Soviet Union's departure (Picard 1994: 92–3).

One author insists that it was not the end of the Cold War in Europe, but the Gulf War instead, that was to shape events thereafter. He describes this war as a 'cataclysmic indigenous event' (Karsh 1997: 288). But was it indigenous? The claim is cast in doubt by the extent to which Iraqi actions may themselves have been influenced by the changes in the wider international context. More importantly, the suggestion has to be qualified when regarded from the point of view of the international coalition that took the war to Iraq in turn. It is surely impossible to understand what galvanized it to action without some reference to the perceived hiatus left behind by the end of the Cold War. This was the context in which a forceful response was felt to be all the more necessary. Lawrence Freedman maintained at the time that one aspect of the war was 'the series of precedents created during the Gulf Crisis for collective international action against flagrant violations of international law' (1991: 208). The implications of this extended far beyond the Middle East alone, and were really about the credibility of the international order as such. This must make us wary of jumping out of the frying pan—where the end of the Cold War determines all things—simply to end up in the fire—where a local and indigenous determinism brooks no challenge.

At any rate, what the end of the Cold War had already prefigured was given further substance by the outcome of the Gulf War. Hitherto radical Arab regimes, and dissidents from all aspects of US policy, chose to side with Washington's venture. Nowhere was this more striking than in the case of Syria, as President Assad struck his own accommodation with the new realities (Hinnebusch 1994: 120, 128). Additionally, the PLO emerged with its Arab reputation badly tarnished by the sympathies it had expressed for Saddam's stance on Israel. In combination, these factors gave momentum to the negotiations that culminated in Oslo. If the disappearance of the Soviet Union left the Arab states with fewer options, it also made the point that the USA no longer needed to be so generous to *its* regional clients. To that extent, 'Israel appears to realize that the end of the Soviet "threat" increases US influence in the region, including its leverage over Israeli decision making' (Goodman 1993: 13–14). At the very least, it encouraged a re-evaluation of Israel in the eyes of the United States (Murphy 1994: 83).

And yet not all of the forces that contributed to Oslo could be so automatically assigned to the ending of the Cold War. One critical variable that was to have an impact both on the PLO and other Arab leaders, as well as on Israeli governments, was the Intifada that emerged in 1987–8, before the Cold War's end. This threatened to delegitimize all those who claimed to speak in the name of the Palestinians, while at the same time intensifying pressure on the Israeli authorities. This helped 'sow the seeds for the secret Oslo Rounds' of negotiations (Ahrari 1996b: 27–8). So secret were these that American officials were unaware of their existence, and left 'astonished' at news of the outline agreement (Reynolds 2000: 591). What these sundry local factors confirm is that a Palestinian–Israeli peace had not been the Cold War's to prevent, nor was it thereafter for the post-Cold War settlement to bestow (Karsh 1997: 291).

Once again, however, the key feature of Middle East politics that impacted on the quest for a post-Cold War settlement was the association between Soviet and American power. It is commonplace to suggest that US policy interests in the Middle East have, for decades, suffered from a serious contradiction. These interests centre upon oil, and Western access to it, and upon the support of Israel. Repeatedly, the latter dimension has threatened to impede the attainment of the former goal. What maintained some uneasy, if unconvincing, equilibrium between the two was the portrayal of the Soviet Cold War threat as a rationalization for American measures in pursuit of both. The consequence of the end of the Cold War was that this contradiction had become all that much more exposed, without the Cold War overlay to conceal it. To that extent, US policy has been forced to accept the burden that its now undisputed regional mastery has thrust upon it. This was to place 'resolution of the Arab–Israeli conflict at the heart of US policymaking', during the subsequent Clinton era (Murphy 1994: 93). The Gulf War entailed the honouring of many debts, including America's debt to itself to resolve this internal contradiction. It is this realization that has, however fitfully, driven America's role in the process from the famous handshake on the White House lawns in September 1993, through to the Clinton search for a second settlement at Camp David in 2000.

But it would be naive to make a settlement of the complex of Arab–Israeli issues the proper test of whether or not there has been a post-Cold War settlement in the Middle East. By that test, the region must surely fail. However, the test is inappropriate. Just as, during the Cold War, the superpowers could neither withhold nor bestow a Middle East peace, so in the post-Cold War era this remains outside the gift of the United States. The post-Cold War Middle East settlement has been much more modest, and, in this respect, shares similarities with that in East Asia. It was not about achieving peace in the Middle East, but about the political architecture within which such peace was to be sought. For many years before the end of the Cold War, this had already become a largely American affair. What the end of the Cold War has permitted is for this to become more widely tolerated. That hitherto *de facto* regime for the Middle East has now become institutionalized in a way that would have been inconceivable during the Cold War, even if there remains on the ground vocal dissent to this structure. The Middle East is far from pacified, but there is wider acceptance than ever before 'at the highest levels' about the political forum within which such pacification needs to be pursued, because there is no viable alternative to it. Locally, and on the ground, things are seen very differently. This is an immense liability to the United States, but a fair measure also of the ambivalent nature of its victory in the region.

Peacemaking does not imply that all events in the Middle East are now driven and controlled by the United States. Any such claim would be palpably absurd. Nonetheless, the end of the Cold War has indubitably shaped a new political superstructure for the core regional conflicts. It is not inconsistent to argue that this superstructure is a creation of the post-Cold War peace, without also asserting that it is the critical determining force in the region. It is no less misleading to deny the existence of this new structure of power, than it would be to pretend that it is all encompassing, or finally decisive.

POST-COLD WAR DISARMAMENT

The nature and extent of the post-Cold War distributive settlement can also be explored functionally. This is best done through a brief review of the military aspects of the peace.

If we take the imagery of a post-Cold War peace settlement literally, the one set of measures we would absolutely expect to find would be provisions for a reduction in the military capability of the defeated state. This kind of forced disarmament has been a general practice since the beginning of organized warfare and, we are informed, 'was part of every major peace settlement from the Treaty of Utrecht in 1713, through the Paris negotiations in 1815 and 1919, to the postwar agreements in 1945' (Towle 1997: 1). Such measures are intended to perpetuate the fruits of war by ensuring that the new distribution of power will not soon be unsettled. Has this been a feature of the post-Cold War settlement? Ostensibly, it might appear not to have been so. 'Indeed, about the only thing that *had not* changed very much by 1991', we are told, 'was the balance of weaponry' (Mueller 1995: 3). Is this an apposite verdict?

We must begin by enquiring whether the kind of arms control that did take place with the end of the Cold War was tantamount to the disarmament that occurs at the end of wars. As the historian of this type of forced disarmament makes clear, it appears as a distinctive *genre* of disarmament, separate from its negotiated variants, and from more recent instances of voluntary arms control. What sets it apart is the element of coercion: its military restrictions are imposed by the victor upon the vanquished at the end of war. The objective is not to attain some abstract quality of stability or equilibrium, but to perpetuate that very disequilibrium that has already been manifested in the result of the war. However, the absoluteness of this distinction is itself problematic. Towle (1997: 14) offers the example of the Washington Treaty of 1922, which was resented by the Japanese military and 'seen by them as just as much an example of forced disarmament as those which take place after defeat in war'. Accordingly, the view that the major arms control agreements at the end of the Cold War should not be regarded as part of a peace settlement, on the grounds that they were negotiated, is less automatically conclusive than might otherwise be thought.

Similar objections are equally suspect. There is the already encountered line of analysis that the eclipse of Soviet military power was not an accomplishment of the West, but rather an outcome self-inflicted by Soviet and Russian economic failure. Even so, its subsequent enshrining in treaties with the West gave it a symbolic standing, not as a unilateral act, but as an attribute of that bilateral relationship. Certainly, this is what has evoked amongst the Russian military the subsequent misgivings that the country had been subjected to 'unequal treaties' at its moment of weakness.

More problematic still is the notion that, far from humiliating the Soviet Union, Western policy was so mindful to avoid doing so that, if anything, it hid from Soviet eyes the full scale of its own failure. As with the Armistice in November 1918, this gave rise to a potent myth that the country had not been defeated, but was instead to be sold out by the politicians. The theme in the history of post-war disarmament to which this properly relates is the requirement for a modulation of the military aspects of the peace, so as not to impede its quest for fundamental political transformation in the defeated state. As regards 1815, the point has been made thus: 'Louis XVIII would be undermined by a vindictive peace while conversely a reformed French monarchy would provide the best guarantee against the sort of revolution which brought Napoleon to power' (Towle 1997: 42). The relevance of this to the contemporary Russian case is abundantly clear. Any attempt to strip the Soviet Union of its military strength would have been profoundly humiliating, especially since Soviet status was almost exclusively bound up with its military might. Such action would thereby have ensured the re-emergence of those very forces that could best resist any desirable transformation of the political system. Western policy thus faced a perplexing dilemma: the danger from the Soviet Union could be averted either by changing its political complexion, or by depriving it of the military means to pose a threat. But pursuit of the latter was likely to undercut the former while, at the same time, there could be no absolute confidence in the former, without implementing the latter also as an insurance. This was not the first time that this dilemma had been faced. Peacemakers, we are reminded, 'try to influence the future behaviour of a defeated state by both altering its constitution and diminishing its power' (Towle 1997: 232). The two goals never sit comfortably with each other, and the case of Russia after the Cold War is no exception in this respect. As the record was to demonstrate, the shifting agenda of arms cuts was to be set as much by 'constitutional' developments within the Soviet Union, as it was by Western assessments of the military balance as such.

These nuances aside, the summary judgement that can be advanced is that the end of the Cold War did indeed result in a punitive military settlement, both in the conventional and the nuclear domains. How solid is the evidence in support of such a claim?

The prime example of disarmament in the conventional sphere was the Treaty on Conventional Forces in Europe (CFE) of late 1990. Nominally, of course, this should be regarded as part of the European settlement alone. However, although strictly limiting Soviet forces in Europe, it necessarily also had an impact on Soviet military power across the board, not least because of the potential for redeploying excess equipment out of the Treaty area, and beyond the Urals.

On the face of it, the CFE Treaty contributed to a substantial, and asymmetrical, reduction of Soviet conventional forces. In its quest for some kind of parity, the Treaty required 'hugely disproportionate' cuts on the Soviet side (McInnes 1994: 12). 'The effect is to force large cuts in east European and especially Soviet forces', was one summary assessment, 'while leaving NATO's inventory relatively unconstrained' (IISS 1990/1: 247). This outcome was magnified by the other dramatic consequences of the end of the Cold War, while the talks were still under way. These eroded the USSR's negotiating position yet further, leaving it 'little to bargain with, but much to bargain for' (C. Kennedy 1994: 59). As a result of the treaty, the Soviet Union shifted from being the 'dominant military power' in the region, to one 'facing military inferiority' relative to NATO (C. Kennedy 1994: 41). These provisions bear all the hallmarks of the kind of settlement that would normally be imposed on a defeated state after a war. The details reinforce such a perception. According to the calculations of two specialists, the former Warsaw Pact states would have to destroy 33,268 weapons, whereas 'NATO countries could limit their net reduction to just 97 weapons' (Dean and Forsberg 1992: 86). Indeed, these same calculations produced some striking alternative figures, if 'real' reductions were taken into account. These made allowance for the full impact of the end of the Cold War, including the disbanding of the Warsaw Pact, and the unification of Germany. On this basis, Dean and Forsberg suggested that on the Soviet/East European side, there 'will thus be an overall reduction of 131,366 items of WTO [Warsaw Treaty Organization] equipment, rather than merely the 33,268 formally attributable to the treaty' (1992: 86–7). At the same time, NATO would be able to improve the quality of its military holdings by the policy of 'cascading' equipment, excess to its limits, from the central front to the NATO flanks (Croft 1994b: 34–5).

A similar picture emerges if we look at the Soviet role in the arms trade. The end of the Cold War resulted in a dramatic diminution in the Soviet/ Russian capacity to sell weapons abroad. Had this been imposed formally in a treaty as a way to limit future Soviet influence, or as a form of economic punishment, it could scarcely have been made more dramatic. In the few years after the end of the Cold War (1990–7), the US share of the global arms trade rose from 27 to 45 per cent while, over the same period, the Soviet/Russian share fell from 29 to 5 per cent (Huxley and Willett 1999: 23).

The pertinent question, of course, is whether these military limitations on Russia can reasonably be regarded as equivalent to the formal constraints of a peace settlement. There would appear to be at least three potential objections to viewing them in this light: the problem of chronology; the fact that they were negotiated and voluntary; and the objection that they were driven by changes in the WTO, rather than as requirements of the West.

The first of these objections points to the chronology. There had been conventional arms talks between the Cold War blocs reaching back to the Mutual and Balanced Force Reductions (MBFR) talks that began in 1973. As these had made little headway after many years, new talks were initiated in 1986 under the auspices of the Conference on Security and Cooperation in Europe (CSCE). These became the umbrella for the CFE, which commenced in 1989, before the end of the Cold War (McInnes 1994: 6–9). On this basis, it might be said, it is wholly misleading to view the resulting treaty as an *effect* of the Cold War's termination. The second difficulty is that post-war restrictions on the size of a country's armed forces are imposed unilaterally by the victors. However, in the case of the end of the Cold War, the CFE was a bilateral set of negotiations within which the WTO was an equal and voluntary participant. Even if the material effects of the treaty fell much more lightly upon NATO forces, there remained an equal obligation to comply with that treaty. This was quite unlike, say, the implicit linkage between the scaling back of German forces in 1919, and a more general undertaking by other states also to reduce their armed forces. And thirdly, as is apparent above, the full scale of the WTO reductions was an unintended side effect of the course of events. It was not something demanded and imposed by the West. Thus one survey concludes that the significance of CFE lies in the fact that 'it both formalizes and extends unilateral force reductions to which the USSR and its erstwhile allies committed themselves over the course of the last two and a half years' (IISS 1990/1: 247). The treaty thus did little more than sanctify, for instance, the cuts that Gorbachev had already announced at the United Nations in December 1988 (McInnes 1994: 13). That is quite different from a punitive Western-imposed peace.

There is some force to these objections, but they are not finally compelling. The issue of chronology is the least telling of the three. The CFE mirrored the wider logic of the end of the Cold War and traced its trajectory. It was both a token of recognition of the forces that were leading to radical change and, at the same time, part of the process for bringing this about. If Gorbachev was to accomplish his wider goals of accommodation with the West, on which his domestic reforms depended, then he needed to make concessions of this kind. Whether they were offered as a means to induce the end of the Cold War, or as a payment in kind when that war was over, is largely immaterial. The logic was the same in either case.

Nor is the complaint that the reduction was negotiated itself decisive. As noted above, there can be degrees of coercion even within a nominally 'voluntary' accord. In the same way, there are elements of negotiation implicit in what may appear to be a coerced settlement. What lends the defeated state some bargaining power is the degree of residual will of the victor to enforce the military restrictions, as, say, in the case of Iraq after the Gulf War. The distinction then between voluntary accord and exacted imposition is far from absolute. It thus follows that, whilst the Warsaw Pact countries agreed to participate in the CFE talks, they did so in full awareness of the pressures and constraints which surrounded their overall strategy. The Soviet Union may have opted to negotiate, but this did not make it any the less aware that it was negotiating from a position of weakness.

Finally, it may be true that Soviet force reductions occurred for a number of reasons, and that their eventual scale had much to do with the wider dynamics unleashed by the end of the Cold War. But the fact that their extent was driven for other reasons does not in any way diminish the significance of the fact that the cuts occurred at all. Whatever the specific nuances surrounding them, these reductions were all derivative from the central logic of the ending of the Cold War, in one sense or another. Objectively speaking, they were the price the Soviet Union had to pay to end the Cold War, albeit that a supplementary charge subsequently fell due when the war did, indeed, come to an end. One analyst's judgement was that the treaty 'merely codified the breakdown of Soviet power' (C. Kennedy 1994: 62–3). Another reflected that the treaty's importance lay precisely in the transitional role that it played, since it was 'as much a part of the new European security order as it was of the old' (McInnes 1994: 6). In their own separate ways, both are making the same point that the treaty was fundamental to the ending of the Cold War, and to ushering in the settlement that would serve as the basis of the new order. It is this link between the new and the old that is traditionally fulfilled by a peace settlement.

A similar picture emerges in the nuclear sphere. The Strategic Arms Reductions Treaty (START) I was signed as the Cold War formally expired. To be sure, its provisions were far less unbalanced than the kinds of cuts embodied in the CFE. START had more the appearance of a treaty between two equals. And yet, underneath this seemingly greater symmetry, two fundamental points stand out. START required cuts in that very category of nuclear forces—land-based heavy missiles—to which the Soviet Union had long been the more committed. START I was to eliminate half of the Soviet SS-18 fleet 'long regarded as the most threatening element of Soviet nuclear forces' (IISS 1989/90: 196). To that extent, regardless of the precise numbers involved, the very principle at stake amounted to a substantial Soviet concession. Secondly, the context needs to be borne in mind. Any reduction in nuclear weapons entailed a major sacrifice for the Soviet Union at a time when its conventional forces were becoming less of an asset, both in numbers and in effectiveness, as the war in Afghanistan had made strikingly clear. If anything, its nuclear status meant more to the USSR in 1990 than at any other time: the reductions that it was to accept were all the more significant when regarded against that background. It is scarcely surprising that the process of nuclear disarmament evoked, in due course, a Russian military backlash for that very reason.

The potential problems in viewing the START process as part of a global peace settlement need not be reviewed in detail. They simply rehearse the points already made above. If anything, the issue of chronology is the more telling in this setting. START was initiated under President Reagan at the height of the Second Cold War. In that sense, it was mere happenstance that it came to its culmination in 1990, a reflection of its slow and painful gestation. This history also accounted for its modest effects. It was common to point out that, while implementing real numerical cuts, the treaty was diminished by the substantial passage of time since the negotiations had begun. The result was that 'post-START arsenals will possess approximately the same number of warheads as when the negotiations began in 1982' (IISS 1989/90: 195). The cuts in the scale of the Soviet arsenal would assuredly have been much deeper, had they been part of a post-Cold War peace settlement, rather than simply a lingering hangover from the Cold War itself.

But START I was not the end of the process, and START II was much more radical in the cuts proposed. Of course, these were again to be imposed upon both sides, not simply upon the Soviet Union. What drove them, however, was unquestionably the political fallout from developments within the USSR that compelled a more active policy of disarmament of Soviet nuclear forces. If scrapping some of the post-Cold War redundancy in the American arsenal was the price that had to be paid to bring this about quickly, it was a negligible price to pay. The two events which compelled a more proactive course of nuclear disarmament were, first of all, the attempted coup in Moscow in August 1991 and, secondly, the disintegration of the USSR itself at the end of that year. The first held out the grim prospect of the nuclear arsenal falling once more into the hands of hardline anti-Western leaders in the Soviet Union; the second, the even grimmer prospect of nuclear proliferation to the untried hands of leaders in the new post-Soviet republics.

The START II process initially took the form of reciprocal but unilateral initiatives, as both Bush and Gorbachev, followed later by Yeltsin, in turn announced more radical cuts to their nuclear forces. While START I had sanctioned totals of 6,000 warheads apiece, the ensuing auction in reverse talked the total down to 4,500, and promised to drive it still lower. It envisaged the final banning of all multiple-warhead land-based ballistic missiles.

We can then regard START II, and the associated policy of staunching nuclear proliferation, as part of a second phase of nuclear settlement after the Cold War. The logic of START II was the traditionalist one of reducing the military resources of defeated states. Since the coup had destroyed faith in the permanence of this new Russian revolution, it seemed wise to take as many as possible of these weapons out of the hands of the former enemy— just in case. At the same time, and through 1995, Western diplomacy was exercised by the need to return nuclear forces held in Ukraine, Belarus, and Kazakhstan to a centralized command in Russia, and to subject them to the constraints of existing treaties.

The best evidence that this phase can be regarded as a set of Western impositions, rather than as voluntary agreements between equals, is to be found in the subsequent Russian reaction to them. This became a major element in the general Russian disenchantment, after 1992, with its hitherto pro-Western phase of policy. Thereafter, nuclear arms control fell victim to the new 'national interest' mood that emerged in Moscow, above all as regarded START II ratification (Lepingwell 1995: 71, 90). Most significantly, the bitter feeling in Moscow that it had been pushed into unduly unequal treaties surfaced in the even higher profile that was to be accorded to its nuclear doctrine. This affirmation emerged in 1993, when a new military doctrine edged away from a policy of no first use of nuclear weapons. As one observer noted, 'the role of nuclear weapons in Russian doctrine has not declined . . . and their missions have in some respects even been extended' (Lepingwell 1995: 73). These statements may have been symbolic, but the symbolism was highly significant in the context.

We can then conclude that the nuclear peace settlement came in two phases. The first was modest and conservative, and reflected an outdated set of considerations. The second was more radical, driven by the urgency of the political changes in the Soviet Union. It was this latter phase that encouraged a backlash in Russia, on the perception that Russia had been driven to concede too much to the West to bring the Cold War to an end. However, regardless of Russian objections to the specifics of the treaties that marked the passing of the Cold War, the more significant aspect of the nuclear peace settlement was the greater asymmetry that it induced, not in terms of numbers, but as regards the opportunities for the exercise of unilateralism. The clearest symbol of this is the relative impunity with which the United States has since dangled the prospect that it might take steps to breach the Anti-Ballistic Missile (ABM) treaty of 1972, in pursuit of some kind of national missile defence system. It is this growing sense of freedom to dictate its own terms, since enjoyed by the United States, that is the best measure of the nuclear peace settlement that had been put in place.

The end of the Cold War can thus be traced regionally, in Pacific Asia and the Middle East, as well as functionally, through its provisions for military disarmament. It would be inaccurate to pretend that in any of these areas there was a radical redefinition of the pertinent issues, simply in response to the end of the Cold War alone. Neither, however, can it sensibly be maintained that business continued as usual in any of these areas. What the ending of the Cold War did was to set in place a set of new political structures that impinged directly upon the calculations of the various players. Although varying in the degree of formality with which it was to be established, each can appropriately be considered an intrinsic aspect of the post-Cold War global terms of peace.

6

GLOBALIZATION AND PEACEMAKING

'If stated without qualification', comments one historian, 'globalization is just cold war victor's history' (Reynolds 2000: 3–4). Any such claim does need to be qualified, as globalization is a much more complex phenomenon than this would have us believe. It is not simply the triumphant outcome of the Cold War, nor is it the West's portrayal of those events. Nonetheless, Reynolds is right to point to one strand within this story, and to make some connection between globalization and the victory in the Cold War. The best way in which this relationship can be broached is by regarding globalization as a significant dimension of post-Cold War peacemaking. While the West did not control globalization, and could not subject it to its political will, it was supportive of some forms of globalization, and wished to see them more widely established. The end of the Cold War afforded the opportunity to embed them in the terms of the settlement.

Globalization was fundamental to this recent phase of peacemaking since it occupied a strategic position both within the distributive, and the regulative, realms of the settlement. It also represented a key element of continuity within the post-Cold War order. At one and the same time, globalization marks the great turning point symbolized by 1990, while also drawing our attention to some fundamental dynamics that have persisted between the Cold War and post-1990 periods. It is, in many ways, and for these reasons, a key architectural feature of the post-Cold War settlement. The purpose of this chapter is to substantiate this somewhat grandiose set of claims by demonstrating the ways in which globalization has contributed to the distributive settlement after the Cold War.

GLOBALIZATION AND THE END OF
THE COLD WAR

It may seem bizarre to imply any association whatsoever between global-ization and peacemaking. We have been warned, correctly, by one specialist in the field that 'equations of globalization and peace might prove to be dangerously complacent' (Scholte 2000: 211). To begin then, we must first clarify the specific nature of the claim that is being made. It is certainly not that globalization is an inherently pacifying process, destined to make the world more peaceful, although this is an assertion that some of its pro-ponents have been happy to make. If it is the case, as in some versions, that the 'globalization story in many ways contains the one about democratic peace' (Buzan and Little 1999: 92), then the one might be taken to lead automatically to the other. However, as it is equally common to attest that globalization means 'the intensification of economic polarization between and within states' (Thomas 1999: 243), we should be cautious about rush-ing to such optimistic conclusions. More modestly, therefore, the sugges-tion being made here is that, if we are to consider the end of the Cold War as issuing in a phase of peacemaking, then globalization has been an intrinsic part of that process. This is regardless of how peaceable or other-wise is the world that eventually emerges from it. If we should not conflate globalization with peace, neither should we confuse peace with peacemak-ing. What peacemaking and globalization share in common is that neither is an end-state. Each is instead a process of becoming, and denotes a transitional phase, leading to some indeterminate condition in the future. Peacemaking may or may not issue in a period of peace; in the same way, globalization is a movement indicating change from one condition to another. What unites the two is this very fluidity that is such a central characteristic of both.

As argued at the outset, peacemaking combines elements of the distri-butive and of the regulative: both are to be found recurrently in historical examples of peace settlements. There are other instances of the hybrid nature of peacemaking elsewhere in this book. However, it is in the case of globalization that this dual nature is most clearly revealed, and any categorical separation of its distributive and regulative aspects is most difficult to achieve. For this reason, it makes sense to view the discussion of globalization in post-Cold War peacemaking as a convenient bridge that links the second and third sections of the book together. Accordingly, the distributive aspects of globalization will be considered in the present chapter, and its regulative aspects outlined in the one to follow.

There are two parts to the argument that need to be grasped at the outset. They demonstrate, in combination, the ways in which both the distributive and the regulative dimensions of peacemaking are implicated in the processes of globalization. The first builds upon the analysis of Ikenberry (1999). He has distinguished between the two settlements that succeeded the Second World War—the containment order and the wider project for the development of a Western liberal order. The former, of necessity, was focused upon the rivalry with the USSR. The latter, although facilitated by the former, was distinct in that its object was not to challenge Soviet power, but rather to solve the contradictions within the Western capitalist and democratic bloc. 'The two settlements', Ikenberry insists, 'had distinct political visions, intellectual rationales, political logics, and (as has become clear lately) historical trajectories' (1999: 125–6). This last point is manifest in the sense that the first settlement has now collapsed, whereas there is no reason to question the continuing survival of the second. In that way, Ikenberry's distinction helps clarify one of the issues that is central to the ongoing argument. It reveals the subtle combination of discontinuity and continuity, given the erosion of the one settlement but the endurance of the second. In addition, it allows us to see, in material terms, how that disjunction might be associated with the distributive and regulative peace. It offers the possibility of conceptualizing a change in the distributive settlement, coupled with a basic reaffirmation and continuation of the regulative settlement. But whilst Ikenberry presents these as two separate and distinct orders, each with its own consequent trajectories, the argument of this chapter is that they are best seen as the distributive and regulative dimensions of the same post-Cold War settlement.

The other important part of the argument is the connection that needs to be drawn between the international and domestic aspects of the peace settlement. It is natural to assume that peace settlements, historically, have concerned themselves with international distribution and regulation: they are instruments that adjust the territories, resources, and conventional relations *between* states. In fact, any such assumption would be mistaken. Peace treaties are as often concerned to impose arrangements *within* states.

This is where the parallel with globalization is noteworthy, and intriguing. The author has previously argued at length (Clark 1997, 1999) that any balanced understanding of globalization requires us to see it as something which integrates the domestic and the international, so much so as to counsel against any strict analytical separation between the two domains. It is therefore remarkable that very much the same needs to be said of peacemaking itself: when peacemakers seek to implement their visions of future order, they invariably do so in a way that integrates the domestic characteristics of states, with the international settlement amongst them. This is the point that emerges most clearly from the work of Maier:

Without resolving in which direction the lines of causal influence flow, I am convinced that International orders . . . have domestic socio-political corollaries. These are often implicit and less visible than the provisions for disarmament or frontier changes that peace treaties make explicit. Nonetheless they remain important. Indeed, my starting point is that ambitious efforts to assure stabilization, such as the peace settlements after great wars, either implicitly or explicitly build upon domestic arrangements within participating countries, as well as upon the specific agreements negotiated between them. (1996: 1)

In short, this chapter needs to engage with both themes. It confronts the issue of continuity and discontinuity raised by the different historical lineage of the distributive and the regulative peace. It explores also the manner in which settlements integrate their proposals for international order with what they envision for the sundry domestic orders as well. The topic of globalization affords the rare opportunity to bring all these dimensions into revealing juxtaposition with each other.

In short, it offers a convenient point of entry into the exploration of that fundamental issue raised earlier about the links between the nature of the Cold War, the forces that brought it to an end, and the characteristics of the subsequent order. These, to repeat, should not be regarded as distinct questions inviting separate answers, but instead require an integrated perspective that embraces all three. Globalization helps us to grasp the nature of this task, and provides a specific case study of it. It was itself an aspect of the Cold War; it was unquestionably one of the forces that brought the Cold War to an end; and it remains an essential feature of the contemporary order. It thus has the potential to shed light on all three phases. By doing so, it teases out the theme of continuity and discontinuity. At the same time, it invites us to combine the dimensions of international and domestic order, since a transformation of some states has been part and parcel of globalization in general, and of the post-Cold War peace settlement in particular. In these sundry ways, globalization holds an important key to an understanding of the post-Cold War order.

Globalization was assuredly an issue within the Cold War itself, an end over which the protagonists were to struggle and which, in turn, was to be instrumental in shaping its own future. Within the geopolitical framework of the Cold War, the dynamic core of the global economy was nurtured. It was, simultaneously, an important means of prosecuting the Cold War, a set of developments that could be exploited by the West to enhance its potent advantages over the Soviet bloc. At the very least, the tentacles of its global communications, global society, and global economic institutions reached into eastern Europe from the 1970s onwards. In the event, these were to make a decisive contribution to the final outcome of the Cold War. When the Cold War did reach its conclusion, the measure of the victory was clearly indicated in the renewed scope for further globalization: there was now the real prospect for it to encompass the globe, after the resistance from the Soviet bloc had been defeated. Finally, globalization embodied the fruit of that victory, and was part of the substance required to satisfy the demands of the victors. In its multiple roles within the Cold War—as war aim, means of prosecution, and as condition of peace—globalization has been heavily implicated in the emergence and specification of the post-Cold War settlement.

THE GLOBALIZATION DEBATE

The topic of globalization is now subject to a bewildering variety of debates from which little agreement or consensus has emerged. If, as Falk maintains, it has 'become the most satisfactory descriptive label for the current historical era', then this is so, as he acknowledges, both 'for better and worse' (1999: 1). The term has become popularized, as much as a statement of our perplexity and bewilderment about the present order, as in any confident expectation that the concept can dispel them. Given its eponymously all-encompassing nature, globalization is used to explain everything, at a cost of leaving nothing that is not still shrouded in haze and mystery.

As things stand now, there are many separate strands to the globalization debate, and it is not proposed to engage here with all aspects of it. The main points of contention centre upon a multiplicity of issues: radical and sceptical views as to how much change globalization has brought; judgements as to whether globalization is beneficial or detrimental; whether it is erosive of state power, or inherently dependent upon it; its causality, and the extent to which it is an autonomous social process; whether it is primarily an economic phenomenon, or multidimensional; and whether we should distinguish between globalization, as a general condition, and its specific neoliberal instantiation at the present time. This myriad of controversies is now discussed in a copious literature (Held *et al.* 1999; Scholte 2000; Baylis and Smith 2001), from which globalization emerges with its essential features largely unresolved.

This chapter will not attempt to deal with globalization in the round, nor take sides in these many controversies. Its central preoccupations are the dual themes of continuity and change, and the role of globalization within the distributive peace. This chapter engages with globalization only insofar as it provides a convenient instrument for thinking about both of these matters. Since, as claimed above, globalization is such a prominent feature of both the Cold War and post-Cold War orders, it offers us telling clues as to the fundamental continuities between both. At the same time, since the victory of the Cold War is so often associated with the expanding scope of globalization, it emphasizes the significance of 1990 as a turning point as well. It is this very duality that is indicative of the essence of the post-Cold War peace.

So powerful has become the rhetoric of globalization that it is understood by many to signify the end of any *international* order at all. Thus the hyper-globalist perspective is predicated on the emergence of 'a radically new world order, an order which prefigures the demise of the nation-state' (Held *et al.* 1999: 4). It is for this reason that one writer expresses the opinion that 'the globalized world of the next century will make international order less and less relevant to the main problems facing humanity' (S. Smith 1999: 117). International order assumes the existence of separate and distinct national territories, each of which has identifiable interests when it interacts with other states: the order is largely, if by no means exclusively, one between those states. By contrast, the imagery of globalization stresses the obsolescence of national polities, economies, societies, and interests, and replaces them with patterns of global interaction that dissect those formerly self-contained sovereign territories. The reason why globalization thus becomes central to the post-Cold War peace is that it is seen to further redistribute power away from states. Typically, the view is held that 'globalization and the end of the Cold War have invoked a system in which states have ceased to be the privileged actors of special importance that they were in the old order' (Holm and Sorensen 1995*b*: 10–11). If this image is accepted, the demise of international order follows logically from it. There can be no order between such state units, if they have ceased to exist as meaningful containers of social action.

But should globalization be construed in such a portentous manner? Is this the most accurate reading of its impact? There is an alternative interpretation that recognizes the profound changes which globalization is having upon international order, but without forcing us to abandon the traditional framework altogether. This alternative is based on the idea that globalization represents a transformation in the nature of the state itself, and is best understood as a theory *of the state*, as against a theory *of its obsolescence*. Once this shift is made, it becomes possible to think in terms of international relations between *globalized states* (Clark 1999, 2001). To be sure, these do not conform to traditional forms implied by the 'billiard ball' model, but they allow us to retain the essential framework of continuing relations between state units, albeit substantially modified in their nature.

What does a globalized state look like? According to the dominant view found in the literature, states are everywhere being 'hollowed out', and find themselves in universal retreat in the face of the advancing forces of economic globalization. Their principal and shared characteristic is therefore their growing policy impotence, and it is by this characteristic that the presence of globalization is most readily to be detected. This retreat, in turn, is symptomatic of the structural imperatives of globalization which have acted to undermine the jurisdiction of states, to erode their scope for policy choice, and to negate their sovereignty (Clark 2000). In its specifically economic variant, this argument takes the form that states are compelled by neoliberal hegemony to conform to certain practices (such as low social overheads, and sound financial strategies) that find approval with international markets, otherwise their economies will suffer punishment.

However, there is reason to think that this is a misleadingly simplified or unbalanced interpretation of what is happening. Rather than view the state as the prisoner of hegemonic forces of globalization, impacting upon it from the outside, it may be more accurate to understand the state as undergoing a transformation whereby elements of its identity are changing, possibly for other and separate reasons. It might even be possible to suggest that globalization, rather than the *cause* of this shifting identity, is substantially an *effect* of this process of state transformation. States are not what they are simply because of globalization. Rather, globalization is possible because of what states are already on the way to becoming.

What is the evidence for this? States have undergone profound shifts of direction in recent decades. They are less the sole providers of a whole range of social goods, such as economic benefits, security, human rights, and social identity. Many of these are increasingly provided, or undermined, on a transnational basis. At the same time, and in conjunction with these shifts, states make different demands upon their citizens. For instance, with regard to security, many states no longer 'mobilize' their citizens to the same extent. The historical nexus between citizen rights and military service has, in some respects, been ruptured.

What is important about this interpretation is that it allows for radical change in the character of states, but without jettisoning the entire framework of international order as a result. To be sure, the 'units' that interact are by no means self-contained and exclusive. They have porous borders, and they no longer represent the sole source of agency within the field. States have been joined by other actors, such as transnational social movements, the channels of global production and exchange, as well as by the instruments of global governance. But we remain very far from living in a world in which international order has no meaning at all. The core idea of relations between globalized states allows us to recognize the major changes taking place, without leaping to the premature conclusion that there is no longer such a thing as an international order in which states remain the primary actors. States may now be increasingly globalized but, however paradoxical it may sound, the order between them remains substantially an international one. In this general sense, globalization is itself a theory that combines radical change with substantial elements of continuity.

But how does the notion of post-Cold War peacemaking assist us in locating the meaning of globalization for contemporary order? Traditionally, globalization and the end of the Cold War have been associated in two different ways. According to the first, globalization is deemed to be a preexisting trend that contributed to the erosion of Soviet power, and to the diminished significance of the geopolitical game in which it was engaged. Globalization was thus an instrument of the West in the Cold War that played a role in eventually subverting the very logic of that struggle. According to the second, globalization has been more consequence than cause: the end of the Cold War has set the scene for a geographical spread of globalization, since it has removed the final geopolitical constraints on its previous extent. Accordingly, globalization reveals elements of both discontinuity and continuity in relation to the passing of the Cold War. As part of the ensuing distributive settlement, there has been a post-Cold War division of the spoils in favour of further globalization. Much of this pertains to the economic and political status of central and eastern Europe, as well as to the transformation of the former Soviet Union. At the same time, there has been a reaffirmation of faith in the regulative principles of liberal capitalism, as first enunciated at Bretton Woods, and periodically restated thereafter. The specific territoriality of globalization has been adjusted in the aftermath of the Cold War, but its governing economic principles continue to regulate the global economy, and much else besides. A key element of the settlement is the further transformation in the identity of states—and especially those released from the socialist bloc—towards a globalized form.

These themes are touched upon in a number of writings. They emerge most clearly in the debates about the chronology of globalization itself. According to this, globalization can be seen as having a history that goes back for several centuries. Alternatively, there is the view that it developed only during the second half of the nineteenth century, or is a much more recent phenomenon of the late twentieth century. Obviously, these debates about lineage are merely reflections of more profound disagreements about its nature and essence. However, it is relatively common to date a new wave of globalization (if not its absolute historical origins) from the second half of the twentieth century (Scholte 2000: 74). When this is done, we are compelled to consider its relationship to the end of the Cold War. If globalization coexisted with the Cold War for much of this period, and if globalization is in some sense the defining quality of the present order, then it would appear that the transitions that have accompanied the end of the Cold War cannot be as profound as initial appearances might suggest, at least as far as the history of globalization itself is concerned.

Perhaps one way of grappling with this is in terms of the afore-mentioned argument of Ikenberry (1999). The distinction that he makes is between a 'containment order' that was overturned in 1989, and a Western liberal order that still endures. The latter was 'much more deeply rooted', and was not dependent upon the Cold War (1999: 124). It owed its historical origins to the inter-war period and, above all, to the Depression and the associated collapse of the Versailles order. 'The origin of this order predated the full onset of the Cold War', we are reminded, 'and it was institutionalized at least semi-independently of it' (Deudney and Ikenberry 1999: 180). This makes it much less sensitive to the passing of the Cold War, and able to survive its demise.

From such a scheme, there emerges a picture of one order that collapses, and another that endures, with the passing of the Cold War. It replicates the present argument about change within, but continuity of, the process of globalization. Indeed, as will be seen later, this Western liberal order is part of what is meant by globalization generally, and stands out as one of the key regulative strands of the post-Cold War period.

How then are we to locate globalization within a framework of post-Cold War peacemaking? For our present purposes, the central question is as follows: as part of the distributive settlement, what does globalization distribute?

GLOBALIZATION AND THE DISTRIBUTIVE PEACE

Intuitively, the idea of the end of the Cold War issuing in a territorial redistribution, that itself is driven by globalization, enjoys a certain appeal. However globalization is defined, it is thought to have been most robust amongst the Western group of industrialized states, even if its effects have been felt far beyond. Most of the reasons for dating the process, or its most recent phase, from the 1960s derive from the changes in production and financial organization that developed apace after that date. Thus viewed, globalization might be construed as a spatial process, spreading out from its centre in the Atlantic community, and gradually entwining and incorporating much of the Third World during the 1970s and 1980s. The major impediment to its further reach then became the recalcitrant social-ist bloc. With the sweeping away of that bloc, the weather was set fair for its, now unchecked, global reach. If we then make the argument that the Cold War was, in part, actually about the future course of globalization, then it follows almost by definition that its end would be marked by a territorial settlement that removed the barriers to globalization's future extension. It is precisely such a distributive settlement that would be the appropriate conclusion to the Cold War struggle, marking the victory of globalization as much as it marked the victory of the West.

There are at least three ways in which we can regard globalization as being part of a post-Cold War distributive settlement. These are the cre-ation of a new balance of economic power; the relationship of globaliza-tion to US hegemony; and the reconstitution of the 'identity' of the Second World. These will be considered in turn.

To the extent that there is some implicit suggestion that globalization has been an *effect* of the end of the Cold War, the argument is predicated on the resulting distribution of economic power. While, previously, there had been a part of the world that was relatively immune to the charms of global capitalism, the ending of the Cold War left the globe as a whole open to its embrace. If the Cold War was fought over the scope of the 'Open Door', then the fruits of Western victory came in the form of its extension to all regions. There was now to be no sanctuary where the logic of capitalism could not prevail. In an age when economic access is much more important than territorial possession, it was this distribution that was the more telling one. Whatever the shifts and adjustments in the post-Cold War territorial settlement, these paled into insignificance in com-parison with the key redistribution that was to take place within this map of economic power.

But the logic of globalization has contributed to a more deep-seated redistribution than this formulation alone would suggest. Even before the end of the Cold War, the view was widespread that one of the main symptoms of globalization was the substitution of the former vertical categories of global differentiation, by a novel and more complex pattern of horizontal hierarchies. Notions of discrete First, Third, and Fourth worlds were already becoming questionable by the time the Second World came to an end, but this accelerated a further redistribution away from the existing forms of stratification. Given the centrality of globalization to the contemporary order, it is useful to regard this distributive effect as a key dimension of the post-Cold War settlement:

Hence, in the post-Cold War context, Third World states, far from disappearing, have increased numerically and in terms of geographic spread. Third World status has effectively been globalised. The picture is highly differentiated, but central characteristics of vulnerability to the workings of the global market, and lack of meaningful influence in global governance institutions, are shared by a growing group of states. (Thomas 1999: 229)

The general drift of such analyses is that there has been a deepening polarization, not between states or regions as such (as in demarcations between North and South), but instead cutting across borders. The key distinction is between those people who benefit by being caught up in the processes of globalization, and those who are increasingly left behind by it. This is 'associated with new patterns of global stratification', it has been remarked, 'in which some states, societies and communities are becoming increasingly enmeshed in the global order while others are becoming increasingly marginalized' (Held et al. 1999: 7–8). In sum, as against any assumption that globalization is homogenizing in its effects, it is better understood as polarizing (Bauman 1998: 18; Sjolander 1996: 609; Hoffmann 1998: 4–5). Although such a process disaggregates, and hence is not state-centric in the last resort, it nonetheless leads cumulatively to a greater concentration of power in those states already strong, and to a further erosion of power in those already weak (Woods 2000b: 2–3). Insofar as the economic 'Open Door' was one of the war aims of the Cold War, the economic settlement that was to prevail at its end has further intensified this particular configuration of economic power. This is assuredly one of the prime dimensions of the distributive peace.

The second dimension of the distributive settlement is the complex relationship between globalization and US hegemony. This is a much-debated issue, and a range of commentators has insisted that we must distinguish between the two. However much American power might have been causally related to, and responsible for the intensification of, the process of globalization, it is a fundamental mistake to think of globalization as being no more than an expression of American power. Whatever the role of the United States in aiding and abetting globalization, it is now something beyond the power of the USA alone to shape or control.

This debate captures some key elements about the contested status of the ending of the Cold War, both as regards globalization and American power. The view of American victory in the Cold War is echoed most clearly in the accompanying judgement that a new distributive settlement, enshrining American interests, has now been effectively set in place. There are paradoxical aspects to this situation, and it is these paradoxes that most clearly illustrate what it is that is novel about the post-Cold War situation. In one version, what the new settlement has done is to widen the scope for American unilateralism:

For the United States a rule-based order has often meant the extension of American rules and procedures to the rest of the world. This was a natural by-product of the hegemony enjoyed by the United States during the postwar years. However, this era is over. In the present, more globalized system, the US risks looking not so much like a leader . . . but as a heavy-rider on the system, eroding multilateralism through its own forceful rebellion against rules when they are not in its interests. (Tussie and Woods 2000: 65)

Such a conception tends to emphasize the post-Cold War settlement as an expression of power, and accords well with notions of globalization as an instrument of redistribution. It is further bolstered by the evidence that globalization has been contested for the very reason that it does indeed embody American values and interests (Huntington 1996: 59).

A distinction can be drawn between this and slightly different versions of the argument. These place a greater distance between American power and the contemporary order. Whatever the origins of this order, it is now divorced from that power and is, at least to a degree, 'owned' by much wider sections of international society. At this point, the impositions of a distributive settlement begin to merge into the more subtle variants of a regulative order that evokes degrees of consent, while remaining far from wholly divorced from applications of power. It is this latter version that is well described by Buzan and Little (1999: 99):

Some argue that international society is not Western but Westernistic. This latter view is based on the understanding that the originally Western ideas on which international society rests . . . have now become effectively universal . . . What one sees through this lens is neither a subtle form of Western imperialism nor a new kind of socio-economic imperialism. It is in part, both.

At stake in these debates is both the magnitude of American power, and the manner in which it relates to the current forms of order. Those who see American power as essentially undiminished in the 1990s are happy to argue that it has been expressed through a classically imposed distributive settlement at the end of the Cold War. Those who believe that American power is now subtly changed, and possibly reduced, are more likely to discern a relationship between power and globalization that works at one remove. Falk typically holds that 'there is no effective economic hegemony of the sort provided by the United States in the post-1945 period'. In consequence, we now have a form of order that embodies 'new mechanisms of co-ordination and compromise' in which, by definition, US power can no longer nakedly have its own way (Falk 1999: 25). At this point, subtle forms of regulation take on the task that enforced distribution is no longer able effectively to perform.

There is thus considerable uncertainty concerning two issues about the impact of the end of the Cold War: whether or not American power has increased or decreased; and whether globalization is more, or less, closely associated with this American power as a result. The answers to the two questions are ambiguous in both cases. Those who calculated in strictly zero-sum terms came, unsurprisingly, to the conclusion that the collapse of Soviet power represented a net additional gain to that of the United States. Those who understood that American power was a compound of two separate things—not only the physical capacity, but the political will to make use of it—took account of domestic political dynamics and reached a less certain verdict in consequence. The loss of a clear and present danger from the Soviet Union, it was concluded, might diminish the ability of the US political system to mobilize its physical resources.

The same dilemma can be expressed in terms of the distinction between the distributive and regulative peace. There can be no doubt that the post-Cold War settlement, as a distributive peace, has resulted in a very substantial reconfiguration of power in favour of the United States and its allies. However, it would be wrong to imagine that the full force of the Cold War victory was to be expressed in this distributive settlement alone. Indeed, mindful of the ambivalence of American power, there were good reasons to inscribe the terms of peace preponderantly within the regulative, rather than the distributive, settlement. This, in turn, makes greater sense of the symbiosis between globalization and American power. The very evidence of growing dissociation between the two, as indeed the case for a decline of American power itself, rests on a fundamental misrepresentation of what has actually happened. Precisely because the regulative settlement was paramount, at least in the initial stages, the role of the United States in shaping and sustaining it was less apparent. That, after all, is precisely the function that regulative settlements are designed to perform.

This is closely related to the third provision of the distributive settlement. It has previously been mentioned that, occupying the middle ground in peace settlements, is the quest to impose a new identity on the defeated states. This is a grey area because it is fundamental to the regulative settlement, but clearly also has distributive consequences as well. Just as Japan and West Germany were 'transferred' to the Western side after the Second World War by domestic reconstruction, so it is possible to see the economic balance of power at the Cold War's end adjusted by the change of identity in the former Second World. While economic transition to market economies was fundamental to the process of locking the former communist states into the global economic order (and hence intrinsic to the regulative settlement discussed below), it was also a way of bringing about a major shift in the balance of power. The introduction of economic measures of marketization and privatization was a way to ensure the durability of the new post-Cold War order, but it was also a critical measure of redistribution within the political economy of power. The aspiration to integration in the globalized economy on the part of the former eastern Europe marked this shift in the distribution of power. Those states that had not been able to participate in the Marshall Plan in 1947–8 had now become eligible for material assistance. They were deemed to be members of the global economy, whether or not there would actually be any financial aid forthcoming for their economic reconstruction. This redistribution defined their new eligibility, even if it did not prescribe any entitlement to benefit from it.

At the same time, the demise of the Second World effected a new distribution of economic power in the sense that it brought to an end a hypothetically opposite pole of attraction. While the command economies of the East had long ceased to provide plausible alternatives, the mere geopolitical existence of the socialist bloc continued to give some rudimentary protection to those other parts of the world that were reluctant to succumb to Western ways. With the disappearance of the Second World, this vestigial international protection was also removed.

In all three senses, globalization was present at the creation of the post-Cold War order. It was implicated in the distributive settlement in these important ways: the demographic map was redrawn to describe proximity to the centres of global activity; the nexus between globalization and American power was renegotiated into a more subtle variant; and the geo-economic map was recast to display the conversion of the former socialist states. These distributions wrought in the name of globalization were every bit as significant as the territorial makeover of Europe, or the settlements in other regions of the globe. Indeed, the implications of this set of transitions were truly global, and this is the proper measure of the distributive aspect of the settlement.

It must be remembered that there is something unnatural about peace settlements. They are attempts to freeze, and perpetuate, a particular status quo. The problem is that they deal with situations that are dynamic, not static. As one historian of peacemaking has observed, 'any peace depends upon immobility, and this is not the normal state of living societies' (Russell 1986: 224). The particular distribution of power at the end of a war is subject to erosion and change, and will not sustain itself in the long term. Thus, if the most important fruits of victory appear to be the material distributions to which they give effect, the deeper reality is to be found in those associated safeguards set in place to give them a degree of permanence. What is so striking about globalization is that it fulfilled both functions at the end of the Cold War. It provided the material gains that the victorious coalition could rightfully claim as its proper due. Over and above this, it also implanted within that distribution an encoded gene: its task was so to govern the future behaviour of the states that were a part of it that the resulting order would not quickly be dismantled. This was the double task of globalization. It would be performed by effecting a new global balance of economic power, but also by encouraging a transformation of key states within it. This blending of the distributive with the regulative aspects of the peace can be illustrated by the case of Russian transition.

THE ECONOMIC PEACE AND
RUSSIAN TRANSITION

In addition to military restrictions, peace settlements imposed on those states defeated in war have normally entailed measures of economic recompense, in the form of indemnities and reparations. Yet on the face of it, any attempt to portray the economic aspects of the end of the Cold War as a kind of peace settlement faces even greater difficulty than does the military aspect. In part this is due to the extent to which the peace seemed to imply economic liabilities for the victors, rather than for the vanquished. It is also because the settlement had less to do with any kind of indemnity in the narrow sense, and was more concerned with a radical reconfiguration of the Soviet economic system as a whole. This was the true price that the USSR had to pay for losing the Cold War.

Nonetheless, a consideration of 'the economic consequences of the peace', in the case of the post-Cold War settlement, is instructive and scarcely an unprecedented suggestion. As the full exposure of post-Soviet transition to Western preferences became apparent in the early 1990s, commentators adopted a language that was little removed from such a framework. Typically, Brzezinski (1992: 33) alluded to the reality that 'the economic and even the political destiny of what was not long ago a threatening superpower is now increasingly passing into de facto Western receivership'. This conjured up parallels with Germany in 1945, and reminds us that it is not unprecedented for victorious powers to inherit economic liabilities to their defeated antagonists. The reason that the more punitive types of Morgenthau Plan, entailing the pastoralization of Germany, were not adopted in 1945 was precisely that the Western powers would have been left to pick up the economic and humanitarian costs of its implementation. Economic peace settlements traditionally take the form of extraction, but they may entail elements of economic obligation and encumbrance as well. It is a fair measure of Russian weakness, and of Western control, that by 1999 Russia was indebted to the tune of some $150 billion (Rutland 1999: 198). The accompanying degree of political dictation was also more obvious than some commentators felt comfortable to acknowledge. 'One of the real and many paradoxes of the West's approach to economic reform in Russia', is one such rueful comment, 'was that while it made great play of the need for more economic choice, it put an enormous amount of pressure on Russian decision-makers to go down one particular path' (Rutland 1999: 191). For these reasons, the suggestion that we have witnessed a post-Cold War economic peace is not so fanciful.

What the true nature of that peace settlement has been is open to various interpretations. The little that we can say with confidence is that, if the ambition was for a successful transition to a flourishing market economy, based on a robust liberal polity, then so far the peace has failed. There are few bright prospects for the immediate future. 'The great trek to capitalist normality', in one considered judgement, 'had led to decline and despair' (Rutland 1999: 183–4).

But what were the goals of transition? We can be sure that they were not an economic settlement designed merely to produce a degree of reparation for the West's costs in prosecuting the Cold War. The only sensible framework within which to approach the economic consequences of this particular peace is one that sees it as designed to bring about a radical transformation in the very identity of Russia: it was about Russia's soul, not about the bill it was required to pay. In less apocalyptic language, the punitive aspect of the settlement resided not in its forms of economic extraction, but rather in its quest for economic conformity. The Soviet Union was above all to be made to pay for the Cold War, not by economic reparations as such, but by abandoning its mischievous economic system, and adopting in its place the mantle of respectable liberal capitalism. Of course, revealing the vestiges of Wilsonianism with which it was imbued, even this was not an end in itself, but a means to a yet grander end still: a durable post-Cold War order. Recalling the comments of Strobe Talbott, a member of the Clinton administration, one author reminds us that 'reform in Russia was not just about Russia but the shape of the new international order waiting to be born in the wake of the Cold War' (Rutland 1999: 183). A failure to become effectively engaged in this reform carried with it the risk that 'domestic weakness would breed political extremism and disorder in the nuclear super power' (Gould-Davies and Woods 1999: 1). On the outcome of this attempt at transformation then depended not only the political fate of Russia, but also the viability of the international order itself.

In pursuit of these goals, just how punitive was the peace to be? And were these aims consistent with each other? There are two ways in which the issues might be viewed. The first is the interpretation that the West punished Russia by what it did; the second that it punished it by what it failed to do. These interpretations are elsewhere referred to, respectively, as 'we messed up Russia', on the one hand; and 'we lost Russia', on the other (Gould-Davies and Woods 1999: 3). The first emphasizes the severity of the 'shock therapy' policy, and is often presented in quasi-conspiratorial terms. In this version, the true nature of the punitive peace is to be found in the intention 'to eviscerate the Russian economy while bringing its natural resources to market at the cheapest possible price' (Rutland 1999: 184). There was also a political and military logic associated with this argument, captured in Havel's dictum that a weak Russia is less of a problem for the rest of the world than a strong Russia (Rutland 1999: 200). The shortcoming of this position, in its more extreme formulations, was that such a Western policy, if implemented, was bound to bring about the very political recidivism in Russia that it was designed to avert.

The second view changes the emphasis, by describing the punitive quality of the peace in terms not of extraction, but of what the West refused to bestow by way of assistance:

Western countries had one big chance to make a difference, at the beginning of 1992 . . . President Boris Yeltsin appealed to the West for help, but in vain. The IMF concluded a minor agreement in July 1992, but by then Russia's reformers had already been defeated, in part because they had counted on the West's help. (Aslund 1999: 71)

In this sense, the International Monetary Fund (IMF) became the fig leaf that hid the nakedness of policy underneath. President Clinton was happy to have the IMF make the running because it symbolized Western 'commitment'—without any real obligation to come up with the resources. This Machiavellian aspect of the economic peace is well captured in the suggestion that the IMF 'permitted the US to push Russia in a direction it hoped it would go, but without having to fork out huge sums of money itself' (Rutland 1999: 189). Thus was Russia punished by a refusal to bestow the resources that might have made some difference.

At the heart of any assessment of the nature of the economic peace is the complex interaction between these economic and political goals. We have already encountered a similar dilemma in the case of military disarmament: the punishment of the new political regime in the defeated state may serve only to damage it, thereby bringing about political relapse, as in inter-war Germany. And yet without confidence in the viability of the new regime, it may be wise to take precautions just in case. The same complex interplay operated between the economic and political objectives of the post-Cold War peace. It was a fundamental goal of the peace at the end of the Cold War that the Soviet Union be transformed to a market economy, with privatized forms of ownership. However, there was always the risk that the attempt to bring this about, hastily and without some social protection, could have damaging political consequences. And so critics of the shock therapy condemned it for failing to ensure continued popular support for economic reform. This failure, in turn, exposed the entire endeavour to political backsliding (Weisskopf 1995: 486). Brzezinski had already drawn attention to this potential clash. 'Any attempt to create simultaneously a free-market economy and a political democracy that does not carefully seek to minimize the social pains of the needed transition', he warned, 'could precipitate a destructive collision between these two objectives' (1992: 49).

In the aggregate, what has the attempted transformation of Russia meant for the distributive settlement? It has resulted in a double move. Certainly, strategies of transition have contributed to the disintegration of the Second World, as a meaningful element within the global distribution of power as a whole. That was the first move. But the Second World has not been reconstituted as part of the First. The net effect, as one disenchanted observer notes, has been to relegate 'these states to the ranks of Third World rather than First' (Thomas 1999: 228). This was the second move. Since this much could have been foreseen of any 'shock therapy', the policy itself can reasonably be viewed as part of the post-Cold War distributive settlement.

One can then assess the wisdom of the economic settlement that has been arrived at in respect to its consistency with the wider political goals of the peace. Whether by attempting too much too quickly, or whether by not doing nearly enough, the West has failed to encourage the economic transition that it had sought. This may be more problematic for the Russians than for anyone else. But with this failure, there also collapsed the ambitions for the wider post-Cold War political order that was to accompany it. It may not be so straightforward to dismiss this as a problem for the Russians alone. To understand why this should be so, we need finally to bring together the central themes of globalization, transition, and the distributive aspects of the peace settlement.

GLOBALIZATION, TRANSITION, AND INTERNATIONAL DISTRIBUTION

To grasp fully this perspective on the post-Cold War peace, we must return to the theme introduced at the outset, namely the linkage between the international and domestic dimensions of a settlement. When peace was sought after 1945, it was not simply in terms of a reconfiguration of international boundaries, and military balances of power. What was more profoundly reconfigured was the nature of national societies to ensure that there could be no repetition of those policies of the 1930s that had destroyed the international economy and, with it, the best hopes for international peace and stability. And so the peace settlement that was pursued after 1945 was one which refashioned the nation-state, in such a way that there would be built in to its very nature a compromise between the requirements of its own internal stability, and the wider needs of international economic stability. The post-1945 peace settlement had thus sought to found an international distribution upon a form of domestic regulation. The international order would derive from the reformulation of the state, rather than good state behaviour being imposed from the outside by international institutions alone.

From this perspective also, there is a remarkable continuity between the post-1945 peace and that of 1990. The post-Cold War regulative peace, as will be seen, was to be concerned, above all, not with deepening the external structures of globalization as such, but rather with internalizing them in the shape of new globalized state forms. It was less the intention of the peace that globalization should impose uniformity and convergence from the outside, than that those converging states would from the inside perpetuate conditions conducive to the beneficent workings of globalization. It is in this very specific sense that the failures, to date, to transform the nature of Russian society and economy represent a continuing challenge to the wider order that the West had sought after 1990 to implant.

This logic revealed some return to its Wilsonian roots. While Wilson's 'great experiment' is normally thought to reside in an international organization to effect peace, it was much more subtly understood by him as an encouragement to the emergence of good types of state that would, in turn, make that international organization workable. The emphasis was to be placed on the changing characteristics of states, rather than simply upon the reform of the international structures within which they would operate. The same was to be true of the new phase of globalization to be stimulated by the end of the Cold War. It would induce a stable order within which economic activity, democratic norms, and liberal beliefs would all be greatly enhanced. But this would be done not by creating a structure of globalization that would entrap the states from the outside but, instead, 'regulate' their behaviour by developing within them a set of new characteristics. This was above all the expectation for those states undergoing transition to liberal market economies.

There is a widespread assumption, albeit mistaken, that since globalization appears to be associated with a diminution of state powers, then this must result from impersonal forces operating from the outside to enmesh and constrain its performance. The much simpler truth is that globalization is supported by states themselves, and is a symptom of their own changing nature. Thus we are usefully reminded that 'in a globalizing world states play a crucial role as stabilisers and enforcers of the rules and practices of *global* society' (Cerny 2000: 121). Of course, some states play a more crucial role in this process than do others. '"Strong" states', it has been suggested, 'are also those which can control—to some degree—the nature and the speed of their integration into the world economy' (Woods 2000*b*: 11). They lead by example, and the emulation which they encourage is itself an extremely powerful source of socialization. One opinion is that the most effective way to conceptualize globalization is as a 'basic change in the way in which major institutional actors think and operate' (Biersteker 2000: 150). This claim can be thought to apply to the whole variety of actors, but assuredly must embrace the states themselves. As such, a redefinition of how states 'think and operate' can be encouraged and spread by state example. This is what was to lie at the heart of the post-Cold War settlement.

It would be wholly inaccurate to imagine that this was a trend inaugurated only at the end of the Cold War. It was already powerfully under way long before then. As earlier suggested, this process was itself an important part of the causal story that brought the Cold War to an end. But in its aftermath, the opportunity was taken to reaffirm the basic tenets of this credo: globalized states participating in an open economic order would be the best guarantee of international peace, prosperity, and stability. In case this was too altruistic a message, it took the precaution of appealing to more self-interested motives as well. The states that would do best in this new order, and benefit most from it, were those which most successfully reinvented themselves in accordance with its prescriptions. To be a traditional state in a globalized order was a recipe for failure, but to be a globalized state in this order was to place oneself in the mainstream of activity, and regain a measure of control over one's destiny. In the ultimate paradox, submission was to be the only meaningful route left to national self-assertion. It is this similar point that is captured in Cerny's observation that 'rather than simply being undermined by inexorable structural forces, the competition state is becoming increasingly both the engine room and the steering mechanism of an agent-driven *political* globalization process' (2000: 138). If there is indeed such a political process at work, then the great symbolic turning point of the end of the Cold War must be understood to be a potent demonstration of it.

Why then is it helpful to construe all of this as an exercise in peacemaking? There are two central claims that need to be made in conclusion. The first addresses the concern that international order is treated too much as if it were 'out there'. 'My worry', S. Smith (1999: 103) elaborates, 'is that too much of the literature on international order presents it as something inherent in the world, as a "given".' To the extent that the worry is real, it is particularly appropriate with regard to the tendency to describe the present order as being one forged by an operative globalization 'out there', and over which we have no control. It thus induces the caution that states shape and 'construct' globalization, rather than simply the other way around (Palan 2000: 140). Moreover, placing this construction of order within a peacemaking framework is then helpful in reminding us of the provisional and contingent nature of that process. Peacemaking seeks to inaugurate a certain kind of order, but with no assurance of success. It is this very provisional quality that is so much the hallmark of the post-Cold War era.

Peacemaking, too, and as already mooted, encapsulates a dual process of international and domestic change. Indeed, its contingency is in large measure a consequence of the dependence of international distribution upon the successful implementation of domestic regulation: if the latter fails then the former can collapse with it. In integrating these two dimensions, peacemaking draws the close parallel with the manner in which contemporary globalization needs also to be understood. In these multiple ways, globalization has been both a key item on the agenda of the post-Cold War distributive peace, and also a key instrumentality for perpetuating the redistribution that had been drawn up in its name.

In sum, locating globalization within a framework of peacemaking is helpful on a number of counts. Above all, it makes sense of the end of the Cold War within the continuing process of globalization. Evidently, globalization did not begin with the end of the Cold War. But just as evidently, the end of the Cold War remains a significant milestone within its development. How are we best to cope with this ambivalence without simply compounding the sense of confusion and uncertainty that already prevails in the analysis of the post-Cold War order? The device of the distributive and regulative functions of globalization, as integrated dimensions of a post-Cold War peace, does better than most. It allows us to distinguish between the specific changes introduced in the post-Cold War economic distribution of power, and to afford great emphasis to them, while retaining a balanced awareness of the degree of continuity inscribed in the regulative peace. Having won the war, the victors were determined not to lose the ensuing peace, and the transformations associated with globalization were, paradoxically, the best available guarantee of continuity that was available. Globalization would become the keeper of the peace, of whose terms it was already a fundamental part.

Globalization does not belong to anyone, or to any state. It is not the property of the USA, nor of its close associates. Nonetheless, it is no accident that many of its current forms have developed as they have. These reflect degrees of deliberation, intention, and political agency. The moment of the passing of the Cold War was one such episode, and the terms of the peace settlement were a classical example of this kind of intervention. It is through such instrumentality, historically, and after great wars, that certain forms of development have been encouraged, and yet others thwarted. The post-Cold War peace was to be no different in this respect.

It is therefore illuminating to regard globalization as part of this settlement. Certain trends within it were actively fostered, particularly with regard to the incorporation into the global economy of the former socialist bloc. Much of this distributive settlement was self-implementing, once the communist regimes fell from power. The move to market economies seemed, at that stage, to be a natural one in the aftermath of the failure of communism, as few other options appeared to be available in any event. However, agents of Western governments, and of the international financial institutions, played their prominent part in the form that this transition was to take. To the extent that they did so, they contributed to the appearance of an enforced peace, however voluntary the switch to market economies might otherwise have appeared. Distributively, the conversion of the previous command economies had the effect of making the world safe for future measures of globalization.

This chapter has explored the part played by globalization in bringing about the post-Cold War redistribution of power. The next will consider the part it was to play, in association with a framework of multilateralism, in preserving it.

III

THE REGULATIVE
PEACE

III

7

MULTILATERALISM AND THE GLOBAL ECONOMY

What was the meaning of the end of the Cold War? 'The triumph of the West was not only a victory of democracy or the market system', is one assured verdict, '*it was also a triumph of Western multilateralism*' (Morgan 1993: 345). The implication of this is that the heroic assessments of the end of the Cold War, as by Fukuyama (1989), have missed the point. Liberal capitalism was less significant in the post-Cold War settlement than was the principle of multilateralism. In fact, to the extent that the prospects for democracy and markets have been enhanced by the end of the Cold War, it is for the reason that they are expressions of a more deeply rooted social principle: multilateralism itself.

It is the function of this chapter to explore the sense in which this was the case. It will address again the question of the continuities within the post-Cold War order, as it is within the regulative settlement that these are most striking. Multilateralism—and one specific embodiment of it in the form of the global economy—was the cornerstone of the regulative settle-ment that was to be reaffirmed at the end of the Cold War. In that sense, it represented not a novel dimension to the post-Cold War order but a restatement, in novel conditions, of a set of principles that had already been present during most of the Cold War. How was multilateralism to regulate the post-Cold War peace? The chapter will deal with a number of principal issues in answering that question. What is the meaning and form of this multilateralism? How is it associated with US power and purposes? How specifically has it featured in the measures enacted at the end of the Cold War? It is claimed that, as a result of the events of 1989–91, governments are now willing 'to undertake unprecedented adventures in multilateralism', and that the term is hence now 'out front' (Morgan 1993: 333). If that is so, what is its significance for the nature of the post-Cold War order?

WHY DOES MULTILATERALISM MATTER?

Before we can assess the role of multilateralism in the post-Cold War peace, we need to give the concept some meaning. It is most helpful to approach this in the way elaborated by Ruggie. According to his formulation, multilateralism is a 'foundational architectural principle' (1993*b*: 25). Rather than focus on its specific instances, we can regard it as a general constituent principle instead. Multilateralism can then be applied in a number of contexts, as in the global economy, to be discussed below. It can be considered also in other settings, such as the liberal rights regime and collective security, as will be addressed in the following chapters. There is a thread of multilateralism that runs through all of these, and it is this general organizing principle, regardless of its specific substance, that is the concern of this chapter. Otherwise expressed, it is the principle of multilateralism that is the foundation upon which other aspects of the post-Cold War regulative settlement have been constructed. We might then echo the distinction made elsewhere: we are here concerned with the institution of multilateralism, rather than with multilateralist institutions (Caporaso 1993: 54).

What is the nature of this organizing principle? Ruggie has described it as being 'mildly communitarian' (1996: 4–5). This is potentially confusing, as it might imply that the principle applies only to a select group, and is not universal in scope. In fact, its meaning is exactly the opposite, inasmuch as the principle is the accepted norm of the entire society. It is exactly because multilateralism requires the implementation of ground rules in a non-discriminatory way that it is universal for all those who subscribe to it. The application of these rules, within the multilateralist group, is inherently 'indivisible' (Morgan 1993: 333). Ruggie elaborates:

In its pure form, a multilateral world order would embody rules of conduct that are commonly applicable to all countries, as opposed to discriminating among them based on situational exigencies and particularistic preferences. Such an order also would exhibit a greater degree of indivisibility among the interests of countries than do alternative forms. Greater indivisibility, in principle, entails two further effects: it increases the incentive to pursue interests via joint action, and permits each country to calculate its gains and losses from international transactions in the aggregate. (1996: 20)

This is the principle formulated in the abstract. In practice, it describes a code to govern certain substantive areas of international life. Economically, Ruggie explains, it means 'the prohibition of exclusive blocs, spheres, or similar barriers to the conduct of international economic relations'. Applied to security, it entails 'equal access to a common security umbrella' (Ruggie 1993b: 12). Elsewhere, he extends the same logic to other spheres, and concludes that a multilateralist order is one which affirms 'anti-imperialism grounded in self-determination', and also 'anti-statism grounded in human rights' (Ruggie 1996: 22). As can be seen, the recurring theme of the principle is universality, non-exclusivity, non-discrimination, and indivisibility. By implication, any such international order is one integrated into a single whole, within which all states have an equal opportunity to participate in its various activities, even if it stops short of any principle of equality as to actual enjoyment of its benefits. It is this formal quality, rather than any emphasis on distributive outcomes, that has led one commentator to depict multilateralism as 'nothing more than the internationalization of the liberal conception of the rule of law' (Burley 1993: 144).

As will be seen below, these *motifs* were to recur in the high-profile American rhetoric unveiling the post-Cold War order. It was to precisely this foundational architectural principle that appeal was made to encapsulate what was 'new' about the order in process of creation. Thus it has been claimed of the New World Order that it embodied a 'quite explicit commitment to an open world market economy', and that it was to be managed 'by a series of interlocking multilateral institutions' (M. Cox 1993a: 88). There was nothing remarkable in the enunciation of these principles. The only matter of puzzlement was the claim that they were tantamount to a qualitatively 'new' world order when, in fact, they stood for a return to a core set of values that had animated the American vision of international order throughout the entire Cold War period.

This marked continuity is the most intriguing aspect of the post-Cold

War order. How are we to capture its essence? This will be done in the argument below by claiming that multilateralism was the keystone of the regulative order that emerged in 1990. In order to substantiate this argument, it is first of all necessary to establish why multilateralism should be seen as an important element of continuity linking the Cold War order to the one that emerged in its aftermath.

MULTILATERALISM AND CONTINUITY

'And when President George Bush today enunciates a "new world order", remarked Ruggie (1993*b*: 7), 'the notion evokes and is entirely consistent with the American postwar multilateralist agenda'. And so the claim to continuity is readily established. With it, comes a highly significant implication. This is best developed by placing 1990 in the context of the precedents of 1919 and 1945. It has been suggested that the reason why wars are so important, and magnify the critical role of the subsequent peacemaking, is that they 'destroy the old rules and institutions of order' (Ikenberry 2000: 17). In what sense is this true of the outcome of the Cold War?

It is illuminating, in hindsight, to contrast the peace settlements of 1919 and 1945. In 1919, the previous political order found itself in disrepute as the Wilsonian rhetoric pledged an abandonment of the old autocratic power politics, and its replacement by new forms of collective security. At the same time, there was a nostalgic wish for a return to the seductive certainties of the old economic order that appeared, in retrospect, as the golden age to which all aspired to revert. Arguably, things were the other way round in 1945. For all the seeming failures of collective security in the inter-war period, there was a reaffirmation of faith in it in 1945, with a pledged resumption of its main articles, however much revised by power political concerns. In contrast, there was no wish for a return to the economic circumstances of the 1930s, since there was no normalcy to which the economic order could revert. What was required was a new blueprint for managing this sphere of life. The 'rules and institutions' of international economic order would have to be developed *de novo*.

In comparison, what is so striking about 1990 is, of course, exactly the continuing salience and support accorded each of the pre-existing orders, the political and the economic. The importance of this is that there was a set of ideas, regarded as still viable, that could be carried forward from the Cold War to the post-Cold War order. As has been astutely observed, '"Old" international institutions ... have not been discredited', and '"Old" ideas have not been delegitimized' (Weber 1997: 248–9). This is a remarkable feature of the 1990 settlement, and its consequences must not be overlooked. At the very least, the endurance of these precepts, from one order to the next, may well have ensured that, despite the major shifts of 1990, 'multilateral norms and institutions have helped stabilize their international consequences' (Ruggie 1993b: 3). In short, without this element of continuity, the impact of the end of the Cold War might have been much more damaging for the international system as a whole.

This is not intended to imply that multilateralism followed a consistent and unidirectional trajectory, across the entire post-1945 period and into the post-1990 era. The course of multilateralism has fluctuated repeatedly in accord with wider strategic and geopolitical circumstances. Keohane (1990: 740) is thus correct to remind us that 'the rise of multilateral institutions has not been linear', and there were substantial threats to blow it off course in the 1980s. Indeed, its early post-war history was chequered. The economic order which emerged from the Second World War bore the scars of its 1930s paternity, reinforced by wartime exigency, and it was this that the United States attempted to reshape in accordance with its multilateralist vision (Leffler 1992: 8). Mechanisms such as the Marshall Plan were thus configured to bring about that desired end, and 'the concept of multilateralism' was to be central to it (R. W. Cox 1987: 214). At the same time, the very onset of the Cold War, and the need for the United States to shore up its emerging Western allies, obliged it to modify its own programme and to allow significant departures from multilateralism, strictly conceived. The non-implementation of much of the Bretton Woods system until the late 1950s is illustrative of this kind of concession (Gilpin 1971: 59).

What all this suggests is that multilateralism has survived, albeit variably, across the period. Although it is a point of continuity between the Cold War and post-Cold War orders, we are reminded that multilateralism has fluctuated in its importance, and in its degree of implementation. But there is a yet more radical diagnosis that gives multilateralism an even more central role than this might suggest. According to this, there is a strand of American foreign policy, interwoven with the key ideas of multilateralism, that has remained consistent throughout, from 1945 until the present. That strand has not been ruptured by the end of the Cold War, for the very simple reason that it was not itself shaped by the Cold War exclusively, but developed in separation from it.

There is now a solid body of commentary which, while differing in the specifics of the argument, is agreed upon this key point: what lends continuity to the post-Cold War order is nothing less than the remarkable continuities in American foreign policy itself. Since this key platform had little to do with the Cold War, we should not be surprised to discover that the passing of the Cold War has left little changed as a result. Cumings's simple analogy captures the spirit of the argument admirably. 'It is as if two horses were running around a track', he mused, 'one broke its leg, and the other kept on running anyway' (1991: 195–6). The mistake too many have made was in assuming that the second horse was running *because* of the first.

There is now a chorus of voices in support of this broad outlook. It draws parallels between the New World Order of 1990, and that of 1945 (Kurth 1991: 4). It insists that America's 'post-war grand strategic aims were essentially unconnected to the superpower rivalry', and thus survived intact at the Cold War's end (Layne 1998: 9). It picks up on the theme that multilateralism had more to do with America's strategy for dealing with its friends, than with its strategy for dealing its foes. Hence fundamental continuities into the post-Cold War era have been obscured by the undue regard accorded the role of the Soviet Union, whereas they are 'illuminated by examining the containment of its allies' (Schwarz 1997: 25). This echoed Cumings's much earlier, but similar, assessment. 'The Cold War had consisted of two systems: the containment project . . . and the hegemonic project', he had suggested, and concluded that 'both the hegemonic project and the allied-containment system survive today' (1991: 213). This directs our attention squarely to the issue of American power, and the nature of the regulative settlement that it sought to establish in 1990. This, in turn, invites reflection upon the role of multilateralism as the underlying principle of that settlement.

How are we to move beyond the endless, and seemingly sterile, debates about the current status of American power? We seem to have reached a dead end on the two strands of the discussion—as to whether American power is *necessary* to sustain multilateralism, and whether it is *capable* of doing so.

MULTILATERALISM AND AMERICAN POWER

It is commonplace in the literature to present the growth of post-1945 multilateralism as a whole as the implementation of an American grand design. In accordance with the corporatist interpretation, this international policy was the projection of US values and institutions onto the international realm: it was the internationalization of the 'New Deal regulatory state' (Ruggie 1993*b*: 30; Hogan 1987). More generally, it is repeatedly contended that multilateralism has been profoundly expressive of American material interests. Given the geography of the United States, and the lack of direct threats to its security, its objectives tend to be 'milieu goals', rather than national interests narrowly defined in response to direct threats to its territorial security. The goal of creating a liberal and multilateral international order is the best expression of this set of American interests. 'Given its size, wealth, and geographical position between the two great oceans', is one such opinion, 'the United States inevitably has global commercial interests that are best served when barriers to trade are few and when economic relations among states are governed by law' (Mead 1991: 378).

To these traditional reasons for its advocacy of multilateralism have now been added the particular incentives that have accompanied the end of the Cold War. Above all, the demise of the structure of superpower conflict during the Cold War has left the United States more reluctant to accept, on its own, the responsibilities of order maintenance. In such a context, it is more than ever convenient that the costs be shared across a range of actors, operating through international institutions. From this perspective, multilateralism is appealing to the United States precisely because it permits a degree of demobilization of the US effort. Accordingly, it has been suggested that 'multilateralism ... has increased its attractiveness for the United States, as Washington has become not only more conscious of the limits of American power but also rather weary of its leadership role' (P. Williams 1995: 217–18).

What this reveals is that our understanding of contemporary multilateralism is caught up in powerful ambiguities and paradoxes resulting from its relationship to American power and purposes. Has multilateralism now become more entrenched because of the unchallenged nature of

American power? Or, conversely, has it been championed as a device that would allow some disengagement of America's role, in keeping with the modulated decline of its power base?

There are some important issues that need to be clarified at the outset. To insist that there is a highly significant association between US power and the development of post-1945 multilateralism is not, of course, to make the claim that there have been no tensions between the two. Nor is it to suggest that the United States has been, in practice, the unswerving supporter of multilateralism in all its manifestations. Nothing could be further from the reality. As Ruggie usefully clarifies, multilateralism is a 'set of abstract principles', and we must remember that 'no American leader . . . has ever proposed to institute these principles in their pure form' (1996: 21). Indeed, throughout the 1980s, the United States had become noticeably guarded about the political dimensions of multilateralism, as expressed through the likes of the United Nations. Some commentators spoke of a 'crisis of multilateralism' at this juncture, brought about by a 'tendency on the part of the United States and some other powerful countries to reject the United Nations as a vehicle for international action' (R. W. Cox 1996: 498). Even with the end of the Cold War, it should not be imagined that the United States, as a matter of policy, rushed to embrace multilateralism in all its forms. Its response has been much more selective and ambivalent. The holy citadel of free trade came under increasing attack within the United States, as the erstwhile geopolitical rationales for giving allies wide access to US markets seemed to dissipate (Sanders 1991: 244).

In short, the standing of multilateralism was deeply ambiguous as the Cold War came to an end. It could be called upon to serve American purposes of both engagement and disengagement. Accordingly, it was an object of attack from opposite ends of the political spectrum, both from those who saw it as a 'cover for an American strategy of abdicating international responsibilities', and from those who feared it would simply encourage others 'to rely excessively on Washington' (P. Williams 1995: 220). This ambiguity was engendered precisely because hitherto 'Cold War multilateralism in the West had a focus and a purpose that were clearly defined' (P. Williams 1995: 219). These had now been lost, and the intellectual case for multilateralism had to be made afresh.

Underneath these ambivalent assessments of multilateralism in the post-Cold War era lay deep-seated differences in the interpretation of

America's role in sustaining it. Was multilateralism an outgrowth of genuine international consensus, or merely a convenient expression of American power and preferences? How substantial was the legitimacy that underpinned the multilateral order, or did it rest on nothing more solid than Washington's capacity to impose it, albeit by arm-twisting negotiation? The issue can be tackled by an initial exploration of the role of multilateralism in the distributive and regulative peace.

The image of the post-Cold War period as a phase of peacemaking, equivalent to the epochal events of 1919 and 1945, is explicit in the portrayal of it as a historical endeavour 'to try to win yet another post-war peace' (Ruggie 1996: 2). Central to this idea of winning the peace is the notion of a postwar regulative settlement. Its function was not merely to enunciate the new distribution of power and territory, but to try by other means to sustain the settlement that had been put in place. It is within this understanding of the post-Cold War regulative peace that multilateralism had a key role to play. The moment of victory in the Cold War would inevitably be transient, but if the benefits of that victory were to be preserved for the longer term, then the means had to be devised to lend them greater permanence. Multilateralism was not only part of the material victory of the Cold War, but also part of the means for sustaining it. In that sense, it appeared in the distributive settlement, but was also an instrumentality for ensuring its longer-term viability. How was multilateralism to regulate the post-Cold War order?

A regulative peace can be construed as a fusion of two discrete forms. The first of these derives from a practice of hegemony, and makes appeal to power, widely defined, as the principal source of regulation. The latter, in contrast, derives its efficacy from legitimate authority and may be described, in the language of one theorist, as regulation by constitutionalism (Ikenberry 2000). The puzzle that needs to be answered is then whether the post-Cold War peace is sustained by hegemony, or by a form of constitutionalism. In turn, we need to explore both the hegemonic and the constitutional accounts of multilateralism.

According to the hegemonic interpretations, multilateralism is simply the expression, and chosen instrument, of dominant American power. With the emergence of its unrivalled power position at the end of the Second World War, the United States found itself able to impose its own preferences for the new order. Given the collapse of the international security order in the 1930s, and that this had been responsible for engulfing the United States in global war, American leaders sought to construct a new order that would prevent any such recurrence. Their diagnosis of the 1930s led to the obvious conclusion that the economic and security orders were defective above all in their flagrant disregard for the principle of multilateralism; the creation of a new multilateral order thereby was to become the solution to the failures of the inter-war period. The ability of the United States to impose its vision, in turn, was a clear measure of the unchallenged condition of American power in 1945. That multilateralism was chosen in 1945 was thus a reflection of American *preferences*; that it could be implemented was a reflection of American *power*. For both these reasons, the history of post-1945 multilateralism became inextricably intertwined with American foreign and economic policy.

Such an image also pervades those 'hegemonic stability' accounts that identify the emergence of the post-1945 order with the clear assertion of American primacy (Gilpin 1987; Keohane 1984). It is also to be found in those 'structural' accounts of American power that regard the normative and ideological principles of any international order as an extension of the most powerful state(s) within it. Typically, Susan Strange (1996: xiv) embraced such a structural position in her analysis of continuing American hegemony, when she claimed of regimes in general that they 'have not so much been the result of a coming-together of equals, but the end-result of a strategy developed by a dominant state'. When the regime is in place, this in turn reinforces the power of the hegemonic state, because it becomes a substitute for more direct expressions and uses of that power. The hegemon can, to a greater extent, rely upon the regime to do the work on its behalf.

It is within this kind of framework that the hegemonic view of multilateralism is located. It is an expression of American interests and power, and is there to impose a set of principles that work to the overall advantage of the United States. By the end of the Cold War, such an assessment was emerging in some quarters with regards to both the economic and the political manifestations of the new multilateralism. As to the economic, the critics denounced the multilateral regulation of the 1990s under the Uruguay Round, and the newly formed World Trade Organization (WTO) because these symbolized the 'defeat of the South'. What was so salient about this economic multilateralism was its sweeping away of all the protective discriminatory safeguards for the Third World that had been fought for during the 1970s and 1980s (Bello 1998: 208). In the political sphere, multilateralism became the new expression of American power in the United Nations. With it emerged the problem of whether 'the UN could function as a world organization if it came to be perceived as the instrument of its most powerful member' (R. W. Cox 1996: 498). Insofar as the regulative peace was one that was shaped around the restatement of the principles of multilateralism, the post-Cold War settlement is best understood as a hegemonic one, designed to limit the power of all other states within the system.

But not all accounts of the post-Cold War peace, nor of the role of multilateralism within it, necessarily take this form. There is one sharp alternative to it, best found in the writings of John Ikenberry (1998, 2000). His interest is in how post-war orders come to be formed, and he sees an important aspect of this as residing within the quest for 'institutional' agreements. These have less to do with specific, and substantive, issues but, more fundamentally, concern 'the principles, rules and parameters within which particular bargains are conducted over outcomes' (1998: 154–5). He then claims that order formation, after major wars, can take the form of 'constitution building'. The essential political logic of this exercise is similar to that entailed by the idea of regulation in this book. As Ikenberry explains, it is a political strategy for preserving the fruits of victory for the longer term:

A dominant postwar state has a choice—it can use its commanding material capacities to win conflicts over the distribution of gains; or, knowing that its power position will eventually decline and that there are costs to enforcing its way within the order, it can move toward a constitutional settlement. In this situation, there are incentives for the leading state to agree to limit its power—to insert itself into a constitutional order—in exchange for the acquiescence and compliant participation of secondary states in the postwar order (1998: 148).

The critical effect of such constitutional strategies is that they 'limit the returns to power' (1998: 149). This reveals the heart of the analytic distinction between a hegemonic, and a constitutional, interpretation of multilateralism. According to the former, multilateralism limits the power of all other states apart from that of the hegemon, whereas in the latter it limits the power of all states, including the hegemon. It is for this reason, and emphasizing again the notion of constitutionality as binding upon all states, that it has been asserted that multilateralism serves not only as a means for developing the international order, but 'also as *the source of legitimacy*' (Morgan 1993: 346).

At stake in this is the degree of consensus, compliance, and legitimacy attached to the norms of multilateralism, as distinct from their expression as a form of power alone. This, in turn, is central to the investigation of the role of multilateralism after 1990. Clearly, it is no part of the present argument to assert that multilateralism in the history of international relations is merely an artifice and adjunct of American power. There had been a long history of multilateralism before any emergence of American primacy, as Ruggie himself had readily acknowledged (1993*b*: 24). Nor, for that matter, can it plausibly be suggested that multilateralism has been consistently applied and respected throughout the golden age of American hegemony. At best, there were at times a kind of minilateralism, masquerading as multilateralism, but circumscribed by 'a large number of persistent derogations from its injunctions' (Kahler 1993: 300).

Nonetheless, the relationship between American power and multilateralism continues to lie at the heart of much that is confusing and problematic about the post-Cold War order. Its ambivalence may be captured in the following grounds on which one critic has chastised Washington for its failures of policy in the post-Cold War period:

In short, the United States has repeatedly created a major dilemma for itself and the world order it has championed in that it has struck the pose as the world's principal order keeper but has shied away from the risks and costs that posture inevitably entails. Washington has made this dilemma more serious than it needs to be, in part because it has systematically opposed or discredited any realistic alternative to American power. (Schwenninger 1999: 48)

This analysis is suggestive, and reaffirms that American power is central to the discussion. It also neatly encapsulates the dilemmas of the regulative peace. On the two conceptions outlined above, multilateralism plays differing roles. It is either the expression of American power, widely defined to include its penumbra, of which the ideas of multilateralism are themselves a part. Alternatively, it forms part of a quasi-constitutional order. Multilateralism can then be conceived as the 'foundational architectural principle' pervading this post-Cold War constitution. The first liberates

American power, by setting it free to define its own terms of engagement; the second circumscribes American power, to make it acceptable to other states. The unhappy compromise of the post-Cold war settlement to date is that the United States prefers the former because it makes the world safe for the exercise of American unilateralism. The problem with it is that this might heap too many burdens on the USA, and for that reason the alternative holds some appeal also. But, however wary it is of the potential political costs of the former, it remains too wedded to it to make the latter seem genuinely plausible to the rest of the world.

This does indeed leave major problems for the viability of the order. If the objective of a regulative settlement is to sustain the peace in the longer term, then the durability of the peace will depend upon the efficacy of that regulative support. In the hegemonic version, the peace is coterminous with the effective application of American power. In the constitutional variant, the peace will endure as long as there is a reasonable consensus that the provisions of the settlement are tolerably legitimate.

The acute danger, of course, is that the order may fall between the two stools. The spectre that looms is like that of 1919, when there was neither a sufficiently robust regulative order, able to draw on a well of legitimacy, nor the resolution to maintain the peace by the more direct application of national power. If the regulative settlement is weak and vulnerable in this way, it falls prey to the tensions of the distributive settlement itself. The more punitive and discredited the latter, the greater is the pressure exerted upon the regulative constraints. If the regulative restraints are uncertain in their validity, hovering uneasily between hegemonic and constitutional variants, then the prospects become increasingly gloomy for the order to endure without substantial challenge.

There are then benefits in approaching this entire issue within the framework of peacemaking. As we have seen, it is possible to adopt either a 'hegemonic' or a 'constitutional' view of this part of the settlement. The implications of each are substantially different for our assessment of the resulting order, and for its prospects for endurance.

On the one hand, this analytic framework gives a central place to power, but then proceeds to qualify that role by the very indeterminacy that is inescapable between the act of peacemaking, and its resulting order. A peace is an act of power, but its consequences cannot be fully determined by it. A similar point can be made in converse fashion. A regulative order is less directly attached to the specific configurations of power than is a distributive settlement, while remaining still an expression of that power. It is not possible to conceive of peacemaking between victor and vanquished outside a framework of the power differential between them. But if power were all that was at stake, peace settlements could be restricted to the distributive sphere alone. It is precisely because power is a precarious foundation on which to base a peace—since it is costly to exercise, and possibly evanescent—that functional substitutes for it are sought to preserve the peace. The regulative peace is then obviously related to power, but less visibly an expression of it. It is the continuation of the victory by other means. If it performs its task successfully, the distribution of power becomes thereafter a less salient consideration and concern. How then has multilateralism been able to serve the needs of such a regulative peace?

MULTILATERALISM AND THE
REGULATIVE PEACE

Regulative settlements, by their nature, tend to be unlike distributive settlements. They normally do not need to take the form of codified agreements. Instead, they articulate a pervasive climate of ideas. To this extent, a regulative settlement may appear to be more rhetorical than substantial. However, appearances to the contrary, they do set out an important agenda, as they seek to induce and foster specific types of state behaviour.

The post-Cold War regulative peace needs therefore to be approached as a set of norms and beliefs. If it is true, as Ikenberry (1998: 150) attests, that the 'major postwar settlements were all big bangs' in their capacity to shape the new order, then we must look to the realm of ideas, not just power distributions, to map out the changes that take place as a result. Amongst these was unquestionably the governing principle of multilateralism, so much so that it was immediately associated with claims, after the Cold War, about the onset of a new age. Typically, multilateralism was identified as the central theme of the New World Order, and it was vouchsafed that 'this is a concept that is increasingly seen by analysts as one of the keys to managing international relations in the post-Cold War era' (P. Williams 1995: 209). At the very least, it was widely recognized that international institutions had benefited greatly from the new mood after the end of the Cold War (Weber 1997: 229). This required a shift of attention away from the superficial preoccupation with the 'structure' of the international system to deeper issues. Amongst these, there was said to be evidence that the 'rush to international institutions reaffirms international law and multilateralism' (Reus-Smit 1998: 24).

As noted, it is important to stress this act of 'reaffirmation', rather than to place too much emphasis on the introduction of new ideas. During 1990 and 1991, when the project of a New World Order by name remained very much in vogue, these central ideas were rearticulated on many occasions by US leaders and officials. The two themes that stood out in this regulative rhetoric were those of 'indivisibility' and 'cooperation in international institutions'. Together, these can be taken as the main expressions of the multilateralist credo. This was best encapsulated in President George Bush's reference, before the UN General Assembly on 1 October 1990, to the enticing post-Cold War prospect of 'the whole world whole and free' (US Information Service 1991). It was powerfully reiterated by the constant appeal to the idea of 'sharing' tasks and responsibilities within the international community. For example, in his major statement on the New World Order before Congress, Bush articulated his vision as a world in which 'nations recognise the shared responsibility for freedom and justice' (US Information Service 1991). Elsewhere, addressing the War College at Maxwell Air Force Base on 13 April 1991, he expressed his hope for a world 'based on a shared commitment among nations large and small, to a set of principles that undergird our relations' (US Information Service 1991). When he was not speaking of 'sharing', his other preferred idiom was that of partnership. He appealed before the UN General Assembly on 1 October 1990 for 'a partnership based on consultation, co-operation and collective action' (US Information Service 1991). Here we have a set of classical expressions of the mainstays of multilateralism, both as a goal to be sought in its own right, and as a means to a wider purpose. All the key elements of multilateralism are contained therein—inclusion, non-discrimination, equality of participation—as the essential bases of an open and free world order.

Had the American President been alone in depicting this as the essential quality of the new order, his utterances might have been dismissed as solipsistic. But Bush's sentiments found an exponent also in the Soviet President Gorbachev. The symmetry of language was often striking, and nowhere more so than when Gorbachev too singled out the great theme of inclusivity within a single integrated order. He aspired to the creation of 'a single international democratic space' (Gorbachev 1991: 114), and in so doing repeated this principal article of the multilateralist faith.

The second dimension that was regularly to be rehearsed was the role of international institutions as the key architectural feature of the new order. State Department officials set out the prospects for the new multilateralist ideal in some detail:

I believe ... that we need a foreign policy which builds on the pre-eminent achievement of US diplomacy during the Cold War; namely the institutionalized patterns of co-operation among the Western democracies. This co-operation, embodied in institutions such as NATO, the OECD and the GATT, grew out of the fact that for the first time in history all the nations of the West saw themselves as part of a common purpose and sharing a common destiny. What we need to do now is to widen this circle to include the many new members of the Democratic family. (Eagleburger 1991)

The same emphasis on multilateral institutions could be found elsewhere, not least with respect to the institutions of the world economy. Bush himself, addressing the IMF-World Bank on 25 September 1990 in Washington DC, praised these two bodies as 'paradigms of international co-operation' (US Information Service 1991).

As already argued, there was nothing very new about all of this. Rhetorically, however, what was so striking about these presentations of multilateralism during the period of the regulative settlement was the appearance given that a new agenda was being pursued, and as part of a new world order. At the same time, of course, the very appeal of multi-lateralism as the new regulative ideal resided in its already proven track record. It could be presented as something new, in full confidence that it would be welcomed as something that had already been successful. If there was a theme of novelty that had some material basis, then it was the geographical scope to which multilateralism was now considered applicable. This expansion in the purview of multilateralism, not the principle itself, was to be the only novel feature of 1990.

Accordingly, the programme for a New World Order directed attention to the prospect of 'one international system' (M. Cox 1993*b*: 8), in contrast to the subdivided world characteristic of the Cold War. In practice, this meant that the goal of the West, as eastern Europe broke away from the Soviet Union, was not the creation of new zones freed from the Soviet orbit, but left to enjoy their own autonomy. Instead, the post-Cold War goal came to be expressed in more positive terms, not just as liberation from the East but as accession to the West. This sleight of hand concealed a world of policy difference. As the US State Department coyly conceded 'the long-term goal of US policy in Eastern Europe is to encourage the region's economic and political integration into the world, ending the artificial division of the continent' (US Department of State 1989: 3). Eastern Europe was not to be extracted and then left in a void; it was immediately to be reinserted into another framework, the global multilateralism that now stood unchallenged. 'The idea was to use multilateral institutions', notes Ikenberry (2000: 235), 'as mechanisms to stabilize and integrate the new and emerging market democracies into the Western democratic world.'

In a sense, this represented little more than the undoing of the corrupting logic of the late 1940s. It has been pointed out that, with the onset of the Cold War spheres of influence, 'multilateralism did not simply vanish in the early Truman years', but instead was 'pushed down to the regional level' (Ruggie 1996: 45). It had not been abandoned, but merely confined to restricted parts of the globe, such as western Europe. That original, and more inclusive, programme could now be reinstated as multilateralism was once more elevated to the global level. At the same time, genuine forms of multilateralism could replace the subsidiary minilateralism that had previously been its substitute. This was not a new logic, simply the working out of the same logic on an expanded front.

It also revealed the complex interplay between ends and means in the history of post-war multilateralism. The regulative peace that had progressively been put in place after 1945 operated increasingly, as Schroeder (1995: 375) has put it, not by means of coercion but by the implicit threat of exclusion. Behaviour was to be shaped by the inducement of accession to the multilateral order, and unsociable behaviour deterred by the threat of exclusion from it. This was the means by which the Cold War had been fought but also, in the moment of victory, the end that was to be fulfilled as well. This created the opportunity for a new round of accessions to the existing order, rather than its replacement by something new.

Multilateralism had always presented this dual aspect in American policy. As a means, it had been thought the essential modality for achieving a more peaceful and prosperous world order, consonant with particularly American interests. In 1990, however, the rhetoric conveyed the impression also that multilateralism was to be an end in itself, the final apotheosis and consummation of the quest to extend the rules of the game to all potential players within it.

This may, of course, all sound much too benign. Again, it is important to recall the critical perspective on the regulative settlement that has already been encountered. Many see this regulation as an exercise in power that is cynically self-interested and discriminatory, whatever the rhetoric might claim. The victory of multilateralism after the Cold War is thus accompanied by sinister overtones. The critics see this most glaringly in the field of economic development for the South. 'In sum, as the UN system of economic development-related institutions lies in shambles', is one such negative verdict, 'the Bretton Woods system of multilateral bodies governing the world economic system for the interests of the world's rich minority has finally been completed' (Bello 1998: 222).

In which other tangible ways has the post-Cold War regulative settlement come to be implemented? Its substantial incarnations, beyond the climate of ideas reviewed above, are to be found in the activities of the motley multilateral institutions that have carved out for themselves an ever increasing role in global governance. These can briefly be illustrated with reference to international trade negotiations, the setting up of the WTO, and the augmented role of the IMF. A brief survey of these international economic institutions conveniently sets the scene for the following discussion of the role of the global economy in the regulative settlement.

The ratification of the Uruguay Round represented a further institutionalization of multilateralism in the realm of international trade. To be sure, it is erroneous to suggest any direct connection between that trade round and the end of the Cold War. The Round began in the mid-1980s, well before any anticipation of the end of the Cold War, and was not finally agreed until December 1993—well after its end. In that sense it is artificial to see it as part of any settlement of the Cold War. Nonetheless, its significance lies precisely in its reaffirmation of a set of ideas at such a critical juncture, and this was to be of much wider symbolic importance. From the 1970s, and throughout the 1980s, free trade had been subject to various pressures, and many analysts thought the future looked bleak: protection-ism, regionalism, and bilateralism were widely expected to have their final triumph over multilateralism.

It must be conceded that multilateralism has not yet finally escaped the remaining challenges to it (Tussie and Woods 2000). Not least is this so because the United States itself is 'decidedly ambivalent' in its own view of 'multilateral trade rules' (Ikenberry 2000: 272). Nonetheless, the mood by the mid-1990s had become much more upbeat and resilient than a decade before. This was largely because the fruits of the trade negotiations had to be seen in the wider political context of the events surrounding the end of the Cold War as well. Note, for example, the self-confidence in the following ode to multilateral trade:

Those of us who believe in the value of international economic integration—through freedom of trade and open markets—have a good deal to be optimistic about. Perhaps not for a century have political ideas and economic trends so helpfully coincided. The Uruguay Round agreement is successfully concluded. The World Trade Organization is up and running with the few remaining outsiders, notably China and Russia, waiting to join. (Cable 1996: 227)

The Uruguay Round had set out to achieve a number of objectives (Nicolaides 1994). These mainly concerned bringing agriculture and tex-tiles within the scope of the General Agreement on Tariffs and Trade (GATT); placing limits on safeguards as a form of protectionism; covering intellectual property rights and trade-related investment; and other ser-vices. If its successes were modest and limited, they must nonetheless be viewed against the background in which they occurred and, as has been noted, 'the Uruguay Round was conceived as a means of stopping the rising tide of protectionism' (Nicolaides 1994: 243). In short, assessments of the Uruguay Round must bear in mind not only what it succeeded in bringing about, but also what it managed to prevent.

This was accompanied by the creation of the World Trade Organization as the final piece of architecture missing from the original post-1945 multi-lateral edifice. This was agreed as part of the Uruguay Round, and the WTO was formally established at the beginning of 1995. The GATT had never been an actual organization, merely a set of rules, and its replace-ment by the WTO was seen as asserting a much more effective form of discipline in the area of international trade. It was also explicitly a reaffirmation of faith in the multilateralist principle. The new WTO was less subject to veto by individual member states, even if remaining far from an egalitarian institution since it continued to be dominated by the leading members of the 'Quad' (Tussie and Woods 2000: 62). Tellingly, and revealing the impetus behind the new multilateralism, both China and Russia sought to join the WTO, although there were seen to be major impediments to both accessions (Eglin 1997; Sabelnikov 1996).

As processes of transition to market economies were encouraged in the former Soviet bloc, the IMF was given a greatly augmented role as the overseer of this task. Whether or not it was deemed to be up to these, the IMF acquired a new sense of purpose as a major international institution in the 1990s. This befitted its role as the ideological champion of the liberal economy. Indeed, its function has been described as being the 'normative' one of fostering 'liberal internationalism' and, in particular, of encouraging 'market solutions to economic problems, national economic openness, non-discrimination between nationals and foreigners, and multilateral approaches to common economic challenges' (Pauly 1994: 204). The logic here was the same as the logic of the creation of the North American Free Trade Agreement (NAFTA), with regard to Mexico. 'NAFTA was a mechanism', it has been adjudged, 'to insure that Mexico's movement toward market capitalism would continue' (Ikenberry 2000: 241). The rise of the IMF in the 1990s was then confirmed by its role as manager of the various financial crises that occurred later in the decade. Its importance with regard to the former communist bloc was underscored by its unique quality as 'the only nearly universal forum for the discussion of global monetary issues' (Pauly 1994: 207).

The restatement of the principles of multilateralism with regard to these key features of the global economy was not some fortuitous occurrence at the end of the Cold War. It was very much part of a strategy of preserving the post-Cold War peace by including within it states from the former Soviet bloc. Multilateralism was the underlying principle that facilitated the role that the global economy was to play within this wider regulative order.

THE GLOBAL ECONOMY AND THE
REGULATIVE PEACE

The discussion of multilateralism in general slides easily into the discussion of the workings of the global economy specifically, and raises similar issues about the place of the global economy in the regulative peace. As part of the post-Cold War peace settlement, globalization has become one of the principal forms through which regulation has been inscribed. It is a way of protecting and reinforcing the main principles of the distributive peace by enhancing their durability. It is this kind of idea that Woods (2000*b*: 17) expresses when she maintains that 'globalization may well further empower those states which shaped globalization in the first place—reinforcing their capacity to regulate its ongoing impact'. We can see in this statement a potent example of the interplay between the distributive and the regulative dimensions of globalization itself. The former provides the political capacity for the latter whilst, in turn, the latter becomes an important means of enshrining and perpetuating the favourable distribution of power that has already emerged. Globalization is the score card and, simultaneously, the rule-book by which the game is to be played.

What does globalization regulate, and how? The answer to these questions is variously conceived in the existing literature. At the broad end of the spectrum, the regulation is thought equivalent to the panoplies of global governance, and at that point shades into the quasi-constitutional characteristics noted by Ikenberry (2000). In conditions of globalization, much of this governance is private rather than public (Barry Jones 2000: 176–7). At the narrower end, it is restricted to behavioural norms for the conduct of a global economy and, as such, supports a set of 'new and increasingly intrusive international rules' that govern markets and competition (Cable 1999: 54).

The more searching question is with regard to the modality of this regulation: how is it done? At this point, there is a conventional account that is dominant in a vast segment of the existing literature. Its central thesis is that globalization regulates by the manner in which it entraps and constrains the activities of states. It is this thesis that underpins the entire edifice of the 'state in retreat' or 'erosionist' types of argument (Clark 1999).

It regulates by limiting or eliminating the policy choices of states, especially in the economic sphere. The examples cited are myriad and need only be illustrated at this point. In a world of mobile capital, it is claimed, 'it has become more difficult to tax capital'. The consequence is that 'the burden shifts to labour'. Generically, this renders it 'more difficult to run welfare states' (Devetak and Higgott 1999: 488). Elsewhere, the loss of state economic power is best illustrated by their loss of control over national currencies, that most deep-seated and traditional symbol of their potency. The problem now is, as the case of Russia in the 1990s demonstrated, that 'in an increasingly globalized world, not even the most authoritarian government can assure that its money will always be preferred to currencies originating elsewhere' (Cohen 2000: 87). As a result of this 'coercive socialization' (Barry Jones 2000: 97), the global economy in effect dictates the kinds of economic policies to be pursued by states. If they challenge their subordination, they will be punished by global markets for their temerity in doing so. Moreover, that economy's insistence on the free movement of goods has further eroded their policy capacity by weakening their ability to police its darker side. 'The free flow of drugs and the free circulation of crime have accompanied the formation of a global world economy', notes Hoffmann (1998: 83–4). He concludes ruefully that 'governments find it difficult to restore against such "bad goods" the controls they have removed to facilitate the flow of the good ones'. Since the entire global financial system is at risk from a crisis within any member of it, the system takes it upon itself to regulate for orthodoxy in the activities of each and every one of them:

The implication is that globalization requires international organizations to enforce a much deeper level of policy integration or convergence, nudging the international institutions ever more deeply into the preserve of national governments' economic policy-making. (Woods 2000c: 214)

In short, the principal manifestation of regulation is to be found in the demise of state policy autonomy: this is what globalization does, and the sweeping away of the debris of the Cold War has removed any final sources of political resistance to this logic. Evidence for the effectiveness of this erosion of state autonomy can be found also in emerging policies of regionalism. These are pursued in recognition of the inability of the state to follow its own path, and should be seen as 'an attempt to regain some of the regulatory influence lost in the national political space' (Sorensen 1998: 99).

According to this mode of reasoning, what makes it increasingly possible for the global economy to dictate the preferences of the individual state is its destruction of the democratic accountability between government and national constituency. This amounts to the breaking, by what Falk terms 'predatory globalization', of 'the former social contract that was forged between state and society during the last century or so' (1999: 3). Since governments are no longer seen as the initiators of economic trends, they are deemed not to be able to control them and, for that very reason, to be unaccountable for them. Thus is the 'democratic deficit' perceived to be the adjunct of the demise of state power in the face of globalization, as is widely acknowledged. Cable (1999: 31) admits that the 'sense of a "democratic deficit" is most acute where economic integration is deepest'. Gray (1998: 17), more iconoclastically, declares the universal truth that 'democracy and the free market are rivals, not allies'. Others note the paradox that, just when it is most needed for engagement with global issues, 'globalization attenuates the hold of democratic communities over the policy-making process within the territorial state' (Devetak and Higgott 1999: 490). And so on: the voices lamenting this condition are legion, and originate from across the political spectrum (Held 1995; Chomsky 1997: 178; Falk 1999: 161; Self 2000: 158).

Given the failure of these mechanisms of democratic accountability, the global economy is able to penetrate the policy-making of the states, and set the priorities for it. Globalization, thus conceived, is a form of regulation by insinuation. Convergence upon orthodox economic policies is effectively manipulated by the global system operating from without the state, but by instilling within it the economic principles and precepts that national governments must pursue. The end of the Cold War thus marks the final victory of this system, and the triumph is enshrined in the regulative peace that was established as a result. That post-war settlement, although effectively an imposition, was so much portrayed as being in the universal interest that it has been willingly acceded to by all participants. So effective is it in its task of regulation, that its basic principles have been gladly embraced.

There are, of course, critics who simply deny the validity of such accounts on empirical grounds (Garrett 2000: 108). The point here is not to enter these debates as such, but rather to challenge the frameworks within which they have been conducted. As the author has argued elsewhere (Clark 1999), the above outline is a misleading account of globalization and, as such, must also be a misleading account of the post-Cold War peace. To be sure, regulation is a very significant component of that settlement, but it does not work in quite the manner depicted in the foregoing version. It is a distortion to see post-Cold War regulation merely in terms of a constraining global economy on two grounds. First, the constraint does not operate simply from the outside in, as this image tends to imply. Secondly, the regulation penetrates more deeply than the implied loss of economic policy choice alone would have us believe. It denotes a much more fundamental transition of which economic behaviour is but one of the symptoms. The regulation, within this alternative framework, occurs above all by the deep-seated changes in the nature of the state (Clark 1999). These changes were assuredly aided and abetted by the regulative settlement at the end of the Cold War, as the earlier discussion of post-Soviet transformation has established.

THE MULTILATERAL PEACE

These represented some of the specific institutional forms through which multilateralism was to be expressed after the Cold War. However, the specific instantiations are in themselves much less significant than the general behavioural ideal that they collectively embody. What was vindicated and reasserted by the events of 1990 was less a set of unchanging institutions than a set of normative guidelines that would pervade the post-Cold War order. This was to be their culminating moment. The precise distributive settlement deriving from the end of the Cold War held out the prospect of the application of these guidelines to a wider segment of international society than at any time in the past. This, alone, would not have been sufficient to lend historical resonance to the opportunity had it not also been coupled with an appreciation of multilateralism as the quintessential means and end of the Cold War itself. This was the future, and it had been shown to work. Multilateralism had helped to deliver the victory, by revealing the full costs of exclusion from it. It also constituted the prize to which all must now aspire.

Within this conception, how does multilateralism sustain the peace settlement and help to preserve it? Multilateralism, it was believed, would bring material benefits (albeit not equal) to all who participated within it. The significance of this, in turn, rested on the diagnosis, deeply imbued since the 1930s, that no international order could be viable without economic and social stability at its base. However, multilateralism was thought critical not simply with regard to its material effects. Additionally, multilateralism came to be associated in the American mind with other virtues as well. The habit of multilateral participation and cooperation, so it was believed, would foster better international citizenship. The practice of international accommodation and peaceful negotiation would embed democratic norms domestically. It would also be fully consistent with the application of a liberal rights order, itself expressed through increasing codification and regulation. In these various ways, multilateralism was conceived as part of the wider 'democratic peace': if the prescriptions of multilateralism were adhered to, peacemaking would thus translate into the actuality of peace.

Multilateralism was also thought to have a more direct impact on international security. There had already been a marked 'return' to the United Nations in the late 1980s, as the Cold War began to wind down. In its aftermath, the recovery of the original mission of the United Nations became a key plank in the multilateralist platform, seemingly realized in the collective security operation of the Gulf War in 1990–1. Above all, we cannot dissociate this regulative settlement of multilateralism from the final expansion of NATO itself. As argued earlier in Chapter 4, this was not on the agenda at the immediate conclusion of the Cold War. Nonetheless, the logic that was eventually to push in this direction was precisely the logic of the extending sway of multilateralism that was so superabundantly present in 1990 and 1991. If multilateralism was now to enjoy unbridled access in other spheres of international activity, could the logic of expansion long be delayed from that greatest of all success stories of the Cold War, namely NATO itself? What meaning would there be to indivisibility, and what legitimacy to equal access, if participation in this alliance was itself to be denied? It was no part of America's programme for NATO in 1990 that it should incorporate the former eastern Europe. However, the very regulative settlement that the United States had helped put in place was itself to become a powerful restraint against any other outcome.

The other principal instances of regulation will be reviewed in the remaining chapters of the book. These cover the forms of contemporary security, and the agenda for the articulation of a set of universal liberal rights. Again, none of these was born as a result of the end of the Cold War, but each was powerfully rearticulated in consequence of that event. The opportunity was taken further to entrench them as the underpinnings of the new international order. It is to these other components of the regulative settlement that the remainder of the book will now turn.

8

THE COLLECTIVIZATION
OF SECURITY

Insofar as wars provide the opportunity for devising new forms of international order, they focus attention upon the conditions of security in particular. By definition, wars represent the breakdown of the existing security order, and they offer the victors the possibility of putting something more effective in its place. This was demonstrably the case as regards the dominant bipolar security order that had prevailed during the Cold War. With its collapse, an alternative order had to be constructed in its stead. However, bipolar competition between the two superpowers, no matter how highly visible during the Cold War years, was not the only element within that existing structure of security. Did the end of the Cold War necessitate changes in all other dimensions of security as well? The function of this chapter is to review the continuities and discontinuities between the two periods, and in particular to explore the regulative aspects of the peace that was put in place after 1990. The core argument is that the security order was to take a form that became extensively 'collectivized'. What has this meant, and what have been its implications for international security?

This approach to the post-Cold War order—as the result of a peace settlement—provides a helpful insight into the trajectory of that order. Analyses of the post-Cold War order have recurrently held that it is a transient phase. The implication is that it is an order still undergoing formation: we cannot yet describe it clearly because the order has not yet materialized fully. All post-war orders are provisional and transient. Frequently, as has been noted by Michael Howard, there is a 'chill peace' (1993/4: 33), after the phase of peacemaking, before the order either stabilizes into a more acceptable form (as after 1815), or before it begins to erode and decline into something worse (as after 1919). In other words, a peace settlement is no more than a *template* for a type of order. Whether the reality will correspond with that outline, or diverge substantially from it, is an open question. The function of the regulative peace is to foster compliance with that blueprint, but there can be no assurance that this will necessarily eventuate. The process on which we have been adrift since 1990 is not the transformation of a Cold War to a post-Cold War order, but rather the attempted implementation of the post-Cold War peace settlement as an actual and viable form of order.

DISTRIBUTIVE AND REGULATIVE SECURITY

The reason why security can be approached via the distributive and regulative dimensions of peacemaking is that both offer strategies for its pursuit. As regards France's approach to the settlement of 1919, and to judge by the standard accounts of that policy, the French definition of security was framed in largely distributive terms. What was required of the peace settlement to satisfy French needs for security was a distribution of territory and military resources that would strengthen France and weaken Germany. All the regulation in the world—via collective security or international organization—was considered superfluous, if that basic need were not to be met. Others, especially the United States and, to a degree, Britain were more inclined to think of post-war security in regulative terms. For this to be achieved, it was important that the territorial and economic distributions should not be so damaging as to erode the basis for effective compliance with the treaty.

Peacemaking is bound, by its nature, to be principally preoccupied with issues of security, widely conceived. Judgements about peace settlements—as to how punitive or lenient they are—will normally be made on the basis of their distributive provisions, since these are the most visible aspects of the post-war division of spoils. Typically, the wisdom of the current post-Cold War peace has been questioned for its lack of 'magnanimity'. The evidence for this is to be found, one theorist suggests, in its distributive terms: 'the United States is repeating past errors by extending its influence

over what used to be the province of the vanquished' (Waltz 2000: 37)
However, while the regulative dimensions of a peace settlement can provide important sources for its durability, they should not be thought as
themselves immune to the new asymmetries of power created by the war.
Although effective regulation seeks for acquiescence and legitimacy, it is
not wholly divorced from power and coercion. Thus while regulative
arrangements have a logic of moderation, they do not respond to that logic
alone. They too are indicative of the degrees of exaction that the peace may
require. It is the very preponderance that the winning states enjoy that
provides them with the freedom to distance themselves from, and seemingly to mitigate, the distributive impositions of the war. On the other
hand, precisely where wars end in the sharpest power differentials, it may
be possible for the winners to express their superiority by a temperate
distributive peace, and one that instead shifts the major burdens of defeat
onto the vanquished through its stringent regulative apparatus. These
complex themes emerge in a revealing fashion from the security provisions
of the post-Cold War regulative peace.

This is central to understanding the nature of the post-Cold War order,
since orders do not emerge directly from the outcomes of military contests.
They are mediated through the process of peacemaking, and that process
itself leaves an indelible imprint upon the outcome. A military historian
gives us a salutary reminder of this fact. 'Few wars, in fact, are any longer
decided on the battlefield,' he recalls. 'They are decided at the peace table'
(Howard 1999: 130). Decisive military victory, by itself, does not translate
into stable peace. For example, there was indeed a decisive military
outcome to the First World War, but the 'indecision' took shape in the
subsequent negotiation of the Versailles settlement (Howard 1999: 130–1).

For an enduring post-war order to develop, two criteria must be met in
the negotiation of the peace: that the 'defeated people accept the fact of
defeat', and that the defeated states be treated 'sooner or later, as partners
in operating the new international order' (Howard 1999: 132). The former
is largely the provenance of the distributive peace, but it is within the latter
that the regulative settlement is of critical importance. In short, the order
that is consequent upon major wars is not the product merely of the clash
of arms but, importantly, of the political arbitration that yields the final
format of the peace. This political process not only determines the division
of the material spoils at war's end, but is also instrumental in shaping the

nature of the regulative peace itself. Nor is there any necessary correspondence between these two dimensions: a mild distributive settlement may actually make it easier to impose a regulative one that is onerous, or may indeed necessitate it.

One of the key features of peacemaking is the encouragement of a compliant government within the defeated state. Howard sees this as critical to any peace settlement: 'a government must be found in the defeated country that is able and willing to take responsibility for enforcing the peace-terms on its compatriots' (1999: 130). In its absence, the victors must themselves take on direct responsibility for its enforcement. It is at this foundational level that the regulative accords are themselves so influential. Part of the task of creating an enduring peace lies in the construction of an international order that is itself acceptable to an emerging government within the defeated state, and which can help legitimize the regime in the eyes of its own people. The distributive peace, in itself, is unlikely to generate such a positive outcome, although it can certainly have a negative impact if its terms are deemed to be unacceptable.

Finally, by way of introduction to this chapter, it is instructive to concentrate upon those parts of the present security order that can be regarded as part of a peace settlement, as against those that cannot. To be sure, many recent developments in international security have contributed to its present characteristics. Some of these began to emerge as long ago as 1945 (nuclear weapons), many developed during the Cold War period (new security issues), whereas others seem to be peculiarly associated with the end of the Cold War itself. All of these play a significant part in the present security order. But some of these have been the result of complex—and often unintended—processes. These should be distinguished from the parts of the present order that can best be explained as acts of political volition and authorship, and as part of the post-Cold War peace.

Once again, the framework of peacemaking enables us to address this distinction. Not all events at the end of a war are under the control of the peacemakers, and the post-war order is assuredly not the construction of the peace settlement alone. Nonetheless, the settlement is an important intrusion into this process, an attempt to impose political will and direction upon what might otherwise be random and uncontrolled events. Indeed, if anything, the endings of great wars are best understood as affording the opportunity for precisely this kind of political intervention:

new directions can be set, or old ones yet further entrenched. This is the capacity that victory delivers, but its writ is not limitless. The victors may seem particularly potent as the disparities in power are intensified, but this does not render them omnipotent in framing the post-war order. What we then need to disentangle from the general processes of change is those specific aspects of security that have been self-consciously imposed as part of the victory at the end of the Cold War. Which components of the security order derive directly from that peace settlement, and how specifically has the regulative security settlement been configured to shape this outcome?

THE CHANGING FACE OF SECURITY

In order to form some impression of what was 'settled' about security at the end of the Cold War—as opposed to the more general transformations under way—we need briefly to assess the changing face of security. There are, of course, some writers who would dissuade us from imagining any radical change in this area at all. For Waltz, the end of the Cold War may have resulted in the demise of bipolarity, but we should not be searching for changes beyond this. 'The world', we are enjoined, '. . . has not been transformed' (Waltz 2000: 39). Just how fundamental these changes are deemed to be very much depends, in this regard, on the theoretical point of departure. As Rosenau acknowledged, the post-Cold War world is merely 'a new form of the existing order', if it is viewed within a continuing framework of states and anarchy. Alternatively, if the focus shifts to the diminished competence of states within a framework of corrosive transnationalism, this may yield the contrary judgement that what we have now is 'a wholly new order' (Rosenau 1992: 23). How are we to judge between these competing claims?

First, we need some summary overview of the changes in security that seem to be associated with the end of the Cold War, even if not narrowly as the consequence of it. Most commonly of all, writers have linked the passing of the Cold War to a loosening of the security bonds of that earlier period. There is, on this accounting, no longer a single and unified field of strategy, at least not to the extent that had been characteristic of the Cold

War. The obverse of this is that individual states, and possibly entire regions, now enjoy—or have had imposed reluctantly upon them—a greater degree of autonomy and self-reliance than hitherto. What has then emerged with the ending of the Cold War is the loss of that former strategic 'coherence'. In this respect, there has been an 'unbundling' of strategy over that period (Guehenno 1998/9: 8). It is as part of this same general process of liberation that the 'unbundling' of states, internally, has also occurred. What hitherto encouraged or compelled them to 'cohere' has since dissipated, and the internal dissolution of states is a symptom of basically this same strategic trend overall (Crockatt 1995: 368). In short, more states have been left increasingly to their own devices and, for some, this has exacted the high price of state dismemberment.

Additionally, and ubiquitously, analysts of security in the post-Cold War period have become convinced that security should now be defined in terms of threats to 'identity', and this has become the much-favoured focus of security analysis. The emergence, or re-emergence, of ethno-nationalist conflicts and wars has, in that sense, been only the most visible manifestation of a much more general trend. Whether that development had actually begun with the end of the Cold War, or whether it was only at that point that serious attention began to be devoted to it, is very much a moot point (Holsti 1999: 291–2).

This, in turn, can be regarded as a specific instance of a more broadly based transformation in the substance of the security agenda itself. Concisely expressed, the Cold War had narrowed and militarized thinking about security, such that security had come to be regarded predominantly as about military threats to the interests of states. This was now deemed no longer to be adequate to an understanding of the wider sources of threat in the post-Cold War period (Clark 1999), although critiques of this approach had in any case already been developing for many years before the Cold War came to an end.

More particularly, but again not narrowly restricted to the ending of the Cold War, a variety of writers claimed to have distinguished the emergence of new forms of violence and war. The traditional characteristics of war no longer seemed relevant to an understanding of the main expressions of political violence in the world. Above all, war itself was losing most of its defining qualities. War, it was maintained, 'has become de-institutionalized in the sense of central control, rules, regulations, etiquette, and armaments' (Holsti 1999: 304). So much was this the case that some were led to describe the emergence of a category of 'new' wars, to replace that of the old (Kaldor 1999: 2–3). Whether the notion of war retained its relevance at all, given the eclipse of its defining qualities, was thereby left open to serious doubt.

We will shortly address the sense in which there has been a collectivization of post-Cold War security, and the extent to which this might be understood as part of a premeditated and designed peace settlement. But already enough has been said by way of general survey of the condition of contemporary security to suggest that there are potential problems with this line of analysis. At least three need to be aired immediately. The first is how we are to reconcile the notion of collectivization with the aforementioned evidence of diminishing strategic coherence. In a word, why is it appropriate to use the word 'collectivization' to describe a set of security trends that might best be thought of as a type of disaggregation? Do not the two terms describe movements in opposite directions? Secondly, many of these developments within the security agenda, and particularly the emphasis on challenges to identity, might best warrant depiction as the 'individualization' of security, rather than as its collectivization. How then are these two characteristics to be reconciled with each other? Finally, the various symptoms of the new warfare described above might best be captured, as they frequently have been, by the notion of the privatization of war (Kaldor 1999: 92). At the very least, there is a pervasive theme of deregulation running through these accounts of contemporary violence. Endemic to the new forms of warfare is the precise breaching of the very restrictions that hitherto gave war its accepted meaning. 'Behaviour that was proscribed', under the old conventions of warfare, Kaldor insists, is now 'an essential component of the strategies of the new mode of warfare' (1999: 8). War, to that extent, has been stood on its head. But how then do the ideas of privatization and deregulation, on the one hand, square with that of collectivization, on the other? There would appear to be a number of substantial paradoxes that need to be resolved before the argument of this chapter can profitably be sustained. Above all, how are we to advance the contention that there has been put in place at the end of the Cold War a regulative settlement, when the fundamental characteristic of so much of the resultant security order seems to be typified by deregulation, not regulation? Before these paradoxes can be addressed and resolved, we need to explore further the precise sense in which the post-Cold War security order deserves to be described as collectivized.

COLLECTIVIZATION AND COLLECTIVE SECURITY

It might well be thought that collectivization of security is but a coy substitute for a system of collective security, and that the two share essentially the same characteristics. However, the point of this neologism is exactly to make a distinction between the two while, at the same time, acknowledging the family resemblance.

Certainly, there seemed to be good reason at the time to identify the end of the Cold War with a resumption of a comprehensive system of collective security. That was the distinctive mood in the air in 1990–1, especially at the height of the euphoria surrounding the successful military operation against Iraq. The favoured image of the moment was the progression from 1919 to 1945, and then onwards from the end of the Cold War. Here was the third historic opportunity to implement a radically new security order, and this time round the omens seemed much more favourable than during the previous two. 'With the end of the Cold War', was the popular refrain, 'the paralysis that has crippled the United Nations' collective security system for nearly fifty years has been lifted and a third opportunity presented' (Blechman 1998: 289). The third opportunity had arisen because 'enthusiasm for collective security' is a natural expression of the fact that 'an epochal conflict makes peace appear normal' (Betts 1992: 13).

As noted, much of this was triggered by the seeming triumph of the Gulf War. To echo the near universal judgement of the period, this had led to the final release of the potential of the UN collective security system, in a situation in which there were now good prospects for significant cooperation amongst the great powers. At last, the military aspect of collective security was working 'in the way that its founders had intended' (A. Roberts 1995/6: 16). Many drew the highly positive conclusion from the Gulf experience that the 'Security Council has shown that it has the capacity to initiate collective measures essential for the maintenance of peace in a new world order' (Russett and Sutterlin 1991: 82).

That is not to say that there was no scepticism present at the time. The dissenters pointed out that the role of the UN in the Gulf crisis had been blessed by unusually favourable—and almost certainly unrepeatable—circumstances. It came at a high point of Soviet compliance, and was triggered by an act of such naked aggression that even some fellow Arab states had little compunction about siding with the international coalition. But there were also more fundamentalist objections to this mood of triumphalism. Perhaps not quite so much had changed as appeared at first sight. Hoffmann, for instance, was not alone in pointing out that many of the stock objections to collective security still retained force in the aftermath of the Cold War. The balance between self-interest and sacrifice for a collective good remained a difficult one for most states to strike, most of the time. In any case, he doubted if a genuine international order could be constructed on a principle of collective security that, for all its community rhetoric, remained rooted in a form of coercion (1998: 127–8). He worried also that the mood of righteousness evoked in the face of Iraqi aggression could engender an 'unconditional surrender' mentality, itself likely to be contrary to sensible diplomacy (1998: 141). Others railed against the dangers of a naivety, based on the compounding of illusions. They warned that benign conditions were being assumed as the prerequisite for successful collective security, while also imagining that collective security would produce these very conditions. In short, there was a complex tautology at work, whereby collective security was regarded as a benign 'state of affairs', and not as 'a mechanism that brings it about' (Joffe 1992: 44). Others made the same point in highlighting the confusion 'about which is the cause and which is the effect in the relation between collective security and peace' (Betts 1992: 7).

The lonely voices of scepticism in 1990 had become the dominant mood of disillusion within a handful of years. The travails of UN peacekeeping operations in the early 1990s fed the general disenchantment. From having done too little for too long, the UN apparatus was suddenly asked to do too much and too soon. Its organizational, financial, and operational shortcomings were soon exposed to full public view.

The critics basked in the smugness of their prescience: they had told everyone that it would end in tears, and it did over Bosnia, Somalia, and Rwanda, albeit for different reasons in each case. But overall the picture which emerged was that the UN had neither the resources nor the acumen to handle those tasks to which the international community decided to become committed, while at the same time there was too much selectivity in acceptance of these commitments in the first place. Collective security, as its detractors had warned, would inevitably issue in selective security. Symptomatically, this was revealed in response to the unsettled conditions in much of the former Soviet Union, as the Western powers, acting through the UN, betrayed their schizophrenic attitude to peacekeeping in the former republics adjacent to Russia. They fell between the stools of 'legitimizing unilateral Russian intervention', as against making the commitments of men and money that would turn peacekeeping in the area into a genuinely UN undertaking (Ruggie 1996: 91). If there was an increasing disinclination for such tasks on the part of the producers of security, there was also an emerging distaste on the part of the consumers for the selectivity on which the new order seemed to be based. 'There is always a risk', one expert warned, 'that a collective security system will be seen as protecting only certain countries or interests or as privileging certain principles at the expense of others' (A. Roberts 1993: 23). By the mid-1990s, the new collective security had certainly become the victim of such apprehensions.

Running through much of the commentary of the second half of the 1990s is thus the conclusion that the experiment with a revived form of collective security had fallen far short of the aspirations for it, largely because it was selectively and inadequately implemented. This is true, but misses an important point. What had in fact been introduced as part of the post-Cold War peace settlement was a system of collectivized security, not the full system of collective security that so much of the rhetoric seemed to imply. In short, the description of the symptoms is accurate, but the diagnosis of the ailment is at fault. Collective security proved inadequate, to be sure, but it was never seriously pursued in the first place. What was unveiled as part of the New World Order was a unique version of it, with resonances of its Wilsonian antecedents, but conjoined with some new dimensions of international security. We must not then make the mistake of equating the two. The error has been twofold. First, there is the mistaken belief that collective security is coextensive with the entire security structure, which it is not. Secondly, it is mistaken in believing that the kind of collective security that was pursued—and against the benchmark of which it was found wanting—was of the classical type, when it was a materially different variant of it.

In short, collective security is but one dimension of the collectivization of security, and that more general context of collectivization reveals the modifications introduced into traditional collective security practice. Thus A. Roberts (1993: 27) was certainly correct in making the first point that 'collective security may properly be considered, not as a general system of international security, but rather as a form of action that is mobilized occasionally and imperfectly'. In this respect, it was not to become the definitive security mechanism for the system as a whole. Others have alluded to the second point when they suggest, somewhat disarmingly, that 'the visibility of the United Nations and its utility for American interests has rarely been higher' (Weiss and Holgate 1993: 279). This draws our attention to the overlap between the workings of the security system, and Western or American interests. These indicate the significant ways in which the collectivization of security has departed from what might have been expected of collective security as such. It is precisely these limits upon the resort to collective security, as well as the reformulations of that collective security in practice, that provide us with clues as to the nature of the regulative peace that was imposed at the end of the Cold War. This can be described in detail once we have set out a fuller version of the collectivization of security that was consequent upon it.

COLLECTIVIZATION AND THE REGULATIVE PEACE

Attaching the label of collectivization to the post-Cold War security order is intended to signify the profound changes that were under way, going beyond the application of traditional ideas of collective security. It is also to suggest that some of these were to be further entrenched, and consciously so, by the post-Cold War peace.

For some time, analysts of security have drawn attention to various respects in which there has been a trend towards its collectivization. For example, Buzan (1995: 198) posed the general issue when he asked how far interdependence would go 'in shifting the referent object for security away from individual states and toward larger collective entities'. In similar vein, theorists of world security had also been nudging the study of security away from its traditional grounding in the individual nation-state (Klare and Thomas 1994: 3). Others again had spoken of the 'internationalization of security', as exemplified specifically in the case of NATO, but as a general process that had been intensified further by the end of the Cold War. To what developments do these claims about the changing bases of security make appeal?

There are various facets to these generic trends but, cumulatively, they refer to detectable signs of the activation, operationalization, and legitimation of force on an increasingly collective basis. Some of these have been discussed by the author elsewhere (Clark 1999), and the argument presented that these should be understood, not simply as the impositions of a new external security environment, but as the reflection of deep-seated internal transformations in states themselves. They are indicative of the changing and developing societal bargains that lie at the heart of the contemporary state. Since there has always been an intimate relationship between the functioning of the state, and its role as the producer of security, these shifts are powerful symbols of the transformations under way. They suggest that the decline of inter-state warfare is both cause and consequence of the diminished role that the state plays in the provision of security backed by force. Thus, at the one end, Van Creveld draws attention to the decline of a state monopoly in this area. 'Interstate war appeared to be in retreat,' he claimed. 'The right to wage it . . . had been taken away except insofar as it was done in strict self-defense', and states could no longer benefit territorially from the engagement (1999: 353–4). At the other end, some writers have associated this with the erosion of state powers across the international board (Laidi 1998: 94).

At the heart of these diagnoses is the contention that a profound shift is under way, not only in the resort to force, but more particularly in the legitimation of it. In her own account of the development of the new warfare, Kaldor (1999: 4) is assertive on this point. 'The new wars', she testifies, '. . . occur in the context of the erosion of the monopoly of legitimate organized violence.' That monopoly has traditionally, and often definitionally, been enjoyed by states alone and is descriptive of the historical process of state-making, in association with that of warmaking.

Are states actually losing this monopoly? One writer presses the argument in a more careful, and specific, direction. He contends of states that they retain the 'monopoly on the ability to *legitimize* violence', but what they have lost is the 'ability to *monopolize*' resort to it (Deudney 1995: 97). In this version, other actors share and participate in the activity of organized violence, but it is the states that continue to legitimize that usage. Even so, the significant shift here would appear to be that states no longer unilaterally legitimize the resort to force, but increasingly do so on a collective basis. Thus has the analogy been drawn between President Bush's quest for a mandate from the Security Council to expel Iraq from Kuwait, and a request for permission 'in the manner of mediaeval princes appealing to the pope' (Van Creveld 1999: 353). Ruggie (1996: 197) encapsulates the seismic shift in his proposition that 'the use of force is subject to greater collective legitimation'. It is this transition that is an important element within the processes of collectivization presently under discussion.

To be sure, there are many purely practical and logistical reasons underpinning such developments. They need not be detailed, as they are commonly discussed and easily recognized. They relate to the sophistication and cost of military technology, and to the declining capacity of all but the most powerful states to deploy the full panoply of military assets. Especially in the climate of post-Cold War military retrenchment, states have been ever more reluctant to make investments in all-round military capabilities. As a result, some kind of *de facto* military specialization, or division of labour, has begun to appear. The result is that most states are now operationally unable to undertake large-scale forceful operations *except* as part of a collective coalition. This has less to do with the nature and purpose of the state than it has to do with workaday material constraints. But, of course, in the longer term the two begin to press in common directions. As citizens come to perceive the limitations of their individual states, legitimacy may be transferred to collective resorts to war: the acceptability of purpose may follow where the sinews of war are actually to be found.

To the extent that such tendencies are present in contemporary security, they denote a confluence of multiple and complex influences. It would be simplistic, and deeply misleading, to attribute them exclusively to the effects of the end of the Cold War. Nonetheless, even if more diffuse in origin, they were yet mediated through the political processes that accompanied the end of the Cold War. In that sense, they became part of the fabric of the peace settlement, further refined and articulated to meet the needs of the end of the Cold War. It may well be true that these trends reflect the wider impacts of globalization and transnationalization upon international security (Kaldor 1999: 140–1). However, that is no reason to dismiss the adjunct argument that powerful actors at the end of the Cold War attempted to inscribe their own agenda upon these existing tendencies. The victors in the Cold War did not originate or control such developments, but they certainly made an attempt to harness them to their own needs and interests. This is what the post-Cold War regulative peace was about in the realm of security.

At one level, the theme of collectivization that suffused the rhetoric at the end of the Cold War can best be understood as a set of intended constraints—antidotes set in place to regulate the centrifugal disorder that might otherwise be the successor to the Cold War structure. At this level, the argument is straightforward and can be briefly traced. Given the perception of the incipient forms of chaos that might follow the Cold War, a regulative peace was required that would provide a set of safeguards against their unbridled expression. The post-Cold War peace was thus set in place to counteract the subversive and revolutionary forces that would otherwise run free.

In this sense, and returning to the paradoxes listed earlier, it is relatively easy to resolve them. The regulative peace favoured forms of collectivization of security precisely as a counteracting force to the mayhem that would otherwise be unleashed in its absence. Collectivization was thus regarded as the natural prophylactic against the disaggregation, individualization, and privatization of warfare and strategy. It was a mechanism for reasserting a degree of state-centred direction, in the face of those very forces of transnationalization that otherwise threatened to make the system unmanageable.

Collectivization was an antidote to the disaggregation brought by the end of the Cold War. If the Cold War had produced its own patterns of coherence—by establishing a hierarchy of interests, with those of the superpowers at its apex—then collectivization was the chosen means of restoring new forms of post-Cold War coherence. In its absence, chaos loomed. By encouraging social norms of 'shared responsibilities' and 'partnership' (see Chapter 7), the United States sought to institutionalize a less costly form of post-Cold War containment than one that was propped up by the exertion of US primacy alone. The establishment of a viable post-Cold War order would thus become a joint undertaking, led by the United States, but with the burdens allocated more evenly than within a purely hegemonic system.

It was also a way of subverting the worst excesses of the individualization of security. In any case, we must be cautious about employing such terminology. As referred to above, the term is used mainly to denote threats to 'identity', as opposed to reified state interests. This is not, of course, to imply that identity politics are necessarily individualistic: they may very much take collective forms, as some of the most vicious expressions of ethno-nationalist identity politics certainly did throughout the 1990s. But the agenda of collectivization was deployed in the very specific sense of a set of regulatory principles that would privilege collective state action in the management of security, under the auspices of the leading centres of the system. Against the immanent tendencies to explode the boundaries of security and its ordering, principles of collectivization were appealed to as a powerfully conservative force that would preserve its more traditional contours. Once again, the irony of the New World Order lay exactly in the degree to which it reaffirmed a very conservative and traditional ideal, for all its extravagant parading of a novel people-centred order.

Finally, and equally obviously, the post-Cold War settlement was regulative in that it promulgated the ideal of regulated war, in the face of all the pressures to the contrary. The symbolic importance of the Gulf War lay in its epitomizing of this ideal. It was a 'lovely war' in that it was fought by regular armed forces, by the classical instruments of military power, and to a decisive conclusion. Above all, it was not about abstractions, such as identity, but literally about lines in the sand. It was a war to which the armed forces of the United States could wholeheartedly commit themselves, without the profound psychological misgivings that had so hampered them for the previous generation. But if the war was a war of liberation for the American military psyche, it was a war of regulation in terms of what it portended for future agendas of security, and for the conduct of war in its support.

At this first level, then, the seeming paradox between collectivization, on the one hand, and its motley challenges—disaggregation, individualization, and privatization—on the other, readily dissolves before our eyes. The relationship is one of opposition, and the former was set out with the specific intent of encouraging a set of security norms that would either inhibit, or minimize the worst excesses of, the latter. But a regulative settlement is unlikely to be successful in the longer term if it goes entirely against the grain. At a deeper level, we must admit also that collectivization of security was a programme intended to work not just against, but also with, the grain of other profound shifts in the nature of international security. How was this to be done?

The loss of the old Cold War coherence was not to be allowed to be replaced by no coherence at all, and so a fundamental task of the settlement was to establish its own account of what represented coherence in the aftermath of the Cold War. This could not plausibly be couched in traditional statist terms alone. Accordingly, as previously noted, the New World Order appealed to an extant universal society that went beyond the confines of the state system itself. To this extent, the New World Order attempted to harness—as ideological supports for the new order—those ideational transformations that at the same time seemed to threaten the every existence of that new order. The visions of disaggregation, individualization, and privatization all made appeal to those shifts in the nature of international security that were already manifest by the end of the Cold War, and were soon to be even further stimulated by that event. They made allowance for the complex transnational forces at work, and the changing role of the state as a security producer. In these respects, the New World Order betokened a tentative step towards recognition of an emergent global society, beyond the limited scope of the Cold War international society.

This was potentially revolutionary stuff, and intentionally designed to be so. Nothing less would have seemed appropriate for the new age that had apparently just dawned. And yet, the purpose remained deeply conservative. The point of spelling out the nature of this new global society was to explicate the contractual basis that underpinned it, and to articulate the social norms that must govern it: what is a society, global or otherwise, if not an elaborate system of social regulation. In this specific sense, the new world was called into existence to serve as the social supports of the old. It is these specific forms of regulation, within that security settlement, that the chapter must now address.

The important context in which the idea of a regulative peace must immediately be placed is the potential for acute deregulation implied by the end of the Cold War. There was widespread recognition that the collapse of such a powerful system of order as that which had prevailed for the past several decades might well leave a vacuum behind. This was a vacuum that could readily be exploited by those who wished to take advantage of their new freedom and, as such, represented a fragile basis for any future order. As things transpired, there were indeed to be challenges to the norms of the international system as conventionally understood, most notably in the case of Iraq's invasion and occupation of Kuwait. However, the greatest breakdown in regulation occurred in the constituents of the viable state itself. This has led some to question whether, in the aftermath of the Cold War, there was really any vulnerability to the international order as such:

If we include wars of secession, wars of resistance, civil wars, the breakdown of states, massive humanitarian emergencies, and the like, then there is an empirical foundation of the designation of 'zones of turmoil', the 'coming anarchy' and the like. But this is not a problem of world order, which is usually characterized as a problem of the relations between states. It is, rather, a problem of the state or more precisely, a problem of the relations between the state and its constituent communities, and between different communities within states. (Holsti 1999: 294)

The distinction drawn is at best artificial—domestic disorders have a habit of impacting on international relations—but it serves to focus our attention on the potential for dislocation that was immanent within the Cold War's ending. Above all, and from the point of view of the victorious Western powers, one of the least palatable of these consequences would have been the emergence of aspirant regional powers intent on exploiting the new regional autonomy to their own advantage. There was a high risk that ambitious or reckless leaders would make the calculation that the old regulative structure of the Cold War was no longer operative, leaving them at liberty to advance their own security interests within their neighbourhood. It was, of course, exactly such a challenge that Iraq's behaviour in 1990 seemed to exemplify. Accordingly, there can be no serious analysis of the actions that resulted in the outbreak of the Gulf War in 1991 that does not locate these events squarely within the context of the 'deregulatory moment' symbolized by the Cold War's end. It was this situation that Saddam Hussein moved to exploit, and it was about the hiatus of control portended by his decision that Washington and its close allies became sufficiently agitated to mount their military action. Thus viewed, it is fundamental to any account of the post-Cold War peace settlement that the Gulf War be regarded as one of its key provisions.

At this point, regulation went well beyond what until then had taken mostly a rhetorical form, and found expression in the actual use of military force. Thus was coercion inscribed in the terms of the regulative settlement. It was an action that was directed at the state that had breached the conventions of the international system. More importantly, and with wider relevance, the war was intended as a substantial demonstration of the continuing validity of the regulative order as against any would-be subverter of it. At one and the same time, the Gulf War stood for the delegitimation of any use of force not sanctioned by the victorious Cold War coalition, while also promoting the collectivization of the use of force to deter resort to it. There were, as a host of commentators have pointed out, too many departures from the strict model of collective security for us to regard the military action in these terms. But in the wider and looser sense of sponsoring and reinforcing a conception of the international order within which unacceptable social behaviour, and the appropriate sanctions against it, would both be defined as shared responsibilities of the international community at large, there was assuredly a move to a collectivized form.

This new type of social regulation, to inhibit regional adventurism, was not exclusively directed against the Third World, but certainly this was an important part of its remit. There could be no new order if its writ did not extend to those parts of the world where there might be significant challenges to Western interests. It is for this reason that many analysts have drawn attention to what they see as the similarities between the new order of 1990, and other attempts to 'discipline' the Third World. This is the nub of Holsti's sardonic remark that a 'new vocabulary of world order does not successfully hide old ideas emanating from the imperial experience' (Holsti 1999: 286). From this perspective, visions of the 'coming anarchy' (Kaplan 2000) in the South were a necessary adjunct of the articulation of the new regulative order that would serve to constrain, and minimize the damaging impact of, this anarchy. There have thus been widely voiced concerns about what the new security order portended for the South. Some express the fear that 'many Third World issues will be regulated by the major powers' (Grant 1995: 570); others that the revivified Security

Council simply reinforced great power preferences, and exposed the South to a new form of condominium (Kostakos 1995: 66). This entire perspective on the new security order has been nicely captured as follows:

If the post-Cold War world were to be divided along North–South lines, into core and periphery, collective security might amount to a mechanism by which the core would maintain its version of order in the periphery. Even though a core–periphery model is too crude to provide an adequate representation of the present global system, it . . . can serve as a corrective to uncritical assumptions concerning the universality and neutrality of collective security. (Richardson 1993: 49)

As already explained, the lack of 'universality and neutrality' is not some incidental corruption of the collective security ideal, engendered by failed attempts to implement it more strictly and fully. Rather this is endemic to the pattern of order that was instituted at the end of the Cold War. The Gulf War provided a military lesson to deter future delinquents by persuading them of the severe consequences of crossing lines still drawn in the sand, and by emphasizing how these violations would be adjudicated by those in a position to dispose of the international community's power. This was never intended to be collective security, but in its self-conscious delegitimation of the use of all force not sanctioned by the custodians of the new order it was a revealing step towards its collectivization. There would be a shared responsibility to desist from breaches of the prescribed order, and the military supports for compliance would be mediated through collective forms, if not actually initiated or controlled by them.

The reason why such a conception of order can fairly be viewed as intrinsic to the post-Cold War settlement is that, at the moment of its elaboration, the Soviet Union was deemed central to it. While this centrality was assuredly to diminish over the next few years, it was a critical element within the peace settlement itself. Indeed it was the co-option of the Soviet Union into such a security scheme that was a precondition of its shift to a collectivized form. In short, Gorbachev undoubtedly saw an accommodation with the United States as part of his overall strategy for the reconstruction of the Soviet system, and thus as a means to an end. However, from the perspective of the United States, such an improvement was an end in itself that was to be further codified in the peace. While the Soviet leader saw the thaw in US–Soviet relations as a way of terminating the Cold War, leaders in the United States saw the end of the Cold War as the opportunity to reconstruct that relationship, and the wider security order that derived from it.

While the Soviet Union was to be co-opted as a partner in this system, there can be no doubting that the United States was to enjoy the leadership role, and it is in this respect that the most self-conscious adjustments to collective security were to be made. This was not by happenstance—the unintended product of its practical implementation—but as part of the original design:

What President Bush had done in espousing the principles of the New World Order . . . was not to create a new organization, but to signal the US re-engagement in it, and the renewal of the original assumption of the UN that the great powers would co-operate. But Bush introduced, explicitly, an entirely new element: that the system would work under US leadership. (Wiener 1995: 50)

As argued in the previous chapter, the security order was to be multi-lateral, and to enjoy the special legitimacy that derived from that fact. But it was to be a guided multilateralism, within which the United States would enjoy a large measure of discretion, while sharing many of its responsi-bilities with other states. It was what was to be called 'a camouflaged leadership rather than an imperial one' (E. B. Haas 1993: 97). If the United States was willing to become engaged and for collective action to be initi-ated, then others would be called upon to participate. If the United States was unwilling, then a *de facto* veto would come into effect that would prevent further action. Selectivity was an intrinsic feature of this design, not an incidental by-product of it. Expressed in its crudest terms, it was intended to persuade the international community 'to underwrite a world order largely manufactured in Washington' (Ayoob 1993: 52). So much was this the case that sympathetic observers enjoined the United States to 'expand its commitment to work for a collective-security regime', as a means of enhancing its legitimacy. This would require persuading a wider section of international society 'to participate fully in a multilateral collective-security system', albeit one that was still 'shaped by the US' (Weiss and Holgate 1993: 279).

Part of the key leadership role to be played by the United States within this system was as the sponsor of a set of core values that would be collect-ively embraced. Indeed, the key function of the regulative peace was to set out the basic principles to which states would be invited to subscribe, as part of their admission to the extended security community of the West. The peace established the conditions of membership, and was a way of actively proselytizing on behalf of this cause. The substance of these values will be explored at length in the next chapter. For the moment, it is sufficient to indicate that adherence to them was what the project of collectivization of security was mainly about, and the regulative peace at the end of the Cold War was its foundational document. If it is true that the West has fostered 'an international (cosmopolitan) public sphere which sustains the development of a shared set of values and norms', then the United States has been central to this development. Whereas, in general, the USA 'has been the pre-eminent guarantor of this cosmopolitan sphere and the defender of the peaceful community of states which it inscribes' (Knutsen 1999: 197–8), this role was to be specifically, and powerfully, rearticulated in 1990. This was the bedrock on which the other provisions of the post-Cold War settlement could be laid.

We need also to return to the above discussion of the 'new warfare', and to the theme of the 'two world orders' (Singer and Wildavsky 1993; Kaplan 2000), that have been such features of post-Cold War commentary. The effect of these discussions has been to create an impression of a global divide between those parts of the world enjoying a post-Cold War peace, and those parts ever more traumatized by the breakdown of governance, and by affliction from the new forms of warfare. There is no neat and tidy separation between the two patterns of order, and they do not conform to strict demarcations between North and South. Indeed, in large measure, Western horror at the conflicts in the former Yugoslavia is traceable to bewilderment engendered by an apparently 'Southern' contagion finding its way into the heart of Europe.

How is all of this to be reconciled with the notion of the collectivization of security? There are two ways in which the issue was to be addressed: as a form of exclusion from the security order, and as a means of extending its operative principles. The idea of regulation was consistent with both.

The notion that the post-Cold War security order has been predicated on a principle of exclusion can be supported in the following way. Holsti (1999) has attempted to subvert the entire imagery of the two zones, one of peace and the other of anarchy. He does, however, accept that parts of the world are suffering from disproportionate degrees of state incapacity and social weakness. These are, of course, precisely the conditions that are conducive to the 'new warfare', and it is within these regions that its prime examples are to be located. Holsti's point, nonetheless, is that such 'weaknesses cannot serve as a foundation for challenges to world order'. On this reasoning, there is no need to regulate the new warfare beyond expelling it safely to the periphery of the zones of peace. It is his basic claim that the fundamental security order 'cannot be challenged by rag-tag groups of African teenagers, by minuscule mercenary armies, or by bankrupted national treasuries' (1999: 305). This does not mean that the new warfare can be left safely unregulated. It means that the effects of this warfare are regulated by expelling them to the margins, and by excluding them from the principal workings of the security order. Many people will suffer the dislocation this brings, but the security consequences will scarcely impinge upon the core members of the zone of peace at all.

The second form of regulation is more direct in nature, and works by incorporation rather than exclusion. Its essentials have already been outlined above in the context of the Gulf War. The purpose of that war was to regulate at two distinct levels. First, it was an instrument for disciplining unruly elements who might potentially challenge the West's dominance of the security agenda after the Cold War. It served this purpose because its 'awesome display of military prowess and extraordinarily low casualties fed increased popular expectations about what US power and leadership might accomplish in shaping the new era to follow' (Bacevich 1995: 182–3). Secondly, and more subtly, the war sought to regulate the new warfare by reimposing a traditional framework upon it, and thereby establishing the ground rules in terms of which the West would encounter the zones of instability. Inherent to the new collectivized security was a principle of selection that applied not only to which regions would be engaged, but also to which types of violence would receive a concerted international response.

There is a conspicuous disjunction between social trends in the zone of peace, and the social characteristics of the new warfare. As noted above, the new warfare bursts asunder all the forms of regulation that have been imposed upon traditional wars, and nowhere more so than by its direct impact upon society, placing civilians in the front line. This is in marked contrast to the thrust of military developments within the advanced societies of the West that are moving in the opposite direction, as Freedman has elaborated:

There is thus a contrast between the trend towards the isolation of Western military organizations . . . from the wider society, and the social character of the more likely conflicts. It fits in with the assumption that, for the moment at least, Western countries can choose their enemies and are not obliged to fight on anybody else's terms. Invitations to war need only be accepted on certain conditions: public opinion must be supportive; the result must be pre-ordained; and the conflict must be structured as a contest between highly professional conventional forces. (Freedman 1998: 77)

This is the heart of the attempted regulation of the security order that has been implemented after the Cold War. Its precepts have since been reinforced by the conspicuous departures from them, displayed in some of the more pitiful ventures in peacekeeping during the first half of the 1990s. The West would seek to discipline unruliness elsewhere by the twin strategies of both pushing it to the margins, and by decreeing its own code of engagement with it. The Gulf War, United States and British air attacks on Iraq, the NATO strikes in the Bosnian war, and the conflict over Kosovo, were all manifestations, and reiterations, of this code. They set the limits to, and exclusions from, Western military commitments. In turn, this code sought to constrain those forms of warfare that were otherwise subverting the terms of engagement in which the West enjoyed its unique technological advantages. Warfare would again be regularized by fighting the wars that could be comfortably won, and by ignoring those that could not. Security, it was hoped, would be collectivized by these twin pressures, pushing towards the safe ground in the middle.

This leads us to the final issue, and the one that links up with the chapter to follow. Thus far, the discussion of post-Cold War security has been conducted largely within the confines of what might be termed the traditionalist order-maintenance use of force. This is concerned principally with issues of national interest, balance of power, and acts of aggression that infringe the rules of the states system. However, as is readily apparent, the post-Cold War security agenda has been preoccupied with a whole package of concerns that extended well beyond this, and which raised the prospect of different considerations for state action. This package is concerned with the vexed dilemmas concerning human rights and their enforcement, notably in what is now referred to generically as the issues of humanitarian intervention.

The next chapter will address the normative underpinnings of this agenda, by suggesting that subscription to a set of ideas—broadly, a liberal rights order—was itself a fundamental part of the post-Cold War regulative peace settlement. For the moment, however, this chapter can be concluded by remarking upon a teasing link between the two areas of military intervention. Part of the United States' leadership of the multilateral security order since 1990 has been concerned with its decisions as to when it would commit its military forces to the maintenance of that order. As demonstrated, it has carved out for itself a leadership role that sought to square one particular circle, namely the reconciliation of the need for legitimacy, with a unilateral right to apply a principle of selectivity. As must be apparent, there is no natural consistency between the two. Nor, as is also apparent, has the United States been willing to take on too much of this task. As has frequently been remarked, the great problem of the post-Cold War period has been to persuade the United States to do enough, not to dissuade it from doing too much.

The question that invites an answer is then about the relationship between this role of order maintenance, and the adjunct agenda of humanitarian intervention. Have the two gone together, reflecting the increased capacity of the West to set its own terms and to impose its own agenda, including that of human rights? Or is the latter an undesirable and unsolicited burden that has arisen as a responsibility because, only thus, can the claims to legitimacy attaching to the other role of order maintenance be sustained? Is a degree of 'entitlement' to humanitarian intervention the unavoidable price that has to be paid for the necessary degree of interventionist order maintenance that is practised elsewhere? In a word, could it be that the West has pursued a collectivization of security and has discovered, unhappily, that to make sense of its claims to legitimacy in this sphere, it must also take on other kinds of responsibilites as well? What this would imply is that the collectivization of security has progressed further than was intended, and the West has found itself more regulated by it than it may have wished. To examine such questions, we must next explore the nature of the liberal rights order as part of the post-Cold War regulative peace.

9

THE LIBERAL RIGHTS ORDER

The triumphalism apparent by 1990 about the coming dominance of liberalism, internationally, portrayed this as some kind of providential outcome. It was to be welcomed as an *effect* of the end of the Cold War and it was in this sense, as an *ex post facto* development, that the moment was enthusiastically received. Such a perception, however, distracted attention from two important and complex issues. The first was that any concentration upon the 'liberal moment' as merely an outcome of the end of the Cold War scarcely did justice to the role of liberalism in bringing about that event. It thereby neglected the dimension of continuity within the liberal rights order. Secondly, the notion that liberalism's triumph was a contingent and fortuitous product of a shift in the distribution of power, and of the consequential demise of any serious ideological challenge, was partial at best. It downplayed the extent to which liberalism was consciously and intentionally deployed at the end of the Cold War as an instrument for consolidating its other beneficial outcomes. In short, liberalism was not some incidental condition that emerged in 1990, but a means to achieving other ends in that situation. It is for this reason that it can properly be regarded as constituting a major element of the post-Cold War peace settlement. This was, indeed, the 'liberal peace', if not quite in the sense that that phrase is traditionally employed. It is the task of this chapter to delineate its main provisions.

WHENCE THE LIBERAL RIGHTS ORDER?

For many, the end of the Cold War was accompanied by a mood of intense expectation. This anticipation focused not merely upon a new era of geo-political stability but also, pivotally, upon a sense that liberalism's moment had finally arrived:

Many expected that after the Cold War, there would be peace, order, increasing prosperity in expanding markets and the extension and eventual consolidation of civil and political rights. There would be a new world order, and it would in these ways be liberal. (Hawthorn 1999: 145)

And yet voice was to be given to the doubt as well. 'We can even ask', Latham mused, 'if a liberal order . . . still exists' (1997a: 205–6). He reached this puzzled conclusion on the basis of how seemingly 'ambiguous' things had now become in the aftermath of the Cold War. The complex forces of globalization, intensified if not initiated by the end of the Cold War, were pushing in a variety of often opposite directions, with uncertain implica-tions for liberalism's future. But even globalization itself, others believed, gave added impetus to liberal confidence. It was the vehicle by which the message of liberalism—in its market, democratic, and global governance dimensions—would be effectively communicated and spread. So what then was the reason for any doubt?

As already indicated, the intense emotionalism about the liberal moment was suggestive of novelty—the appearance of a new dawn. How-ever, the important perspective that the liberal order brings to bear, as part of the regulative peace settlement, is exactly an awareness of the element of continuity as well. A liberal rights order was not invented, and imposed, in 1990 as an act of revolutionary faith in the aftermath of the Cold War. Rather was it that liberalism had contributed to that revolution in the first place, and was now to become further entrenched as a means of perpetuat-ing the resultant peace. There were also other striking elements of longer-term continuity, attached to liberalism's role in twentieth-century warfare, which substantiated its claim to being central to the post-war peace. In one rendition of this history, two authors recount the following morality tale:

Just as the Allied victory in World War I had cemented liberal values in Western Europe, and just as the outcome of World War II had spread those values to key parts of Central Europe, the Western triumph in the Cold War finally allowed for the effective penetration of liberalism into the East. (Gitz and van Raemdonck 1997: 241)

This same imagery—of a 'community of liberal-constitutionalist states' expanding in consequence of their emergence 'as the winning coalition after each of this century's major conflicts'—recurs elsewhere (Reus-Smit 1997: 584). This is, of course, a misleadingly sanitized version of the century, from which the Soviet Union has been conspicuously airbrushed as part of the victorious coalition of 1945. Nonetheless, it is revealing insofar as it posits liberalism as a point of continuity in the warfare of the century: liberalism's role in 1990, on this account, was not so radically different from that in 1919 and 1945. There had then already been attempts to deploy liberalism as a specific programme for the reconstruction of states, and for the entire international system, on both of those earlier occasions. The association between liberalism, and victory in the twentieth century's great wars, is thereby clearly made.

To the extent that any such parallel exists, it reminds us of this continuity. It also draws our attention to the continuity between liberalism as a war aim, within the Cold War, and as an outcome of its end, as part of a post-Cold War peace. The liberal order was not one born in the aftermath of the Cold War. It had already been an instrument of that victory—part of the war effort—and was not simply an outcome of its ending. The point is well made in the claim that 'globalising liberalism' was responsible for 'its own victory', insofar as 'the success and spread of liberal institutions and values considerably contributed to the end of the Cold War' (Huysmans 1995: 482). Viewed from this perspective, liberalism was a continuation of the Cold War by other means, namely through the peace settlement itself.

In these ways, the contemporary liberal rights order is not new but develops from a longer lineage. This is not, however, to deny that 1990 represented some kind of epochal moment, merely to place it in context. The powerful emotive appeal of liberalism in 1990 derived from precisely this potent combination—its vindication as an already successful international system, coupled with the fresh impetus that would now be lent to it by the new configuration of global forces. To that extent, liberalism, like multilateralism, could be unveiled as a new set of principles for international order, in the firm conviction that it had already been tried and tested, and would be all the more welcome for being so. The main elements of the liberal order, accordingly, were not invented in 1990, merely reaffirmed in suitably modified form. This became very clear in the context of doctrines of human rights that had, in any case, been a growing element of international order since 1945. It has been said of these doctrines that they are simply a 'version of the liberal position on rights', but whereas their universalism was 'always implicit . . . it is now explicit' (C. Brown 1999a: 105). It is in this limited sense alone that 1990 marks a measure of discontinuity within the strict confines of an ongoing tradition of human rights reflection. There was assuredly a much greater sense of anticipation and expectation that 'the end of the Cold war opens up a possibility for establishing a global liberal order as a common good' (Huysmans 1995: 473). Repackaged it certainly was, but not substantially reinvented, and this lay at the heart of its regulative role in the post-Cold War settlement.

It is the function of this chapter to establish the true provenance of this liberal rights order. The starting point must then be an admission that the 'new' liberal regime cannot be understood merely as the consequence of the end of the Cold War, nor simply as a reflection of the new balance of ideological power. Its fundamental purpose was to serve as an instrument, rearticulated and given a higher profile, in order to preserve these other outcomes. We need then to reverse the order in which we traditionally think about the relationship between these things. It is less the case that the end of the Cold War gave rise to a new liberal rights order; instead, a liberal rights order was consolidated to sustain the other beneficial effects of the end of the Cold War. As part of the peace settlement, this order was a means to an end, rather than an end in itself.

THE LIBERAL PEACE

What is the reason for presenting it thus? On what basis can we argue that liberal rights formed part of a consciously designed peace that would regulate the new distributive settlement? There is, of course, the general objection to such a presentation that has already been encountered elsewhere in this book, and which challenges the argument that the post-Cold War order can be construed largely as an exercise in peacemaking:

We ought not to project back or forward from what may be a unique twentieth century history to assume that the character of all epochs depends on purposeful order-making. As we move into the twenty-first century, it may be that the state-driven order-making model of our recent past will become less relevant. (Latham 1997*b*: 442)

Part of this objection can be readily conceded: orders do not always fulfil the wishes of the peacemakers who strive for them. There are many facets of order that evade the best efforts of the peacemakers to control them and, for that reason, we should not conflate the ensuing order with their designs alone. That, however, is no good reason not to study the designs of the peacemakers at all. It is these that reveal the template of the peace, if not the precise form in which it actually takes hold.

More specifically, there is the potential difficulty that liberalization of political systems, at any rate those in eastern Europe, was offered up at the outset, rather than exacted by the victorious powers after the war was won. It has been remarked, demonstrating this logic, that 'the commitment to liberalise and democratise society was in the first instance a response to internal demands for reform, rather than external harassment or pressure' (Mayall 1993: 168). Thus construed, we are pressed to concede that liberalization preceded the end of the Cold War, and was a condition for its happening, rather than something imposed as a consequence. Chronologically, accordingly, the view that the liberal rights order was, in any sense, part of a *post-war* peace may appear to be problematic.

What this objection misses, however, is any sense of the power dimension at the end of the Cold War. Whatever the reasons for that ending—and liberal pressures from without, as well as limited moves towards liberalization from within, were certainly amongst them—it remains the case that, in the aftermath, there was to be a subtle blending of these ideological trends, with other power political realities. In a word, it became difficult 'to distinguish between the impact on the world system of a victorious liberal internationalism and that of hegemonic America' (C. Brown 1999*b*: 47). Whatever the liberal heritage to date, the West enjoyed after 1990 a vastly greater freedom to articulate its own vision of an international order, crafted around its distinctive liberal position. Indeed, the point can be made all the more forcefully. Instead of the incipient liberalization in the Soviet Union and eastern Europe *before* the end of the Cold War destroying the rationale for regarding it as part of the post-Cold War peace, it actually strengthens the argument. Insofar as the settlement enacted what was already in train in any case, it seemed a fairer and more sensible peace: it was working with the forces of history, and not against them.

This also allows us to note the extent to which the liberal rights order that was to be set in place after 1990 was a liberalism of a kind, and limited in its purview. There had, of course, been many earlier critiques of the entire post-1945 human rights agenda, as being predominantly driven by Western interests and precepts. Tellingly, one author had represented the general Third World perspective on the Universal Declaration on Human Rights in his critical appraisal of it. Insofar as it omitted the 'right to live in a respected, secure, and above all a powerful state', it was a partial document that 'disregarded the power factor' (Von Laue 1987: 319). If that earlier document had failed this particular test, then it could be said that the restatement of the essentials of a liberal rights order at the end of the Cold War did little better in this regard. It came no closer to meeting this exacting condition, for the simple reason that it was underpinned by the realities of the post-Cold War power situation. This reminds us also, as will be discussed below, that peace settlements are significant for what they settle, not only in respect to the vanquished, but also as regards all other participants in the system, including former allies of the victors, as well as the neutrals.

To sharpen the focus of the following discussion, the issue confronting us, baldly stated, is whether 1990 represents a moment of greater ideological convergence and normative change—or whether it merely depicts the new distribution of power, and the concomitant strength to refashion the ideological debate in a particular direction. Does the post-1990 liberal rights regime describe an order, already extant and now more deeply entrenched and pervasive—as the optimists might suggest? Or do we need to remain cynically pessimistic in regarding this liberal moment as little more than a reflection of the unchecked nature of Western power? Even a hardline proponent of Western interests, such as Samuel Huntington, had no difficulty in suggesting that the 'concept of a universal civilization is a distinctive product of Western civilization' (1996: 66). To the extent that this is so, then the greater confidence in the universalization of political forms that accompanied the end of the Cold War may be regarded in just those power-political terms. It is this logic that makes us see it as a definitive aspect of the post-Cold War peace.

We can explore this theme through the specific issue of interventions on behalf of humanitarian abuses. The most authoritative recent exposition of this topic concludes that there is evidence to support the emergence of a more 'solidarist' conception of international society: the practice of humanitarian intervention since 1990 reflects deep-seated normative change that is now impinging upon state practice (Wheeler 2000). However, that author is equally mindful of another reading of the evidence:

The realist answer is that the new practice of humanitarian intervention in the 1990s is a phenomenon of changing power relations. The end of the Cold War dramatically changed the global balance of power with Western states, led by the USA, occupying a hegemonic position in the global political order. (2000: 288)

The crux of the matter is whether humanitarian intervention specifically, and the liberal rights order more generally, should be understood as an expression of such greater normative solidarism, or merely as the consolidation of Western power. This dilemma runs through the entire human rights debate, and will continue to do so as long as 'the distinction between globalization and Westernization is unclear' (Evans 1997: 137).

To be seen as part of a regulative settlement, the new liberal rights order needs to be understood as evidence *both* for normative change *and* for the exercise of state power to foster its development in preferred directions. To divorce it entirely from power would be naive, as many commentators have testified. This liberal worldview, and its great potential for shaping the international order, has been described by many as 'hegemonic' at the present time, an indication of the 'pervasiveness of American power in the broadest sense' (Richardson 2000: 22, 27). But if it is to succeed in regulating and preserving the post-Cold War order, it must aspire to a degree of legitimacy, and thus extend beyond its basis in a direct, and material, exercise of power alone. It is this dual role—as an assertion of power but mitigated by a desire to convince others willingly to subscribe to its precepts—that makes sense of it as part of the settlement that concluded the Cold War. This settlement was not instantly definitive, and has since been refined and modified. But the initial intent to deploy such an order to ensure the integrity and survival of the other elements of the post-Cold War peace can scarcely be in any doubt.

DEFINING THE LIBERAL RIGHTS ORDER

As yet, no attempt has been made to specify the substance of this liberal rights order, and it is to this that the present section turns. This is a necessary preliminary to the detailed argument about how it forms a part of the regulative peace settlement. The main elements of this order will be presented as the following: a concern with the beneficial effects of democracy, and a programme for encouraging its extension; a greater international interest in human rights; and a rhetorical, if not always practical, commitment to self-determination. These are the basic elements that constitute the order that has been elaborated since 1990.

They derive, of course, from the wider traditions of liberalism, and suffer from many of the ambiguities and uncertainties that are characteristic of this family of political theories. Given this diversity, this is no place to expound a systematic account of liberalism in its many forms and variants. However, a brief outline is needed, especially to establish the particularly Western stamp that has been placed on this order.

Even those inclined to be sceptical of it are prepared to admit that, following Fukuyama (1989, 1992), it 'does make some kind of sense to talk of the triumph of Western liberalism' (C. Brown 1996: 30). Be it noted, however, that in this argument the emphasis is placed as much upon the *Western*, as it is upon the *liberalism* itself. The import of this is that the priorities of the liberal agenda are defined predominantly within a discourse about rights. In terms of a pattern of order within the state system, the implication of this, insofar as it is implemented, is that 'a liberal ethos of world order subordinates the principle of state sovereignty to the recognition and respect of human rights' (M. J. Smith 1998: 76).

This makes the second point that rights are defined as attaching to individual human beings. For liberalism, this is the starting point for any political theory: it takes the 'individual as the ultimate and irreducible unit of society and explains the latter in terms of it' (Parekh 1992: 161). It follows from this that rights belong to humans as individuals, and this has always been the predominant Western conceptualization of them. This stands in contrast to competing paradigms of rights that stress their social or collective bases (Felice 1996: 8, 18).

This point of philosophical departure also entails a broad spectrum of liberal positions on the marked inequalities between people that derive, in substantial measure, from their membership of different states. Some conservative versions of liberalism are broadly tolerant of these inequalities, while more radical versions—that take the individual basis of rights literally—are inclined to call for measures of redistributive justice as a precondition of the enjoyment of other forms of rights (Richardson 1997: 7).

But even if these basic liberal beliefs are integral to the post-Cold War order, this does not explain how they are to be reconciled in such a way that a viable international order emerges from them. The reason for labelling this dimension of the regulative peace a 'liberal rights order' is to bring out the contention that it is a composite of several parts. It embraces a conception of liberal internationalism, a high profile for doctrines of individual human rights, and finally, a concern to meld all these into a working international order as well. Not only is the jump from liberalism to order not automatic but, as traditionally conceived, an emphasis on human rights might be thought inimical to the maintenance of international order. In summary, we are faced with the old dilemma of reconciling justice with order. How does the liberal rights agenda seek to achieve this?

This tension arises because the notion of rights is constrained from two opposite directions. It is pressed, on the one side, by its liberal derivation: this defines and circumscribes the rights that are thought to be applicable. From the other side, it is subject to the constraints of what is thought compatible with international order. This, in particular, and as will be developed below, sets limits to policies of humanitarian intervention, as also to the implementation of the principle of self-determination. Human rights is a key concept in the regulative peace, but certainly not as an absolute entitlement. It is the linchpin in the effort to give legitimacy to the post-Cold War settlement, while ensuring that it does not become detached either from power or compelling national interests. We need to look at each of these elements of the liberal rights order in turn, as well as at the interrelationships between them.

The main connection that is created between liberalism and international order is via democratization and the democratic peace. This was the predominant anticipation of the liberal moment in 1990, and assumed that the expansion of the democratic zone of peace would entail a more peaceful world order. This, according to the liberal credo, occurs as a result of two processes. The first is as the consequence of democratic forms *within* states, which are believed to be responsible for generally more pacific behaviour. The second is the percolation of democratic norms through the machinery of the international system itself (Ray 1995: 6; Holden 1996*b*: 137).

The subject of the liberal peace has been the centre of an extensive, and often acrimonious, literature and this is not the place to expose it to detailed scrutiny. The minimum that needs to be said, however, is that there are many potential obstacles to the validity of its claims (Clark 1999: 156–66). In summary form, these might be presented as follows. First, there is the generic critique emerging from within the globalization literature that democracy is itself being increasingly hollowed out, with resultant democratic deficits. To the extent that this is so, it is legitimate to enquire how effective in preserving the peace democracy can be expected to be. There is then, as noted by some authors, a degree of irony in questioning 'the efficacy of the liberal democratic state just at that historic moment when liberal democracy seems to have triumphed on a global scale' (Held and McGrew 1993: 261). In the context of the present discussion, how impressive can be the regulative function of liberalism if one of its main institutional and normative clusters, namely democracy, is itself under great pressure?

Secondly, the issue has been raised as to whether there is a darker side to the democratic peace. The focus of the literature is upon the beneficent impact of democracy on the relations between liberal states. But does this say anything about the relations likely to develop between liberal and illiberal states? Some have suggested that the negative side is a tendency to aggravate relations of this kind. Indeed, there is the claim that it is those same liberal ideas that enhance the peace within the democratic zone that, paradoxically, 'prod these states into war with illiberal states' (Owen 1994: 88). At the very least, 'the frequently aggressive behaviour by liberal states toward non-democracies' (Risse-Kappen 1995: 503) is noted. It is for this very reason—that liberalism is not necessarily an adjunct of a harmonious international order in the round, but may aggravate some relationships within it—that some writers have appealed for adherence to a form of constitutionalism in the relations between liberal and illiberal states. The importance of this is to highlight 'the obligations which liberal states will have to observe in their dealings with non-liberal societies if they are to meet the criticism that any new world order will be a hegemonic order biased towards Western interests' (Linklater 1993: 29). The problem here is that the post-Cold War regulative peace aspired precisely to be a loose constitutional apparatus of this kind, but as part of a post-war settlement could scarcely avoid exposure to such a critique of its provenance.

The third issue does not derive from within the narrow liberal peace argument, but brings us back directly to the great issues of war and peace, and their relationship to the international order. There was the temptation, and it was barely concealed in much of the liberal self-satisfaction at the end of the Cold War, to regard the rash of democratization—its third wave—as being driven largely by the normative supremacy of the democratic ideal itself. What this leaves out of account is the extent to which the need for new political forms, in the newly created states, was simply an effect of war and its consequent territorial changes:

After 1989, as after 1918 and 1945, the primary cause of the creation of new states has been the collapse of empire rather than popular nationalist revolt, let alone any widespread conversion to liberal principles of constitutional self-government. (Fawn and Mayall 1996: 214)

This puts a number of key issues usefully into perspective. It downplays the role of liberalism as some kind of irresistible force that naturally and spontaneously carved its image upon the new international order after 1989. At most, it was the handmaiden of that process, with war's impact on empires taking the leading role. For the same reason, it reminds us that liberalism was to be an artifice of the peace, much as it had been designated as such in 1919. It was a tool of the peacemakers as they sought to shape the resulting order, not simply an agent in its own right, acting in pursuit of its own agenda.

Fourthly, there has been extensive debate as to whether it is liberalism that generates the peace or whether, in a reversal of the causal chain, liberalism is parasitic upon the peace that is already in existence. This has been a popular refrain amongst neorealists, for example, who maintain that the peace is caused by structural factors and, in turn, this may be conducive to the embedding of democratic government. The relationship does not work the other way round (Layne 1994: 44–5). In one critical respect, this kind of argument is right, even if for the wrong reasons. What was to be integral to the regulative settlement at the end of the

Cold War was indeed an attempt to shape a peaceful order that would encourage democratic systems to take hold and flourish. To that extent, the reasoning behind the neorealist objection was, in fact, acted upon. But this was not to the exclusion of the obverse relationship. There persisted also a firm conviction that a liberal rights order, with democratic political systems as the emerging norm, would indeed contribute to the attainment of peace.

Both versions of the belief were, of course, to be called seriously into question as the 1990s unfolded. Neither the peace, nor associated democratic forms, took hold as readily as had been anticipated. Yugoslavia was the great test case for both. Accordingly, Western failures in dealing with that tragedy 'dealt a brutal blow to the idea that the democracies possessed the capacity, or the will, to enlarge that zone of pacification and cooperation created inside the Western political community' (Pfaff 1993: 5). Neither the peace, nor democracy, could gain any effective purchase on that situation. But the fact that this was one of the areas in which the peace settlement failed is no grounds for denying the existence of the peace settlement in the first place.

The components of the liberal rights order come together, secondly, in terms of differing conceptions of human rights, and how to implement them within a state-centred system of order. There has been some modest optimism about the human rights record since the end of the Cold War. The period, we are told, has 'so far brought an incremental deepening of the global human rights regime' (Donnelly 1999: 88). On the broad issue with which this chapter is concerned—namely whether the liberal rights order is sustained by greater normative convergence, or merely by a greater disparity in power—Donnelly comes down, with appropriate qualifications, in favour of the former. The much-remarked Vienna Conference on Human Rights in 1993—generally offered as an example of the profound disagreements about conceptions of human rights—he sees as pointing in the opposite direction, and indicative of 'normative deepening'. Despite the widespread attention paid to divisions over gender and cultural aspects of rights at that event, he is of the contrary opinion that 'Vienna actually represented a dramatic decline in ideological conflict over human rights and a clear victory for advocates of the universality of international human rights obligations' (Donnelly 1999: 88–9). In terms of actual practice, he has also emphasized the various ways in which the end of the Cold

War decreased traditional geopolitical incentives for the superpowers to support rights-abusing regimes (Donnelly 1993: 133). This is echoed in Wheeler's more recent contentions about the 'tendency to invoke humanitarian justifications by Western governments to legitimate their use of force'. This is indicative, he believes, of the development of solidarism, the characteristic of which is a responsibility for 'guardianship of human rights everywhere' (Wheeler 2000: 14, 11–12).

The sceptics remain wholly unpersuaded, and raise two issues in particular that are especially germane to the present discussion. The first concerns the liberal hallmark of the human rights regime. The second, also associated with this, concerns the relationship between rights and society. As to the first, the pervasive issue, as already mentioned, is whether the human rights regime reflects its distinctive Western liberal origins. The emphasis within it is upon culturally particular definitions of individual rights, as against social and collective expressions of them. Where this has engendered anxiety and resentment is in those 'other' countries that regard this as a back-door form of social reconstruction, designed to soften up their societies for further penetration by Western political, cultural, and economic systems. This is not to deny the role of the liberal rights order as part of the regulative peace, but to say instead that its role in this regard is so transparent to its opponents as to undermine any quest for legitimacy. It is too overtly a unilateral enactment to maintain any pretence to be a genuinely cooperative enterprise.

The second focus is upon the seemingly chicken-and-egg relationship between society and rights. For Western liberals, the latter come first and can be discussed in abstraction because of their primacy. It is the fact that they do not attach to any society in particular that lends them their universal quality: for this reason they are, by definition, human rights. Those who espouse this position feel no need to be defensive about the global credentials of these rights since 'liberalism's concern for the ethical life of individuals is not a merely Western ideal' (Hoffmann 1998: 245). Given this priority, the related belief tends to be that, if we start with rights, we can build genuinely liberal and civilized societies on top of them. Even a global society is a meaningful objective of this kind of quest. Others dissent, and wish to reverse the relationship. Just as the detractors from the liberal peace maintain that peace supports democracy, and not vice versa, so there is a school of thought—broadly communitarian—that starts with an existing society before entering into any discussion about rights. We cannot sensibly debate rights, or specify their contents, in an asocial context (Bellamy and Castiglione 1998: 160; Thompson 1998: 188). This is the assertion that 'rights have no separate ontological status; they are a by-product of a particular kind of society' (C. Brown 1999a: 120). On this reckoning, we cannot build a society starting with rights: rights exist only where there is already a society. The problem then for a regulative peace that is centred upon a notion of human rights is that it cannot artificially generate a genuine global society.

The debates and controversies about the significance of human rights in the post-Cold War order mostly reflect these deep-seated issues. In turn, they pose major problems for the legitimacy towards which the regulative peace has aspired. Again, these need not be set out in any detail, but will merely be illustrated with regard to the particular concerns of this chapter. Despite Donnelly's optimism, noted above, it has been heavily qualified. He admits that most of the 'impediments to establishing effective inter-national human rights policies ... remain essentially unchanged in the post-Cold War world' (1992: 258). Even more dismally, he reckons the old problems have been joined by new ones, and particularly by the threats from nationalism (1993: 152).

As yet, however, the messianism at the heart of the liberal project remains essentially intact, and to that extent remains the regulative ideal of the post-Cold War peace. C. Brown informed us some years ago that the 'assumption that universal norms and values will triumph over those based on particular local contexts is a feature of contemporary liberalism in almost all its forms' (1995: 92). For all the seeming setbacks to this belief during the 1990s, this regulative ideal is as firmly in place today as it was when unveiled in 1990. The principle has been breached, to be sure, but it is far from being abandoned or in retreat. The belief that a liberal pro-gramme of rights will soften the edges of international conflict, and lend legitimacy to the West's custodianship of the post-Cold War order, remains deeply entrenched. There should, however, be no illusion about the basis of this hope. It did not rest alone upon a confidence that this was a spon-taneous and natural evolution, whatever the triumphalism of 1989–90 might have suggested to the contrary. It rested instead upon the conviction that this had to be fostered and encouraged by the West, if the other elements of the post-Cold War peace were to be held in place. If the liberal rights order disintegrated, much else would erode with it, including many of the benefits bestowed by the distributive settlement.

The third dimension of the problem is the relationship between order and self-determination. Again, as with human rights in general, a right to self-determination does not always sit comfortably with a viable international order, all liberal rhetoric notwithstanding. The key question since 1919, and one reformulated in 1990, was how a liberal commitment to self-determination, and a definition of this as an actual right, was to be reconciled with practical concerns for statehood, and for an effective international system. A proliferation of small states—especially if weak, vulnerable, and containing remaining minorities—would place endless pressure on the international order and thus, as a right, had to be circumscribed in practice. As part of the immediate settlement of the Cold War, the principal policy of the West was to hold together, first the Soviet Union, and subsequently the federal state of Yugoslavia. In this respect, there is little evidence of a commitment to self-determination, and it might appear puzzling that it should be regarded as one of the pillars of the new liberal rights order.

The contradiction is more apparent than real. A degree of public commitment to self-determination, as a fundamental principle, was inescapable in the context of the end of the Cold War. It was precisely the infringement of that principle during the Cold War years that had offended so much. In a sense, the Cold War came to be about its denial. For that reason alone, there was bound to be an exhilarating moment of reaffirmation when the Cold War came to an end. In any case, self-determination was inextricably bound up with other elements of the liberal canon. It connected closely to the liberal agenda for democratization. 'The attempt to link democracy to self-determination', it was pointed out, 'is a development most notable in the rhetoric surrounding the debate over a post-Cold War "New World Order"' (Fawn and Mayall 1996: 196). It was also intertwined with human rights, in the sense that 'nations have moral rights, of which the most important is the right to self-government' (Graham 1997: 5). Accordingly, it was impossible to move forward on any part of the liberal front without moving forward on all parts of it simultaneously. Self-determination, as a result, was catapulted forward as part of this general momentum.

Of course, as many have commented, there is irony in the fact that self-determination is itself a universal principle that issues in a particular result. The principle is itself cosmopolitan, in that it purportedly applies to all human beings, but the consequence of its application is the vindication of 'a communitarian principle' (J. Williams 1996: 54). It is this apparently unholy alliance that may be responsible, as the same author suggests, for the 'resulting mess'.

What contributes to the mess is the constraints that are generally observed in the practice of self-determination, no less so at the end of the Cold War than in 1919. It can never be pursued to any logical conclusion without profound damage to other elements of the international order, including a wholesale fragmentation of existing states. For that very reason alone, the end of the Cold War was met by virtually no encouragement on the part of Western leaders for the secessionist aspirations within the former eastern Europe. Secondly, however, when new states did begin to emerge in any event, principle had to be further tempered by expediency by the non-application of the liberal tests for self-determination. To this extent, the problems of the post-Cold War period reflected the troubled prehistory of this principle in the inter-war period:

In view of the failure of historical attempts to deal with the problem of minority rights and secessionism within the liberal theory of international society, it is not surprising that an unambiguous application of a democratic test of self-determination has not occurred in the post-Cold War era. (Fawn and Mayall 1996: 197)

It had been hoped that these other liberal tests would themselves act as some kind of constraint on the extent of the new self-determination. They did not. However, since there could be no dilution of the actual principle of self-determination itself, especially in the heady atmosphere surrounding the end of the Cold War, the implicit tensions between this liberal norm, and other concerns about international order, could scarcely be disguised. In sum, it would have represented a greater contradiction to deny self-determination in principle than it was to limit its application in practice. This was the best the post-Cold War peace could do to square that particular circle.

LIBERAL RIGHTS AND THE
REGULATIVE PEACE

It remains to spell out the implicit argument concerning the regulative function of these sundry norms and principles. Richardson captures the essence of the ensuing analysis:

The 'end of history' image, then, may be seen not as a momentary aberration of post-Cold War euphoria but as a pointer to the distinctive character of international liberalism at the beginning of the new millennium. It underpins an optimistic view of the world as one regulated by liberal norms in which the aspiration to achieve world peace through the spread of liberal democarcy is close to achievement. (2000: 31–2)

In this final section, the manner of that regulation will be traced through an exploration of liberalism's pervasive influence upon the post-Cold War peace. It needs to be stressed at the outset that its impact was exercised, not as a separate and independent force, but rather through its mutual reinforcement of the previously discussed themes of multilateralism, and collectivization of security. These, taken as a whole, are the defining features of the post-Cold War settlement, and it is through their combined agency that the victors in the Cold War have aspired to preserve the resulting peace. Once again, the regulative power of liberalism, and the degree of legitimacy attaching to it, was believed to derive from its continuity from an earlier period but, as Richardson suggests, this was reaffirmed in 1990 into a subtly new version of its core beliefs.

Intrinsic to this vision of liberalism is its relationship to a distinctive form of economic activity. We have already encountered some aspects of this in the account of the regulative functions of globalization. The important perspective to emerge was the concept of liberal capitalism as an inseparable unity of political and economic forms. Certainly, the amalgamation of the two sets of beliefs—liberal polity and liberal economy—had always been fundamental to post-war American thinking about the preservation of 'democracy and capitalism in the United States' (Deudney and Ikenberry 1999: 192). But the symbiosis between the two was reformulated much more starkly at the end of the Cold War, in a way that privileged the economic order. In short, the rhetoric of the period affirmed the unity of the two spheres, while also adjusting the balance between them. 'The economic liberals argued that the essential need was to recognise the market order as an independent institutional order whose boundaries democracies must not interfere with', is how Gamble (1996: 127–8) interprets this. The effect is that the 'market order was now openly understood as an international order'. Both liberal democracy and liberal capitalism would bolster the existing order but, where necessary, the former would be required to accede to the needs of the latter. While the rhetoric maintained that liberal democracy and capitalism were both fully compatible with each other, and indeed co-requisites, the compatibility would if necessary be guaranteed by modulating the political system, so that it would not interfere with the workings of the economy. Economic neoliberalism, from this point of view, entailed a degree of political deregulation as well. As argued in Chapters 6 and 7, however, this deregulation is a characteristic of complex transformations within states, and not simply of the global economy impacting upon them from the outside. Liberal capitalism regulates the peace by encouraging new state priorities that are, in turn, fed into these shifting domestic compacts.

This does not mean that the traditional liberal agenda of encouraging the enhancement and expansion of the liberal peace has become unimportant. On the contrary, the Kantian perspective became all that much more pertinent in 1990, precisely because of the Hegelian moment with which it appeared to be conjoined (Clark 1999: 162). The former purported to explain why peace would deepen, and the latter to explain why its compass would geographically widen. Once both were in place, there could be greater confidence about the sustainability of the international order into the future. Russett expressed the hope and expectation in his claim that 'if enough states become stably democratic in the 1990s, then there emerges a chance to reconstruct the norms and rules of the international order to reflect those of democracies' (1993: 138).

The same point can be made with a slightly different emphasis. According to it, the democratic peace

presents the currently prevailing international order as Washington would like to have it appear—as essentially benign, so long as the American model continues to win greater acceptance. Here the image of the democratic peace merges with that of the end of history. Those who do not conform with the prevailing norms are presented as culturally and historically retarded. (Richardson 2000: 25)

In this alternative account, the liberal peace develops less as the unfolding of some natural and immanent process, and more as the consequence of political intervention. To the extent that a liberal peace takes hold and expands, this will be as a result of the regulation that has been actively fostered through the set of liberal principles since the end of the Cold War. These principles seek to regulate not simply the international behaviour of states, but the very nature of the states themselves, as the best guarantee of their compliance with the norms of the new order.

Another way of making the same essential point is to suggest that the regulative function of the post-Cold War peace is actively to construct an expanding security community, and liberalism serves as the key instrument of this project. This, in turn, leads the discussion back to the vexed issue of the relationship between democracy and community. Can democracy help generate a community, or is it possible only where such community already exists? The resolution of this dilemma lies at the heart of the debates, not only about the liberal peace itself, but also about the possible extensions of democratic practice into the wider sphere of global governance. The prevailing assumptions about the New World Order were undoubtedly that this was a moment when espousal of shared liberal norms could help forge a new world community, and that liberal democratic practice would contribute to that process. In President Bush's words 'a world based on a shared commitment . . . to a set of principles that undergird our relations' (Jones 1996: 82) would help generate a real community, and liberalism would be instrumental in bringing this about. In the beginning was democracy, and community would issue forth from it. But it is precisely this instrumental view of democracy that is rejected by many, as has been particularly evident in the discussions of the various projects for transnational or cosmopolitan democracy (Clark 1999: 155–62). The generic objection, deriving from communitarian first principles, is that 'organizational forms by themselves cannot create a democratic society' (J. Thompson 1998: 186). If this is the case, then a liberal community cannot be created by artifice, either within individual countries where the societal consensus does not already exist, or across the machinery of international governance because this is not embedded in 'the commitment to community which democratic citizenship requires' (1998: 186).

The most visible material manifestation of this liberal regulation since

1990 has, of course, been the practice of humanitarian intervention. Under its umbrella, 'intervention by the liberal democracies is justified partly in terms of maintaining order but more in terms of correcting flagrant violations of human rights' (Richardson 2000: 25). There can be little doubt that this development has been directly attributable to the end of the Cold War, as writers on the subject have testified. They note a 'fundamental transformation' resulting from the interventions in post-Gulf War Iraq to protect the Kurdish and Shia communities, and in the wake of UN Security Council Resolution 688 of April 1991 (Ramsbotham and Woodhouse 1996: 69). Wheeler likewise confirms a 'key normative change' towards the 'enforcement of global humanitarian norms' (2000: 289). How does all of this relate to the post-Cold War regulative peace?

The regulation was intended to operate in three interlinked ways. In combination, these would serve to create a virtuous circle of reinforcement that would intensify liberalism, the democratic peace, and the sustenance of the post-Cold War order. The first of these instruments was the overt reliance on force as a means to ensure compliance with the liberal rights order. That order not only decreed a set of liberal norms to be observed in international society, but also legitimized the use of force for their enhancement and protection. It validated a new version of just-war theory, insofar as it permitted a 'reordering of international relations in accordance with considerations of human rights', and the application of force towards that end (Coates 1996: 206–7). The use of that force would, of course, be contingent upon the distribution of power, and hence upon the role of the United States in wishing to mobilize it. As C. Brown correctly makes clear, the matter of the 'promotion of liberal values in the world, the protection of human rights . . . will only happen if the US is prepared to make it happen' (1999*b*: 48). It is in this sense—not so much in the articulation of the norms, but in the creation of the licence for their enforcement—that the liberal peace is important as a means of regulation.

Secondly, and as should in any case be clear by now, the post-1990 liberalism was a credo not only for the regulation of international behaviour but also, and more basically, for the regulation of the nature of states themselves. If it was true that international order would be respected by certain kinds of states, then the best way of preserving that order was by the prescription of the preferred model of state in the first place. This would generate a series of states more compliant with the existing order.

Hence, liberalism was to be an instrument for the active socialization of states, by holding out to them the costs in lost sovereignty of their failure to conform. The point is implicit, if not quite the intention behind it, in Hoffmann's vindication of a liberal practice of intervention, since a 'state that is oppressive or violates the autonomy and integrity of its subjects forfeits its moral claim to full sovereignty' (1998: 245–6). Good behaviour, and adaptation to the prescribed liberal norms, thereby becomes the means of avoiding this fate.

Thirdly, there would be a reinforcement of the liberal zone by drawing attention to those states that fell outside it. Both on the part of those states acting on behalf of the liberal community, and on the part of those either ostracized or punished by it, there would be fostered a greater sense of this zone's community identity. Indeed, the very practice of intervention on behalf of liberal and humanitarian values would itself underwrite the sense of either belonging to that order, or of falling outside it. Either way, this was intended as a powerful form of socialization of behaviour, by further entrenching the sense of membership of those states which already belonged to it, and of the costs of exclusion to those that remained beyond the pale.

What is already implicit in this comment, and a point that can easily be neglected, is the following. There is a danger that we think of peace settlements as being about the relations between victors and vanquished alone. However, this is demonstrably not the case, especially as regards the regulative dimensions of peace settlements. These seek to regulate relations among the victors, and among other parties, as much as they are impositions upon the defeated alone. This is very much so in the case of the liberal rights order. Here was a set of prescriptions that would continue to constitute the identity of the Western bloc after the end of the Cold War, and to regulate their mutual relations with each other. Not only did it affirm faith in the necessary attributes of good statehood and good behaviour, but regulated both by imposing new rights and duties within the international system as a whole. If anything, the liberal rights order, as part of the post-Cold War settlement, has carried greater implications for relations within the West, and for relations between North and South, than it has for the defeated communist bloc, narrowly depicted. Only within such a rounded perspective can the functionality of the post-Cold War settlement be fully appreciated and understood.

It is thus necessary to reiterate the theme of power in the post-Cold War regulative settlement. In establishing a prescriptive model that was to be encouraged by a system of inducements and punishments, the liberal rights order relied explicitly on power for part of its effectiveness. However, the peace sought also to go beyond the distributive settlement, in creating for itself an acceptable basis in legitimacy as well. This explains some of the paradoxes of that order, as well as some of its most notable shortcomings, and it is to these aspects that the chapter turns in conclusion.

It was because of his concern that the post-Cold War order would be seen to be a naked exercise in Western dominance that Linklater made his appeal for it to take a more overtly 'constitutional' form. His worry, as he expressed it at the time, was that 'it is profoundly important that the powerful democracies do not let their enthusiasm for the triumph of liberal democracy overshadow their moral and political obligations to the periphery' (1993: 38). As suggested above, it was very much a part of the settlement of 1990 that the Western powers collectively be seen to be the mainspring of an expanding liberal community at the core of the international system, but also themselves to be bound by their own prescriptions. This entailed negative duties of desisting from breaches of international norms, as well as positive obligations, to maintain order both in the inter-state sense and also in the wider humanitarian view of it. Whether, since 1990, this constitutionality has survived the test is very much open to question. It is, however, doubtful that any unequivocally affirmative response can be given to it.

Legitimacy is itself derived from multiple sources, ranging from voluntary compliance at one end of the spectrum to veiled resorts to power-based inducements at the other. In these terms, and for all its attempts to make liberal rights the basis of a legitimate order, international practice since 1990 has witnessed a more forthright regulation by means of power rather than by willing compliance alone. If anything, the emphasis has shifted progressively from the latter to the former. In part, and as argued with respect to the fluctuating evolution of the distributive settlement as a whole, this has been as a result of the growing confidence in the West that it needs to pay a lower price to ensure acquiescence with the existing order. As uncertainties about the future of Russia solidified into a reassurance about its marginality, so less needed to be done to give real substance to the regulative settlement to preserve that peace. In a word, there was greater confidence that the distribution of power could be sustained by its own logic, and hence legitimacy had a smaller part to play in the grand design overall.

And yet this is not the whole explanation for what has happened. Another part of the argument must be located in the very paradoxes that emerged in the effort to sustain a liberal order by means of its own inherent appeal. The nature of this is nicely captured by Hawthorn. 'The paradox of a liberal hegemony in the post-Cold War world', he explicates, 'is that it is weak because it cannot convincingly be demonstrated, and in so far as it can be, threatens to undermine the principles on which it is' (1999: 160). This is to say that the very rhetorical style of a liberal rights order leaves it exposed to challenge, and when action is taken to enforce it, it is seen to contradict its own beliefs. This appears a convincing summary judgement on the history of the first post-Cold War decade, and can be illustrated in two respects.

The first is with regard to the formal institutions of global governance, including the United Nations, international financial institutions, and bodies like the G-7. Within them, the dominant Western powers have jealously guarded and further entrenched their own privileged positions, so much so that increasingly consensus has been sacrificed to the need to retain tight political control. Power has become the dominant mode of regulation, and the early aspiration for a more broadly based support has largely been eroded or abandoned as a consequence. It is the recognition of this that has further compelled the proponents of cosmopolitan democracy to set out their case. Simply put, and in Held's (1995: 139) words, 'if the democratic underpinning of the organizations and forces of the international order is open to doubt, so too is the basis of their legitimacy'. To the extent that the liberal rights order has disappointed hopes about an amelioration of the former, it is certainly fair to acknowledge the latter as the necessary consequence.

Secondly, there is the paradox that the greater salience accorded to human rights after 1990 also gave birth to the need for more forceful action in their support. Many have been deeply uncomfortable with this unholy combination of the liberal warrior that has been produced as a result. But it is not the issue of resort to force as such that is at stake, but whether that resort enjoys some legitimate basis or not. In this respect, C. Brown's comments on the opening and closing wars of the 1990s are illuminating, if limited:

Far more than the Gulf War of 1990–91, does it seem likely that NATO's war with Yugoslavia over the fate of Kosovo will be seen as a defining event of the post-Cold War era. NATO, here, has been fighting a liberal's war; that is to say, a war fought predominantly in response to gross human rights violations and threats of genocide. (1999*b*: 49)

The comment is fair enough as far as it goes, but does not go far enough. Both were liberal wars, inasmuch as they were intended to shore up aspects of the liberal rights order. To be sure, there was much greater emphasis on human rights in 1999 than in 1991. But both situations were presented as unacceptable challenges to the order as a whole, and the liberal account of that order extended beyond a concern with human rights alone. They were both, in that respect, important instances of regulative wars, fought to preserve the fabric of the post-Cold War settlement. What then sets them apart is less the degree of the focus upon human rights, and more the extent of legitimacy that was seen to attach to the military operations in the two cases. While both wars attracted their fair share of dissidents and detractors, it is not unreasonable to suggest that the Gulf War enjoyed greater support and legitimacy, across a wider spectrum of international society, than did the war in Kosovo.

There is no doubt a whole range of factors that can help explain this. The Gulf War was seen to be a straightforward inter-state war, and in that sense was about the conventions of sovereignty. This was a cause to which most states could subscribe without undue agonizing. As against this, the campaign over Kosovo had a messy intra-state dimension to it and this, on its own, was sufficient to give some states pause. Most obviously, the Gulf War gained much of its legitimacy from being backed by Security Council resolutions, whereas the same was not achieved in the war against Serbia, even if the Security Council did not support a motion *against* the war either.

Two issues emerge from this discussion. On the relationship between the legitimacy of the wars and their formal backing in the United Nations, we need to determine which was cause and which effect. Was the Gulf War supported in the UN because it was widely regarded as legitimate, or did it become so because it found widespread support in the UN? The same, in reverse, might then be said for the war in Kosovo.

The second issue is whether the response of the international community in the two instances was itself determined by the intrinsic merits of the two cases, or simply a reflection of the generally more soured international atmosphere that had developed by the end of the 1990s.

On these questions, this chapter comes down in favour of the latter interpretation as regards both. The Gulf War, although benefiting from the clarity of its cause, found favour in the international community because there was a supportive constellation of international forces behind the international cooperation to which it gave rise. The relatively benign phase of the post-Cold War armistice was undoubtedly a contributory factor towards this outcome. In contrast, while the war over Kosovo laboured under the anxieties produced by its humanitarian agenda, and under worries about how its military means would benefit its political goals, it was fundamentally the object of this greater international division, rather than the subject of it. Of this, the paramount determinant was that, by 1999, the Western conclave of states rested more securely in its post-Cold War victory, and was more minded to regulate by power, if it could not regulate by legitimacy alone.

In these complex ways, we can see that the liberal rights order was not merely the fruit of victory in the Cold War, but an actual means of preserving the benefits that victory had brought. It also reveals the inconclusive, and partial, settlement that had been imposed by 1991. Just as the nature of the distributive peace was to shift, and become more exacting, during the course of the 1990s, so parts of the regulative settlement were reimposed as the decade unfolded. No single and consolidated peace had been established immediately at the Cold War's end. Instead, and following on the model of 1945, a peace was to be progressively constructed with the passing of the years. In some respects, its terms became harsher with that passage of time.

CONCLUSION

The thesis of this book, succinctly stated, is that we gain considerable understanding of the post-Cold War order if we regard it as a typical phase of post-war peacemaking. In the great historical examples of the past, the end of a period of protracted conflict issued in attempts to impose new distributions of international power, as well as to inculcate wider principles and norms for the conduct of international relationships. This is very much in line with what has occurred also since the end of the Cold War. More-over, and following earlier precedents, the peacemaking has extended into attempts to reconstruct the nature of the defeated states. In those earlier cases—Napoleonic France in 1815, Wilhelmine Germany in 1918, and Nazi Germany and Imperial Japan after 1945—the defeated were to be politically recast in the aftermath of war. Likewise, the former Soviet Union and its socialist allies have been 'pacified' by attempted radical transformations to their political and economic character. Whatever else contributes to the totality of today's order—and there is much else besides—that process of inter-state peacemaking occupies a central place within it.

Whatever our intrinsic interest in peace settlements, we would not be entitled to foist this framework upon the post-Cold War order were it not for the fact that it is manifestly applicable to do so. The end of the Cold War yielded a phase of international politics that bore all the classical hallmarks of the peace settlements reached at the end of previous great wars. The Cold War, to be sure, was not in form a war of the traditional variety, but can be regarded as a war of a kind nonetheless. For more than four decades, the superpowers competed across a host of dimensions—militarily, technologically, ideologically, economically, culturally, and icon-ically (as in space and sport). These competitions had a profound, and often violent, impact on many other societies around the world. Moreover, if wars themselves are regarded as the great catalysts of social and economic change, then the Cold War was certainly not found wanting in this regard. And yet, at the end of the 1980s, this great contest came to a dramatic end. That termination could not itself have been more remarkable, and subsequently influential, had it resulted from the direct defeat in war of one of its protagonists. For those reasons combined, the analogy between the end of the Cold War, and a phase of post-war peacemaking, is so striking as to warrant our adoption of it as the appropriate frame of reference.

There are additional considerations that further vindicate the approach. The ongoing debates about the nature of the post-Cold War order have been much concerned with two puzzles in particular. The first is about the degree of novelty and difference represented by the current order, and is preoccupied by assessments of the elements of continuity and discontinuity within it. Thus far, the debate has directed attention to this issue, but without any consistent framework for its consideration. Writers have started from their individual points of theoretical departure, and have made their judgements accordingly. The second, and substantial, focus of debate has been upon what it is that has been most affected by the end of the Cold War. Has it been the 'structural' context in which international politics takes place, or has it been the 'procedural' norms and institutions that motivate the players who take part in it? Again, the motley views expressed over the past decade or so reflect different theoretical assumptions. However, there has been no common ground on which these views have met or been able to engage with each other. As a result, the respective arguments have passed each other by like ships in the night.

Part of the case for approaching the post-Cold War period as an exercise in peacemaking is then that it provides just such a common framework within which these two sets of issues can be confronted. The device of delineating the distributive and regulative dimensions of a peace settlement allows the possibility that any individual peace will forge its own distinctive combination of aspects of continuity and discontinuity. That combination may, but need not, revolve around the axis separating the regulative and distributive spheres. In the case of the end of the Cold War, the argument takes precisely this form. Most of what we consider to be the areas of greatest change and discontinuity after 1989 are those deriving from the distributive elements of the peace. In contrast, it is within the regulative sphere that the points of continuity are most marked. Similarly, as against the inconclusive deliberations about the new polarity, on the one hand, or upon emergent managerial norms, on the other, peacemaking offers a single frame within which these two aspects are compelled to engage with each other. Peace settlements deal both with the structural aspects of a post-war situation, and with the procedural constraints brought to bear upon it, in a direct and explicit way. This creates the opportunity for a more insightful engagement between the two.

When we adopt the framework of peacemaking, what conclusions emerge as a result? To begin with, we need to consider the nature of the peace settlement that has been set in place. What were its provisions, and what has been settled by it? In terms of the preceding argument, we can best consider the nature of this post-Cold War peace by distinguishing between its distributive and its regulative aspects.

The principal instances of the distributive peace were to be located in Europe, as befitted the centrality of that continent to the Cold War itself. Admittedly, much of the redistribution that there took place was not consciously intended in the first instance. But, in this respect, it was scarcely unusual. The settlement after 1945 came to hinge critically upon the division of Germany, even though that had not been part of anyone's original design. Two conclusions emerge from the distributive peace in Europe. The first is that it came in phases, and has been constructed over a period of time. After a relatively benign 'armistice', the settlement proper moved through a phase of cooperation, before gravitating towards the more robust marginalization of Russia that was the feature of the second half of the 1990s. The second observation, accordingly, is that the settlement has become progressively more severe for Russia as time has lapsed. By the end, it warranted those condemnations of it, as by Gaddis (1998), as a short-sighted settlement that ignored the unhappy lessons of 1919.

The idea that there was such a peace settlement in Europe is largely unproblematic. It is more contentious when applied to other regions, such as Pacific Asia and the Middle East. Nonetheless, the argument can be advanced that there was indeed a wider global settlement for the simple reason that the recession of Soviet power left a need to redefine the political architecture within these various regional settings. That process of redefinition was tantamount to the global terms of peace.

In Pacific Asia, there seemed initially to be much less change as a direct consequence of the end of the Cold War. The reason for this was not that no knock-on effects were experienced there, but rather that these effects were different, reflecting the particular experiences of that region during the Cold War itself. The process of adjustment was a measure of the differing starting points—as between Asia and Europe—from which the adjustment had to take place. Pacific Asia has so far accommodated the changed pattern of post-Cold War international politics by acknowledging the diminished role of Soviet power. The result has been, paradoxically, to entrench the role of the United States which, against many predictions, persists in exercising its pivotal responsibility as a producer of the security framework. There has, as yet, been no devolution of power to the region itself, as Washington appears to have acted on the belief that 'Asia was too important to be left to the Asians' (Mastanduno 2000: 506). This has resulted in no final peace settlement, but in a crypto-peace at best. Too many of its arrangements, including the long-term sustainability of America's role, are overly transient to be regarded as the final architecture for the management of the region's affairs.

The claim that a global peace settlement encompassed the Middle East should not be misunderstood to signify the attainment of a viable peace within that region. A decade after the end of the Cold War, this remains a distant and uncertain prospect. More modestly, the claim that can be asserted is that the political architecture within which such peace is to be sought has been modified to take account of the demise of Soviet power. This was relatively straightforward to accomplish, since Soviet power had already been in sharp decline in the area since the early 1970s. The peace settlement has therefore been instrumental in configuring the modality of international oversight of the key regional problems, especially the complex Israeli–Palestinian issues. That settlement has confirmed and deepened US primacy within this sphere. This leaves untouched the remaining paradox that, while American power may be unchallenged, it is far from all-determining: the fact that nobody else can do it does not mean that Washington can.

The other illustration offered of the distributive peace was from within the functional realm of disarmament. Victors traditionally use peace settlements to magnify and perpetuate a favourable balance of military power. Unsurprisingly, the end of the Cold War was itself accompanied by major accords on conventional and nuclear disarmament. For all that these seem not to fit within the category of post-war 'enforced disarmament', on account of their having been negotiated instead, they are nonetheless revealing of the nature of the post-Cold War peace. On the face of it, the CFE produced the more dramatically asymmetrical outcome. However, while START resulted in a more balanced deal, it saw deep cuts into the category of weapons upon which the USSR had been the more reliant. The extent of the USA's victory in the nuclear area is further revealed in the confidence it has since given to Washington to dangle the prospect of its exercising unilateral freedom of action on national missile defence.

Less evidently, but no less significantly, there were to be aspects of globalization that became integral to the distributive peace. Globalization occupies a strategic place in several of the key arguments advanced in this book. It straddles the distributive and regulative dimensions of the post-Cold War settlement; it represents important elements of both continuity and discontinuity as between the Cold War and post-Cold War orders; and it is an excellent illustration of the interlocking nature of the international and domestic aspects of peacemaking. In its purely distributive function, globalization after the Cold War contributed to the new balance of global economic power; extended the reach of the global economy; and further intensified the complex interplay between its own sundry manifestations and US power. Greater scope for further globalization had been a war aim of the West during the Cold War, and this outcome was manifestly one of its more pronounced distributive effects.

At the same time, globalization was also inscribed in the regulative settlement. It was to be one of the principal mechanisms for keeping the peace, when once it had been made. Throughout the third section of the book, the argument has been developed that multilateralism and the global economy, trends towards a collectivization of security, and the further inculcation of a liberal rights order were all mutually reinforcing aspects of the regulative peace. Each had a substantive agenda of its own and was, to that extent, an end in itself. However, each needs to be understood also as a means to the end of the preservation of the post-Cold War settlement as a whole. It is for this reason that they can be regarded, collectively, as forming an actual part of the peace, but serving a wider purpose within it. Intriguingly, and in sharp contrast to the other great peace settlements since 1815, the regulative settlement in 1990 has been a marked point of continuity with the pre-war order. Whereas earlier settlements sought to inculcate regulative principles that would *transform* international relations for all, the post-Cold War regulative peace has functioned to *conserve* what was already in existence, while bringing the outsiders within its fold.

Of the various components of the regulative peace, the continuities in the area of multilateralism are the most visible. Multilateralism is a general principle for organizing various international functional activities, and is exemplified in such bodies as the United Nations and the World Trade Organization. It is based on ideas of inclusiveness and non-discrimination. As such, and applied to spheres like the global economy, it was reasserted after 1990 as a principal vehicle for perpetuating the results of victory in the Cold War. It derived its inherent appeal from its existing record of success during the post-1945 period as a whole. Its seductive charm was, simultaneously, exploitable in the interests of the dominant Western powers, and became their chosen instrument for preserving the gains they had already won.

Multilateralism in the political and economic spheres found its counterpart in the collectivization of security. This was driven by a complex set of forces, by no means all directly pertaining to the end of the Cold War. Indeed, many of these developments—the emergence of new security actors, and a dilution of the state's monopoly of legitimacy over the use of force—were themselves part of the reason for a reassertion of a 'collective' approach. Given the stimulus which the end of the Cold War also gave these liberating forces, there was a need to re-regulate the resort to violence to push it in more controlled directions. This did not signal a move to collective security as such. What it did signal was an attempt to attach legitimacy to those actions sponsored by the international community, and in effect by its leading members. It would simultaneously further delegitimize all other resorts to force. It did so by operating a self-conscious principle of selectivity that determined which enemies would be engaged, and on what terms. Some enemies could be safely ignored, and were. Others would be engaged only by resort to means that could safely be adopted: if not, then not at all.

This form of regulation related closely to its third component, the liberal rights order. In some respects, one prominent expression of the collectivization of security in the 1990s—namely, humanitarian intervention—was the link between the two. From a managerial perspective, it seemed increasingly illogical to distinguish between international community wars arising out of inter-state conflicts, and community wars in response to intra-state disputes. In consequence, a degree of forceful humanitarian intervention went hand in hand with the reassertion of the more director-ial policy of order-maintenance in general that the collectivization of security already betokened. This sat comfortably with the other elements of the liberal rights order. It constituted a social pressure for the develop-ment of certain kinds of polities that would best uphold the emergent international order itself. By so doing, they would help keep the peace that the Cold War had delivered. If needs be, this could be supported by armed action, either on behalf of a liberal internationalist position (as in 1991 against Iraq), or on behalf of a liberal rights position (as in 1999 against Serbia). The latter form of intervention was a logical extension of the former activity, insofar as the collectivization of security was seen progres-sively to entail the management of rights, as well as the oversight of order more narrowly defined.

What remains to be clarified is the means employed for preservation of this peace, and the implications this might have for the future stability of the post-Cold War order. During the course of the book, a number of themes have emerged as to the nature of peacemaking, and it is appropri-ate to pull these together at this point. Prominent throughout has been the twin categories of distributive and regulative peacemaking. This gives rise to a fascinating—but still largely unexplored—agenda about the complex relationship between the two. What determines how much reliance is placed upon each, and how, if at all, is the severity/lenience of one related to the degree of confidence in the other?

In close proximity to this discussion is a set of questions about the balance between power and legitimacy in creating and sustaining the peace. Is the distributive peace the remit of power alone, while the regula-tive peace is the exclusive domain of concerns about legitimacy? If this is too stark, how might we develop a more subtle appreciation of the relationship between them?

Initially, it needs to be insisted that the two categories—distributive and regulative—are by no means absolute and hermetically sealed from each other. They would be much less interesting if that were, indeed, to be the case. Already, we have encountered many instances that would belie any such claim. At the very least, the recurrent wish to transform the defeated state in the aftermath of war can readily be understood as an instance of both. Changing the character of the vanquished can have decisive implications for the distribution of power; it is also a means of encouraging compliance with the terms of the peace. More broadly, what is distributive in one historical context may more appropriately be viewed as regulative in another. The division of the economic spoils may be thought of as a classic instrument within the distributive peace. However, in 1919, for example, reparations were viewed not just as a demand of the peace, but also as an instrument for keeping it: it was a way of regulating German behaviour in the future in a way that was compatible with French security. In short, those twin categories must be thought of as indicative, and not absolute, for analytical purposes.

More fundamentally, it is misleading to imagine that what distinguishes them is the distributive peace's expression of power, as against the regulative peace's reliance on consensus. The relationship displays much more nuance than this would have us believe. The point can be addressed by looking at a similar tension in Ikenberry's position. On the one hand, he has expressed an optimistic view about the durability of the Western order. 'It is not the preponderance of American power that keeps the system intact', he concludes, 'but its unique ability to engage in strategic restraint' (2000: 270). At the same time, he concedes elsewhere that it is 'useful to think of the ability of the leading state to restrain and commit its power credibly as, paradoxically, a type of power' (2000: 259). On the latter point, Ikenberry is assuredly correct, but it unsettles the earlier claim. If strategic restraint is a way of reducing 'the returns to power', and hence of securing a wider consensus and legitimacy, this alone does not succeed in divorcing the strategy from power: it is simply one form that its exercise can take.

In a word, regulative peacemaking too depends upon power, even when it searches for accommodations that go beyond it. So clearly the issue is not simply to distinguish the distributive from the regulative on the basis of the degree of power or legitimacy upon which each respectively depends. The regulative peace is itself a subtle blend of power and legitimacy. While seeking to found itself upon the latter, it is very far from divorced from the former.

Why then do states prefer one strategy to the other? What conditions determine the balance that might be struck between them? And what might this signify for the post-Cold War order? We can certainly agree with Ikenberry that, since 1815, there has been a discernible trend towards greater reliance upon the regulative aspects of peacemaking, rather than upon the distributive provisions alone. An effective regulative peace has the attraction of appearing to place fewer burdens upon the victorious states for the direct exercise of their pre-eminent position. The more acceptable the peace settlement as a whole is regarded to be, the more compliant will be the defeated powers, and the less vulnerable it is to revisionist challenge.

That much is straightforward, and as a set of political prescriptions has long been well understood. But there are perhaps a number of facets of the post-Cold War peace that place this relationship in a slightly different, and murkier, light. The argument can be illustrated in the following ways.

There has been a tension in Western attitudes towards the construction of that peace. This has resulted from a pronounced ambivalence as to whether its future durability would best be safeguarded by its distributive, as opposed to its regulative, terms. That uncertainty is exemplified above all in the goals of Russian transition. Was the objective of this simply to effect a redistribution of power by bringing Russia, or at least the other states of eastern Europe, across to the Western side? Or was it to so transform the Russian polity that it became itself wedded to the concept of the peace, and willing to ensure compliance with it? The tension that developed as the 1990s unfolded was that measures taken by way of insurance within the distributive peace (such as NATO enlargement) had the side effect of contributing to Russian disenchantment with its own accommodative policy, thereby undercutting its regulatory effectiveness. At the same time, the less threatening Russia seemed to become to Western interests, the less incentive there was to be respectful of such Russian sensitivities. In combination, the tension expressed itself in a drift away from a consensual regulative peace, and towards a more overt implementation of a stringent distributive peace.

In any event, it can equally be suggested that, in 1990, the regulative became the principal strand of the peacemaking, not because this would most distance the peace from power, but because it was within these dimensions that power could most effectively be exercised. The fact that the components of the regulative peace already had a track record of success, proven in the outcome of the Cold War, spoke eloquently on behalf of such a strategy. On this reasoning, the distributive peace was initially restricted to a supporting role, not because it was too overtly power based, but because it was less effectively so. It would appear also that, since 1990, the balance has gradually shifted back towards the distributive peace, on the perception of declining necessity to render the concessions to the defeated that the regulative peace normally brings. It has been repeatedly suggested in the book that the terms of peace have become harsher over time, above all because it was felt safe to make them so.

We are then left with two observations that derive from the same essential logic. The first is that the terms of the peace seemed initially to be relatively benign, but this was deceptive. They appeared to be lenient only because the less visible regulative peace had been left to do most of the work. The reason for this preference was not that the regulative settlement was less reliant upon Western power, but because the various soft forms of Western power could most effectively be expressed through its provisions. The second is that, over the decade since, the balance has tilted back somewhat from the regulative to the distributive, with a seemingly more severe peace being imposed as a result. This again tends to be deceptive. It is less important that the peace has become harsher than that there has been a shift in its mode of enforcement. The reason has been that the more direct forms of distributive power could now be resorted to, the less open to challenge did the entire peace settlement appear to be. Consequently, the West has felt more confident in exacting a fuller price, both from Russia and from the system as a whole.

This leads directly to some final assessments about the nature of the post-Cold War peace. How severe has it been? What has been the duration of the peacemaking? And is the peace settlement more significant for the changes it has introduced, or for the profound continuities that it has reinforced?

The book has raised questions about how harsh the peace has been, especially when viewed in comparison to historical precedents. As must by now be obvious, there is no single or straightforward answer that can be given to that question. The harshness, or generosity, of the peace has changed over time, and has been blurred by the shifting balance between its distributive and regulative dimensions. In sum, however, its terms have been exacting, taken as a package, and its distributive provisions in particular have certainly become harsher with the passage of time.

Secondly, this leads to the related conclusion that it is a peace still under construction. The European settlement has been put progressively in place across the decade since 1990. In other regions, such as Pacific Asia, a final settlement is yet to be established, and we have only a partial peace thus far. There was assuredly no single, and all-encompassing, peace conference in 1990, issuing in a comprehensive settlement. Instead, like the settlement after 1945, the peace has been incremental, adding by stages to its existing dimensions, and with resultant changes to its character overall.

Finally, this view of post-Cold War peacemaking permits us to develop a more specific engagement with the troublesome matter of continuity and discontinuity. It is here that the starkest differentiation between the distributive and regulative aspects of the peace is to be discovered. Without doubt, all the best examples of discontinuity are to be found in the distributive sphere. Even in cases where this picked upon an existing trend, the effect of the end of the Cold War was so to intensify and accelerate it as to constitute a major change. The panoply of distributions—in spheres of influence, state unification and dismemberment, military balances, and the new geography of inclusion—has been such as to draw the sharpest possible contrast between the worlds of the Cold War and its successor.

As against this, the strongest continuities are apparent in the regulative sphere. In none of its key dimensions—multilateralism and the global economy, changing patterns of security, nor liberal rights—did the end of the Cold War mark a novel point of departure. On the contrary, in all three areas, these were to be so salient in preserving the peace precisely for the reason that they were already regarded as keystones of the very victory in the Cold War. It was their proven track record as instruments in the attainment of that victory, and as a set of developments from which the vanquished had hitherto been excluded, that their potency for keeping the peace was to reside. In short, the changes that the settlement brought about would be preserved by those very elements that remained constant.

What this finally leaves to be resolved is the great question of the likely future stability of the order that the post-Cold War settlement has bequeathed to us. Again, Ikenberry's optimistic diagnosis perhaps holds some dangers of complacency. '[S]table political orders', he judges, 'tend to be those that have low returns to power and high returns to institutions' (2000: 266). For all the reasons already set out, things are not quite so simple, but above all because the returns to institutions are not wholly separate from, nor independent of, the returns to power. In sum, the regulative peace may seek to distance itself from power, but it can do so effectively only if the victors enjoy the margins of power that allow them to resort to this strategy in the first place: this is itself an expression of a kind of power.

These reflections invite two radically contrasting conclusions overall. Insofar as the entire post-Cold War peace—in both its distributive and regulative dimensions—has been an artifice of overarching power, its stability might be regarded as guaranteed for the foreseeable future. It is supported by accretions of power in all areas—hard and soft—such that it enjoys margins of preponderance in excess of anything attained hitherto in previous peace settlements. The order will not soon be overthrown, because there can be no serious revisionist challenge to it, at least none with any real prospect of success. On this assessment, the order will endure because the distributive and regulative settlements, collectively, trump any resistance to it. Its stability is rooted in the sense, albeit highly limited, in which it is in the best interests of all participants to acquiesce in it. The costs of defection, for its weaker participants, would assuredly be higher than are the costs of continued compliance.

The alternative view is that, because the regulative settlement is itself so transparently reliant upon the high returns to power, the order is unsustainable in the longer term. However subtle and indirect, its provenance in the peace settlement reveals it to be too much an enterprise of political imposition, and too little of genuine consent. In the absence of a regulative peace that is seen to enjoy anything beyond a limited pragmatic value, the order as a whole is left exposed and vulnerable. The regulative settlement has become a continuation of the distributive by other means, and not a legitimate alternative to it. In these terms, the order is sustainable only if future shifts in the distribution of power do not take place. Given the dynamic quality of the relativity of power, this seems most unlikely. It could occur only if, in this particular sense, we had indeed reached the end of history. Since there is no convincing evidence to suggest that this is so, the prospects for the future of the current post-Cold War order must remain deeply uncertain.

They can improve only if there is a greater commitment to a more genuinely legitimate order than has been demonstrated thus far. This, in turn, would require a revision of the post-Cold War distributive peace to be more sensitive to the predicament in which the vanquished Russia now finds itself. It would require, more generally, a revised regulative peace in which the reasonable concerns of disaffected sections of the international community are addressed seriously, and a more effective constitutional limitation placed on the powers of the West as a result. The West may have no short-term interest in conceding any of this, but in the longer term its stake in doing so is overwhelming.

REFERENCES

ACHARYA, A. (1999), 'A Concert of Asia', *Survival*, 41 (3).

ADLER, E., and BARNETT, M. (1998) (eds.), *Security Communities* (Cambridge).

ADOMEIT, H. (1995), 'Russia as a "Great Power" in World Affairs: Images and Reality', *International Affairs*, 71 (1).

AHRARI, M. E. (1996a) (ed.), *Change and Continuity in the Middle East: Conflict Resolution and Prospects for Peace* (Houndmills).

—— (1996b), 'The Peace Process and its Critics: Post-Cold War Perspectives', in Ahrari (1996a).

ALBRECHT-CARRIE, R. (1965), *A Diplomatic History of Europe since the Congress of Vienna* (2nd edn.) (London).

ALBROW, M. (1996), *The Global Age: State and Society beyond Modernity* (Cambridge).

ALLISON, G., and TREVERTON, G. (1992) (eds.), *Rethinking America's Security: Beyond Cold War to New World Order* (New York).

ANDERSON, J. (1997), *The Limits of Sino-Russian Strategic Partnership*, Adelphi Paper 315 (Oxford).

ANTONENKO, O. (1999/2000), 'Russia, NATO and European Security after Kosovo', *Survival*, 41 (4).

ARBATOV, A. (1997), 'Russian Domestic Politics, Foreign Affairs and Geopolitical Considerations', in Carlton and Ingram (1997).

ARCHIBUGI, D. (1998), 'Principles of Cosmopolitan Democracy', in Archibugi, Held, and Kohler (1998).

—— and Held, D. (1995) (eds.), *Cosmopolitan Democracy: An Agenda for a New World Order* (Cambridge).

—— —— and Kohler, M. (1998) (eds.), *Re-Imagining Political Community: Studies in Cosmopolitan Democracy* (Cambridge).

ASLUND, A. (1999), 'Russia's Collapse', *Foreign Affairs*, 78 (5).

ASMUS, R. D., KUELER, R. L., and LARRABEE, F. S. (1993), 'Building a New NATO', *Foreign Affairs*, 72 (4).

Aspen Strategy Group (1995), *The United States and the Use of Force in the Post-Cold War Era* (Queenstown, Md.).

AXTMANN, R. (1998) (ed.), *Globalization and Europe: Theoretical and Empirical Investigations* (London).

AYOOB, M. (1997), 'Defining Security: A Subaltern Realist Perspective', in Krause and Williams (1997).

—— (1993), 'Squaring the Circle: Collective Security and the System of States', in T. G. Weiss (1993).

BACEVICH, A. J. (1995), 'The Limits of Orthodoxy: The Use of Force after the Cold War', in Aspen Strategy Group (1995).

BAGINDA, A. R., and BERGIN, A. (1998) (eds.), *Asia Pacific's Security Dilemma: Multilateral Relations amidst Political, Social and Economic Changes* (London).

BALDWIN, D. A. (1997), 'The Concept of Security', *Review of International Studies*, 23 (1).

—— (1993) (ed.), *Neorealism and Neoliberalism: The Contemporary Debate* (New York).

BALL, D. (1996a) (ed.), *The Transformation of Security in the Asia/Pacific Region* (London).

—— (1996b), 'Introduction', in Ball (1996a).

BARRY JONES, R. J. (2000), *The World Turned Upside Down: Globalization and the Future of the State* (Manchester).

—— (1995), *Globalisation and Interdependence in the International Political Economy: Rhetoric and Reality* (London).

BAUMAN, Z. (1998), *Globalization: The Human Consequences* (Cambridge).

BAYLIS, J., and SMITH, S. (2001) (eds.), *The Globalization of World Politics: An Introduction to International Relations* (2nd edn.) (Oxford).

—— —— (1997) (eds.), *The Globalization of World Politics: An Introduction to International Relations* (1st edn.) (Oxford).

BELL, P. M. H. (1986), *The Origins of the Second World War in Europe* (London).

BELLAMY, R., and CASTIGLIONE, D. (1998), 'Between Cosmopolis and Community: Three Models of Rights and Democracy within the European Union', in Archibugi, Held, and Kohler (1998).

BELLO, W. (1998), 'The Bretton Woods Institutions and the Demise of the UN Development System', in Paolini, Jarvis, and Reus-Smit (1998).

BERTRAM, C. (1995), *Europe in the Balance: Securing the Peace Won in the Cold War* (Washington, DC).

BESCHLOSS, M. R., and TALBOTT, S. (1993), *At the Highest Levels: The Inside Story of the End of the Cold War* (Boston).

BETTS, R. K. (1993/4), 'Wealth, Power, and Instability: East Asia and the United States after the Cold War', *International Security*, 18 (3).

—— (1992), 'Systems for Peace or Causes of War? Collective Security, Arms Control, and the New Europe', *International Security*, 17 (1).

BIERSTEKER, T. J. (2000), 'Globalization as a Mode of Thinking in Major Institutional Actors', in Woods (2000a).

BLECHMAN, B. M. (1998), 'International Peace and Security in the Twenty-First Century', in Booth (1998).

BLOOMFIELD, L. P. (1995), 'The Premature Burial of Global Law and Order: Looking beyond the Three Cases from Hell', in B. Roberts (1995).

BOEMEKE, M. F., FELDMAN, G. D., and GLASER, E. (1998) (eds.), *The Treaty of Versailles: A Reassessment after 75 Years* (Cambridge).

BOHMAN, J. (1999), 'International Regimes and Democratic Governance: Political Equality and Influence in Global Institutions', *International Affairs*, 75 (3).

BOLTHO, A. (1996), 'The Return of Free Trade', *International Affairs*, 72 (2).

BOOTH, K. (1998) (ed.), *Statecraft and Security: The Cold War and beyond* (Cambridge).

—— (1991), 'Security and Emancipation', *Review of International Studies*, 17 (4).

—— and SMITH, S. (1995) (eds.), *International Relations Theory Today* (Cambridge).

BOURANTANIS, D., and WIENER, J. (1995) (eds.), *The United Nations in the New World Order: The World Organization at Fifty* (Houndmills).

BOWKER, M., and ROSS, C. (2000) (eds.), *Russia after the Cold War* (Harlow).

BRACE, L., and HOFFMANN, J. (1997) (eds.), *Reclaiming Sovereignty* (London).

BRENNER, M. (1995a) (ed.), *Multilateralism and Western Strategy* (Houndmills).

—— (1995b), 'The Multilateral Moment', in Brenner (1995a).

BRESHEETH, H. (1991), 'The New World Order', in Bresheeth and Yuval-Davis (1991).

—— and YUVAL-DAVIS, N. (1991) (eds.), *The Gulf War and the New World Order* (London).

BROWN, C. (1999a), 'Universal Human Rights: A Critique', in Dunne and Wheeler (1999).

—— (1999b), 'History Ends, Worlds Collide', *Review of International Studies*, 25 (Special Issue).

—— (1996), ' "Really Existing Liberalism", Peaceful Democracies and International Order', in Fawn and Larkins (1996).

—— (1995), 'International Political Theory and the Idea of World Community', in Booth and Smith (1995).

BROWN, S. (1994), 'World Interests and the Changing Dimensions of Security', in Klare and Thomas (1994).

—— (1992), *International Relations in a Changing Global System: Towards a Theory of the World Polity* (Boulder, Colo.).

BRZEZINSKI, Z. (1995), 'A Plan for Europe', *Foreign Affairs*, 74 (1).

—— (1992), 'The Cold War and its Aftermath', *Foreign Affairs*, 71 (4).

BULL, H. (1977), *The Anarchical Society: A Study of Order in World Politics* (London).

BURLEY, A-M. (1993), 'Regulating the World: Multilateralism, International Law, and the Projection of the New Deal Regulatory State', in Ruggie (1993a).

BUSZYNSKI, L. (1996), *Russian Foreign Policy after the Cold War* (Westport, Conn.).

BUZAN, B. (1995), 'Security, the State, the "New World Order" and beyond', in Lipschutz (1995).

—— (1991), *People, States, and Fear: An Agenda for International Security Studies in the Post-Cold War Era* (London).

—— and LITTLE, R. (1999), 'Beyond Westphalia?: Capitalism after the "Fall" ', in Cox, Booth, and Dunne (1999a).

—— and SEGAL, G. (1994), 'Rethinking East Asian Security', *Survival*, 36 (2).

—— HELD, D., and McGREW, A. (1998), 'Realism vs Cosmopolitanism: A Debate', *Review of International Studies*, 24 (3).

CABLE, V. (1999), *Globalization and Global Governance*, Chatham House Paper (London).

—— (1996), 'The New Trade Agenda: Universal Rules amid Cultural Diversity', *International Affairs*, 72 (2).

CAMILLERI, J. A. (1995), 'State, Civil Society, and Economy', in Camilleri, Jarvis, and Paolini (1995).

CAMILLERI, J. A.(1993), 'Alliances and the Emerging Post-Cold War Security System', in Leaver and Richardson (1993a).

—— and FALK, J. (1992), *The End of Sovereignty? The Politics of a Shrinking and Fragmenting World* (Aldershot).

—— JARVIS, A. P., and PAOLINI, A. J. (1995) (eds.), *The State in Transition: Reimagining Political Space* (Boulder, Colo.).

CAPORASO, J. A. (1993), 'International Relations Theory and Multilateralism: The Search for Foundations', in Ruggie (1993a).

CARLTON, D., and INGRAM, P. (1997) (eds.), *The Search for Stability in Russia and the Former Soviet Bloc* (Aldershot).

CARPENTER, T. G. (1991), 'The New World Disorder', *Foreign Policy*, 84.

CARR, E. H. (1939), *The Twenty Years Crisis* (London).

CASSESE, A. (1990), *Human Rights in a Changing World* (Cambridge).

CERNY, P. G. (2000), 'Restructuring the Political Arena: Globalization and the Paradoxes of the Competition State', in Germain (2000).

—— (1996), 'Globalization and Other Stories: The Search for a New Paradigm for International Relations', *International Journal*, 51 (4).

CHAN, S., and WIENER, J. (1999) (eds.), *Twentieth Century International History: A Reader* (London).

CHOMSKY, N. (1997), *World Orders, Old and New* (London).

CHUBIN, S. (1995), 'The South and the New World Order', in B. Roberts (1995).

CLAD, J. C. (1995), 'Old World Disorders', in B. Roberts (1995).

CLARK, I. (2001), 'Globalization and the Post-Cold War Order', in Baylis and Smith (2001).

—— (2000), 'A "Borderless World"?', in Fry and O'Hagan (2000).

—— (1999), *Globalization and International Relations Theory* (Oxford).

—— (1997), *Globalization and Fragmentation: International Relations in the Twentieth Century* (Oxford).

COATES, A. (1996), 'The New World Order and the Ethics of War', in Holden (1996a).

COHEN, B. (2000), 'Money in a Globalized World', in Woods (2000a).

COWLING, K., and SUGDEN, R. (1994), *Beyond Capitalism: Towards a New World Economics Order* (London).

COX, D. (1996), *Retreating from the Cold War: Germany, Russia and the Withdrawal of the Western Group of Forces* (Houndmills).

COX, M. (2000), 'From the Cold War to Strategic Partnership? US–Russian Relations since the End of the Cold War', in Bowker and Ross (2000).

—— (1997), 'Bringing in the "International": The IRA Ceasefire and the End of the Cold War', *International Affairs*, 73 (4).

—— (1995), *US Foreign Policy after the Cold War: Superpower without a Mission*, Chatham House Paper (London).

—— (1994a), 'Rethinking the End of the Cold War', *Review of International Studies*, 20 (2).

—— (1994b), 'The Necessary Partnership? The Clinton Presidency and Post Soviet Russia', *International Affairs*, 70 (4).

—— (1993a), 'Whatever Happened to the "New World Order"?', *Critique*, 25

—— (1993b), 'Towards the New World Order?', *Politics Review*, 2 (4).

—— BOOTH, K., and DUNNE, T. (1999a) (eds.), *The Interregnum: Controversies in World Politics* (Cambridge).

—— —— —— (1999b), 'Introduction', in Cox, Booth, and Dunne (1999a).

Cox, R. W. (1997), 'An Alternative Approach to Multilateralism for the Twenty-First Century', *Global Governance*, 3 (1).

—— (1996), *Approaches to World Order* (Cambridge).

—— (1987), *Production, Power, and World Order: Social Forces in the Making of History* (New York).

CROCKATT, R. (1995), *The Fifty Years War: The United States and the Soviet Union in World Politics, 1941–1991* (London).

CROFT, S. (1994a) (ed.), *The Conventional Armed Forces in Europe Treaty: The Cold War Endgame* (Aldershot).

—— (1994b), 'Negotiations, Treaty Terms and Implications', in Croft (1994a).

CRONIN, J. E. (1996), *The World the Cold War Made: Order, Chaos and the Return of History* (New York).

CROXTON, D. (1999), *Peacemaking in Early Modern Europe: Cardinal Mazarin and the Congress of Westphalia 1643–1648* (Selinsgrove, NJ).

CUMINGS, B. (1999), 'Still the American Century', in Cox, Booth, and Dunne (1999a).

—— (1991), 'Trilateralism and the New World Order', *World Policy Journal*, 8 (2).

DAKIN, D. (1979), 'The Congress of Vienna, 1814–15, and its Antecedents', in Sked (1979).

DANCHEV, A. (1995a) (ed.), *Fin de Siècle: The Meaning of the Twentieth Century* (London).

—— (1995b), 'Introduction: The Sarajevo Century', in Danchev (1995a).

DANIELS, P. W., and LEVER, W. F. (1996) (eds.), *The Global Economy in Transition* (London).

DANILOV, D., and DE SPIEGELEIRE, S. (1998), *From Decoupling to Recoupling: A New Security Relationship between Russia and Western Europe?*, Chaillot Papers 31 (Paris).

DANNREUTHER, R. (1999/2000), 'Escaping the Enlargement Trap in NATO–Russian Relations', *Survival*, 41 (4).

DARK, K. R., with HARRIS, A. L. (1996), *The New World and the New World Order* (Houndmills).

DAVIS, M. JANE (1996) (ed.), *Security Issues in the Post-Cold War World* (Cheltenham).

DEAN, J. (1994), *Ending Europe's Wars: The Continuing Search for Peace and Security* (New York).

—— and FORSBERG, R. W. (1992), 'CFE and beyond: The Future of Conventional Arms Control', *International Security*, 17 (1).

DEUDNEY, D. (1995), 'Political Fission: State Structure, Civil Society, and Nuclear Security Politics in the United States', in Lipschutz (1995).

DEUDNEY, D., and IKENBERRY, G. JOHN (1999), 'The Nature and Sources of Liberal International Order', *Review of International Studies*, 25 (2).

—— —— (1994), 'After the Long War', *Foreign Policy*, 94.

—— —— (1992), 'Who Won the Cold War?', *Foreign Policy*, 87.

DEVETAK, R., and HIGGOTT, R. (1999), 'Justice Unbound? Globalization, States and the Transformation of the Social Bond', *International Affairs*, 75 (3).

DEWITT, D. B. (1993), 'Introduction: The New Global Order and the Challenges of International Security', in Dewitt, Haglund, and Kirton (1993).

—— HAGLUND, D., and KIRTON, S. (1993) (eds.), *Building a New Global Order: Emerging Trends in International Security* (Toronto).

DIBB, P. (1995), *Towards a New Balance of Power in Asia*, Adelphi Paper 295 (Oxford).

—— HALE, D. D., and PRINCE, P. (1999), 'Asia's Insecurity', *Survival*, 41 (3).

DICKEN, P. (1992), *Global Shift: The Internationalization of Economic Activity* (2nd edn.) (London).

DONNELLY, J. (1999), 'The Social Construction of International Human Rights', in Dunne and Wheeler (1999).

—— (1993), *International Human Rights* (Boulder, Colo.).

—— (1992), 'Human Rights in the New World Order', *World Policy Journal*, 9 (2).

DOWNS, G. W. (1994) (ed.), *Collective Security beyond the Cold War* (Ann Arbor).

—— ROCKE, D. M., and BARSOOM, P. N. (1998), 'Managing the Evolution of Multilateralism', *International Organization*, 52 (2).

DOYLE, M., and IKENBERRY, G. JOHN (1997) (eds.), *New Thinking in International Relations Theory* (Boulder, Colo.).

DUNN, J. (1995) (ed.), *Contemporary Crisis of the Nation State?* (Oxford).

DUNNE, T., and WHEELER, N. J. (1999) (eds.), *Human Rights in Global Politics* (Cambridge).

—— COX, M., and BOOTH, K. (1998) (eds.), *The Eighty Years Crisis: International Relations 1919–1999* (Cambridge).

EAGLEBURGER, L. (1991), 'US Must Adjust to Different, Challenging World', Address at George Washington University, 21 Nov.

EGLIN, M. (1997), 'China's Entry into the WTO, with a Little Help from the EU', *International Affairs*, 73 (3).

EVANS, T. (1997), 'Democratization and Human Rights', in McGrew (1997).

FALK, R. (1999), *Predatory Globalization: A Critique* (Cambridge).

—— (1997), 'State of Siege: Will Globalization Win Out?', *International Affairs*, 73 (1).

—— (1995a), *On Humane Governance: Toward a New Global Politics* (Cambridge).

—— (1995b), 'Regionalism and World Order after the Cold War', *Australian Journal of International Affairs*, 49 (1).

FAWCETT, L., and HURRELL, A. (1995) (eds.), *Regionalism in World Politics: Regional Organization and International Order* (Oxford).

FAWN, R., and LARKINS, J. (1996) (eds.), *International Society after the Cold War: Anarchy and Order Reconsidered* (Houndmills).

—— and MAYALL, J. (1996), 'Recognition, Self-determination and Secession in Post-Cold War International Society', in Fawn and Larkins (1996).

FELICE, W. F. (1996), *Taking Suffering Seriously: The Importance of Collective Human Rights* (Albany, NY).

FORBES, I., and HOFFMAN, M. (1993) (eds.), *Political Theory, International Relations, and the Ethics of Intervention* (Houndmills).

FREEDMAN, L. (1998), *The Revolution in Strategic Affairs*, Adelphi Paper 318 (Oxford).

—— (1992), 'Order and Disorder in the New World', *Foreign Affairs*, 71 (1).

—— (1991), 'The Gulf War and the New World Order', *Survival*, 33 (3).

FRIEDBERG, A. L. (1993/4), 'Ripe for Rivalry: Prospects for Peace in a Multipolar Asia', *International Security*, 18 (3).

FRIEDEN, J. A., and LAKE, D. A. (1995) (eds.), *International Political Economy: Perspectives on Global Power and Wealth* (3rd edn.) (New York).

FRY, G. (1993), 'At the Margin: The South Pacific and Changing World Order', in Leaver and Richardson (1993*a*).

—— and O'HAGAN, J. (2000) (eds.), *Contending Images of World Politics* (Houndmills).

FUKUYAMA, F. (1992), *The End of History and the Last Man* (London).

—— (1989), 'The End of History', *National Interest*, 16.

GADDIS, J. L. (1998), 'History, Grand Strategy and NATO Enlargement', *Survival*, 40 (1).

—— (1997), *We Now Know: Rethinking Cold War History* (New York).

—— (1992/3), 'International Relations Theory and the End of the Cold War', *International Security*, 17 (3).

—— (1992*a*), *The United States and the End of the Cold War: Implications, Reconsiderations, Provocations* (New York).

—— (1992*b*), 'The Cold War, the Long Peace, and the Future', in Hogan (1992).

GAMBLE, A. (1996), 'The Limits of Democracy', in special issue of *Political Quarterly*.

GARRETT, G. (2000), 'Shrinking States? Globalization and National Autonomy', in Woods (2000*a*).

GARTHOFF, R. L. (1994), *The Great Transition: American–Soviet Relations and the End of the Cold War* (Washington, DC).

GARTON ASH, T. (2000), *History of the Present: Essays, Sketches and Despatches from Europe in the 1990s* (London).

GEISS, I. (1997), *The Question of German Unification* (London).

GERMAIN, R. (2000) (ed.), *Globalization and its Critics* (Houndmills).

GILL, S. (1997) (ed.), *Globalization, Democratization and Multilateralism: Multilateralism and the UN System* (Houndmills).

GILPIN, R. (1987), *The Political Economy of International Relations* (Princeton, NJ).

—— (1981), *War and Change in World Politics* (Cambridge).

—— (1971), 'The Politics of Transnational Economic Relations', in Keohane and Nye (1971).

GITZ, B. R., and VAN RAEMDONCK, D. C. (1997), 'The Triumph of Liberalism and the "New Europe"', *Global Society*, 11 (2).

GOODBY, J. E. (1998), *Europe Undivided: The New Logic of Peace in US–Russian Relations* (Washington, DC).

GOODMAN, M. (1993), 'Moscow and the Middle East in the 1990s', in Marr and Lewis (1993).

GORBACHEV, M. (1991), 'Perestroika and the New World Order', Nobel Lecture, 5 June (Moscow).

GOULD-DAVIES, N., and WOODS, N. (1999), 'Russia and the IMF', *International Affairs*, 75 (1).

GRAHAM, G. (1997), *Ethics and International Relations* (Oxford).

GRANT, C. (1995), 'Equity in a Global Partnership', *International Affairs*, 71 (3).

GRAY, J. (1998), *False Dawn: The Delusions of Global Capitalism* (London).

GREIDER, W. (1997), *One World, Ready or Not: The Manic Logic of Global Capitalism* (London).

GUEHENNO, J.-M. (1998/9), 'The Impact of Globalization on Strategy', *Survival*, 40 (4).

GULICK, E. V. (1967), *Europe's Classical Balance of Power* (New York).

HAAS, E. B. (1993), 'Collective Conflict Management: Evidence for a New World Order', in T. G. Weiss (1993).

HAAS, R. (1997), *The Reluctant Sheriff: The United States after the Cold War* (New York).

HALL, J. A. (1996), *International Orders* (Cambridge).

—— and PAUL, T. V. (1999), 'The State and the Future of World Politics', in Paul and Hall (1999).

HALPERIN, M. H., and SCHEFFER, D. J. (1992), *Self-Determination in the New World Order* (Washington, DC).

HARADA, C. (1997), *Russia and North-East Asia*, Adelphi Paper 310 (Oxford).

HASLAM, J. (1998), 'Russia's Seat at the Table: A Place Denied or a Place Delayed', *International Affairs*, 74 (1).

HAWTHORN, G. (1999), 'Liberalism since the Cold War: An Enemy to itself?', *Review of International Studies*, 25 (Special Issue).

HEISBOURG, F. (1999/2000), 'American Hegemony? Perceptions of the US Abroad', *Survival*, 41 (4).

HELD, D. (1998), 'Democracy and Globalization', in Archibugi, Held, and Kohler (1998).

—— (1995), *Democracy and the Global Order: From the Modern State to Cosmopolitan Governance* (Cambridge).

—— (1992) (ed.), *Prospects for Democracy*, Special Issue of *Political Studies*.

—— and McGREW, A. (1998), 'The End of the Old Order? Globalization and the Prospects for World Order', in Dunne, Cox, and Booth (1998).

—— —— (1993), 'Globalization and the Liberal Democratic State', *Government and Opposition*, 28 (2).

—— —— GOLDBLATT, D., and PERRATON, J. (1999), *Global Transformations: Politics, Economics and Culture* (Cambridge).

HERRMANN, R. K. (1991), 'The Middle East and the New World Order: Rethinking US Political Strategy after the Gulf War', *International Security*, 16 (2).

HINNEBUSCH, R. A. (1994), 'Egypt, Syria and the Arab State System in the New World Order', in Jawad (1994).

HINSLEY, F. H. (1967), *Power and the Pursuit of Peace* (London).

HIRST, P. (1997), 'The Global Economy—Myths and Realities', *International Affairs*, 73 (3).

—— and THOMPSON, G. (1996), *Globalization in Question: The International Economy and the Possibilities of Governance* (Cambridge).

HOBSBAWM, E. J. (2000), *The New Century* (London).

—— (1994), *Age of Extremes: The Short Twentieth Century 1914–1991* (London).

—— (1990), *Nations and Nationalism since 1870: Programme, Myth, Reality* (Cambridge).

HOFFMANN, S. (1998), *World Disorders: Troubled Peace in the Post-Cold War Era* (Lanham, Md).

—— (1995/6), 'The Politics and Ethics of Military Intervention', *Survival*, 37 (4).

—— (1995), 'The Crisis of Liberal Internationalism', *Foreign Policy*, 95.

HOGAN, M. J. (1992) (ed.), *The End of the Cold War: Its Meaning and Implications* (Cambridge).

—— (1987), *The Marshall Plan: America, Britain, and the Reconstruction of Western Europe, 1947–1952* (Cambridge).

HOLDEN, B. (1996a) (ed.), *The Ethical Dimensions of Global Change* (Houndmills).

—— (1996b), 'Democratic Theory and Global Warming', in Holden (1996a).

HOLM, H-H., and SORENSEN, G. (1995a) (eds.), *Whose World Order? Uneven Globalization and the End of the Cold War* (Boulder, Colo.).

—— (1995b), 'Introduction: What has Changed?', in Holm and Sorensen (1995a).

HOLSTI, K. J. (1999), 'The Coming Chaos? Armed Conflict in the World's Periphery', in Paul and Hall (1999).

—— (1996), *The State, War, and the State of War* (Cambridge).

HOLTON, R. J. (1998), *Globalization and the Nation-State* (Houndmills).

HOOGVELT, A. (1997), *Globalisation and the Postcolonial World: The New Political Economy of Development* (Houndmills).

HOWARD, M. (1999), 'When are Wars Decisive?', *Survival*, 41 (1).

—— (1993/4), 'Cold War, Chill Peace', *World Policy Journal*, 10 (4).

HUGHES, B. B. (1993), *International Futures: Choices in the Creation of a New World Order* (Boulder, Colo.).

HUNTINGTON, S. P. (1996), *The Clash of Civilizations and the Remaking of World Order* (New York).

HURRELL, A. (1999), 'Power, Principles and Prudence: Protecting Human Rights in a Deeply Divided World', in Dunne and Wheeler (1999).

—— (1995), 'Explaining the Resurgence of Regionalism in World Politics', *Review of International Studies*, 21 (4).

HUXLEY, T., and WILLETT, S. (1999), *Arming East Asia*, Adelphi Paper 329 (Oxford).

HUYSMANS, J. (1995), 'Post-Cold War Implosion and Globalisation: Liberalism Running Past Itself?', *Millennium*, 24 (3).

IISS (Annual), *Strategic Survey* (London and Oxford).

IKENBERRY, G. JOHN (2000), *After Victory: Institutions, Strategic Restraint, and the Rebuilding of Order after Major Wars* (Princeton).

—— (1999), 'Liberal Hegemony and the Future of the American Postwar Order', in Paul and Hall (1999).

—— (1998/9), 'Institutions, Strategic Restraint, and the Persistence of American Postwar Order', *International Security*, 23 (3).

—— (1998), 'Constitutional Politics in International Relations', *European Journal of International Relations*, 4 (2).

—— (1996), 'The Myth of Post-Cold War Chaos', *Foreign Affairs*, 75 (3).

—— (1995), 'Funk de Siècle: Impasses of Western Industrial Society at Century's End', *Millennium*, 24 (1).

INOGUCHI, T. (1995), 'Dialectics of World Order: A View from Pacific Asia', in Holm and Sorensen (1995a).

JACKSON, R. H. (1990), *Quasi-States: Sovereignty, International Relations and the Third World* (Cambridge).

—— and JAMES, A. (1993) (eds.), *States in a Changing World: A Contemporary Analysis* (Oxford).

JACOBSON, J. (1998), 'The Soviet Union and Versailles', in Boemeke, Feldman, and Glaser (1998).

JAMES, A. (1986), *Sovereign Statehood: The Basis of International Society* (London).

JAWAD, H. A. (1994) (ed.), *The Middle East in the New World Order* (Houndmills).

JERVIS, R. (1991/2), 'The Future of World Politics: Will it Resemble the Past', *International Security*, 16 (3).

JOFFE, J. (1992), 'Collective Security and the Future of Europe', *Survival*, 34 (1).

JONES, P. M. (1996), 'Is There Any Moral Basis to the "New World Order"?', in Holden (1996a).

KAHLER, M. (1993), 'Multilateralism with Small and Large Numbers', in Ruggie (1993a).

KALDOR, M. (1999), *New and Old Wars: Organized Violence in a Global Era* (Cambridge).

—— (1998), 'Reconceptualizing Organized Violence', in Archibugi, Held, and Kohler (1998).

KAMP, K.-H. (1998), 'NATO Enlargement: Debating the Next Enlargement Round', *Survival*, 40 (3).

KANET, R. E., and KOZHEMIAKIN, A. V. (1997) (eds.), *The Foreign Policy of the Russian Federation* (Houndmills).

KAPLAN, R. D. (2000), *The Coming Anarchy: Shattering the Dreams of the Post Cold War* (New York).

—— (1997), *The Ends of the Earth: A Journey at the Dawn of the 21ˢᵗ Century* (London).

—— (1994), 'The Coming Anarchy', *Atlantic Monthly*, 277.

KAPSTEIN, E. B. (1994), *Governing the Global Economy: International Finance and the State* (Cambridge, Mass.).

KARSH, E. (1997), 'Cold War, Post-Cold War: Does It Make a Difference for the Middle East?', *Review of International Studies*, 23 (3).

KEAL, P. (1993), 'Nuclear Weapons and the New World Order', in Leaver and Richardson (1993a).

KEGLEY, C. W., and RAYMOND, G. A. (1999), *How Nations Make Peace* (Houndmills).

KENNEDY, C. (1994), 'The Soviet Union and CFE', in Croft (1994a).

KENNEDY, P. (1993), *Preparing for the Twenty-First Century* (London).

—— (1988), *The Rise and Fall of the Great Powers* (London).

KEOHANE, R. O. (1990), 'Multilateralism: An Agenda for Research', *International Journal*, 45 (Autumn).

—— (1984), *After Hegemony: Cooperation and Discord in the World Political Economy* (Princeton).

—— and NYE, J. S. (1971) (eds.), *Transnational Relations in World Politics* (Cambridge, Mass.).

KEYLOR, W. R. (1998a), *The Legacy of the Great War: Peacemaking, 1919* (Boston).

—— (1998b), 'Versailles and International Diplomacy', in Boemeke, Feldman, and Glaser (1998).

KISSINGER, H. (1995), *Diplomacy* (New York).

—— (1977), *A World Restored* (London).

KLARE, M. T., and THOMAS, D. C. (1994), *World Security: Challenges for a New Century* (2nd edn.) (New York).

KNUTSEN, T. L. (1999), *The Rise and Fall of World Orders* (Manchester).

KOFMAN, E., and YOUNGS, G. (1996) (eds.), *Globalization: Theory and Practice* (London).

KOSTAKOS, G. (1995), 'UN Reform: The Post-Cold War World Organization', in Bourantanis and Wiener (1995).

KOTHARI, R. (1997), 'Globalization: A World Adrift', *Alternatives*, 22 (2).

KRAMER, M. (1999), 'Ideology and the Cold War', *Review of International Studies*, 25 (4).

KRAUSE, K. and WILLIAMS, M. C. (1997) (eds.), *Critical Security Studies: Concepts and Cases* (London).

KRAUTHAMMER, C. (1991), 'The Unipolar Moment', *Foreign Affairs*, 70 (1).

KUPCHAN, C. A. (1998), 'After Pax Americana: Benign Power, Regional Integration, and the Sources of a Stable Multipolarity', *International Security*, 23 (2).

—— and KUPCHAN, C. A. (1995), 'The Promise of Collective Security', *International Security*, 20 (1).

—— —— (1991), 'Concerts, Collective Security, and the Future of Europe', *International Security*, 16 (1).

KURTH, J. (1991), 'Things to Come: The Shape of the New World Order', *National Interest*, Summer.

LAIDI, Z. (1998), *A World without Meaning: The Crisis of Meaning in International Politics* (London).

—— (1994) (ed.), *Power and Purpose after the Cold War* (Oxford).

LATHAM, R. (1997a), *The Liberal Moment: Modernity, Security, and the Making of Postwar International Order* (New York).

—— (1997b), 'History, Theory, and International Order: Some Lessons from the Nineteenth Century', *Review of International Studies*, 23 (4).

LAYNE, C. (1998), 'Rethinking American Grand Strategy: Hegemony or Balance of Power in the Twenty-First Century?', *World Policy Journal*, 15 (2).

—— (1994), 'Kant or Cant: The Myth of the Democratic Peace', *International Security*, 19 (2).

—— (1993), 'The Unipolar Illusion: Why New Great Powers will Rise', *International Security*, 17 (4).

—— and SCHWARZ, B. (1993), 'American Hegemony—Without an Enemy', *Foreign Policy*, 92.

LEAVER, R., and RICHARDSON, J. L. (1993a) (eds.), *The Post-Cold War Order: Diagnosis and Prognosis* (St Leonards, NSW).

—— —— (1993b), 'Introduction: How Certain is the Future?', in Leaver and Richardson (1993a).

LEBOW, R. N. (1999), 'The Rise and Fall of the Cold War in Comparative Perspective', in Cox, Booth, and Dunne (1999a).

—— (1995), 'The Long Peace, the End of the Cold War, and the Failure of Realism', in Lebow and Risse-Kappen (1995).

—— and RISSE-KAPPEN, T. (1995) (eds.), *International Relations Theory and the End of the Cold War* (New York).

LEFFLER, M. P. (1992), *A Preponderance of Power: National Security, the Truman Administration, and the Cold War* (Stanford, Calif.).

LEGRO, J. W. (1997), 'Which Norms Matter? Revisiting the "Failure" of Internationalism', *International Organization*, 51 (1).

LEPINGWELL, J. W. R. (1995), 'START II and the Politics of Arms Control in Russia', *International Security*, 20 (2).

LIGHT, M., WHITE, S., and LOWENHARDT, J. (2000), 'A Wider Europe: The View from Moscow and Kyiv', *International Affairs*, 76 (1).

LINKLATER, A. (1998), *The Transformation of Political Community* (Cambridge).

—— (1993), 'Liberal Democracy, Constitutionalism and the New World Order', in Leaver and Richardson (1993a).

LIPSCHUTZ, R. D. (1995) (ed.), *On Security* (New York).

LYNCH, A. (1992), *The Cold War is Over—Again* (Boulder, Colo.).

LYONS, G. M., and MASTANDUNO, M. (1995) (eds.), *Beyond Westphalia? State Sovereignty and International Intervention* (Baltimore).

McGREW, A. (1997) (ed.), *The Transformation of Democracy?* (Milton Keynes).

—— and BROOK, C. (1998) (eds.), *Asia-Pacific in the New World Order* (London).

—— and LEWIS, P. G. (1992), *Global Politics* (Cambridge).

McINNES, C. (1994), 'The CFE Treaty in Perspective', in Croft (1994a).

MACMILLAN, J., and LINKLATER, A. (1995) (eds.), *Boundaries in Question: New Directions in International Relations* (London).

MAIER, C. S. (1996), 'The Social and Political Premises of Peacemaking after 1919 and 1945', unpublished paper, symposium on 'Altered Strategic Landscapes in the Twentieth Century', Yale University.

MAK, J. N. (1998), 'The Asia-Pacific Security Order', in McGrew and Brook (1998).

MALIK, M. (1998), 'Security in the Asia-Pacific: From Bilateralism to Multilateralism', in Baginda and Bergin (1998).

MANN, M. (1997), 'Has Globalization Ended the Rise and Rise of the Nation-State?', *Review of International Political Economy*, 4 (3).

MARANTZ, P. J. (1997), 'Neither Adversaries Nor Partners: Russia and the West Search for a New Relationship', in Kanet and Khozhemiakin (1997).

MARR, P., and Lewis, W. (1993) (eds.), *Riding the Tiger: The Middle East Challenge after the Cold War* (Boulder, Colo.).

MARTEL, G. (1998), 'A Comment', in Boemeke, Feldman, and Glaser (1998).

MASTANDUNO, M. (2000), 'Models, Markets and Power: Political Economy and the Asia-Pacific, 1989–1999', *Review of International Studies*, 26 (4).

—— (1999), 'A Realist View: Three Images of the Coming International Order', in Paul and Hall (1999).

—— (1997), 'Preserving the Unipolar Moment: Realist Theories and US Grand Strategy after the Cold War', *International Security*, 21 (4).

MAYALL, J. (1993), 'Non-Intervention, Self-determination and the New World Order', in Forbes and Hoffman (1993).

MAYER, A. J. (1968), *The Politics and Diplomacy of Peacemaking* (London).

—— (1959), *The Political Origins of the New Diplomacy* (New Haven).

MAZOWER, M. (1998), *Dark Continent: Europe's Twentieth Century* (London).

MEAD, W. R. (1991), 'The Bush Administration and the New World Order', *World Policy Journal*, 8 (3).

MEARSHEIMER, J. (1994/5), 'The False Promise of International Institutions', *International Security*, 19 (3).

—— (1990), 'Back to the Future: Instability in Europe after the Cold War', *International Security*, 15 (1).

MIALL, H. (1994) (ed.), *Redefining Europe: New Patterns of Conflict and Cooperation* (London).

MIKOYAN, S. A. (1998), 'Russia, the US and Regional Conflict in Eurasia', *Survival*, 40 (3).

MILLER, J. D. B., and VINCENT, J. (1990) (eds.), *Order and Violence: Hedley Bull and International Relations* (Oxford).

MORAVCSIK, A. (1997), 'Taking Preferences Seriously: A Liberal Theory of International Politics', *International Organization*, 51 (4).

MORGAN, P. M. (1993), 'Multilateralism and Security: Prospects in Europe', in Ruggie (1993a).

MOYNIHAN, D. P. (1993), *Pandaemonium: Ethnicity in International Politics* (Oxford).

MUELLER, J. (1995), *Quiet Cataclysm: Reflections on the Recent Transformation of World Politics* (New York).

MURPHY, E. C. (1994), 'The Arab–Israeli Conflict and the New World Order', in Jawad (1994).

NIBLOCK, T. (1994), 'A Framework for Renewal in the Middle East', in Jawad (1994).

NICOLAIDES, P. (1994), 'The Changing GATT System and the Uruguay Round Negotiations', in Stubbs and Underhill (1994).

NIKITIN, A. (1997), 'NATO Enlargement and Russian Policy in the 1990s', in Carlton and Ingram (1997).

NYE, J. S. (1992), 'What New World Order?', *Foreign Affairs*, 71 (2).

—— (1990), *Bound to Lead: The Changing Nature of American Power* (New York).

OSIANDER, A. (1994), *The States System of Europe 1640–1990: Peacemaking and the Condition of International Stability* (Oxford).

OWEN, J. M. (1994), 'How Liberalism Produces Democratic Peace', *International Security*, 19 (2).

PALAN, R. (2000), 'Recasting Political Authority: Globalization and the State', in Germain (2000).

PAOLINI, A. J., JARVIS, A. P., and REUS-SMIT, C. (1998) (eds.), *Between Sovereignty and Global Governance: The United Nations, the State and Civil Society* (Houndmills).

PAREKH, B. (1992), 'The Cultural Particularity of Liberal Democracy', in Held (1992).

PAUL, T. V., and HALL, J. A. (1999) (eds.), *International Order and the Future of World Politics* (Cambridge).

PAULY, L. V. (1994), 'Promoting a Global Economy: The Normative Role of the International Monetary Fund', in Stubbs and Underhill (1994).

PFAFF, W. (1993), 'Is Liberal Internationalism Dead?', *World Policy Journal*, 10 (3).

PICARD, E. (1994), 'The Middle East after the Cold War and Gulf War', in Laidi (1994).

PIERRE, A. J., and TRENIN, D. (1997), 'Developing NATO–Russian Relations', *Survival*, 39 (1).

RAMSBOTHAM, O., and WOODHOUSE, T. (1996), *Humanitarian Intervention in Contemporary Conflict* (Cambridge).

RAVENHILL, J. (1993), 'The New Disorder in the Periphery', in Leaver and Richardson (1993*a*).

RAY, J. L. (1995), *Democracy and International Conflict: An Evaluation of the Democratic Peace Proposition* (Columbia, SC).

REUS-SMIT, C. (1998), 'Changing Patterns of Governance: From Absolutism to Global Multilateralism', in Paolini, Jarvis, and Reus-Smit (1998).

—— (1997), 'The Constitutional Structure of International Society and the Nature of Fundamental Institutions', *International Organization*, 51 (4).

REYNOLDS, D. (2000), *One World Divisible: A Global History since 1945* (London).

RICHARDSON, J. L. (2000), 'The "End of History"', in Fry and O'Hagan (2000).

—— (1997), 'Contending Liberalisms: Past and Present', *European Journal of International Relations*, 3 (1).

—— (1995), 'Problematic Paradigm: Liberalism and the Global Order', in Camilleri, Jarvis, and Paolini (1995).

—— (1993), 'The End of Geopolitics', in Leaver and Richardson (1993*a*).

Risse, T. (1997), 'The Cold War's Endgame and German Unification', *International Security*, 21 (4).

Risse-Kappen, T. (1995), 'Democratic Peace—Warlike Democracies? A Social Constructivist Interpretation of the Liberal Argument', *European Journal of International Relations*, 1 (4).

Roberts, A. (1999), 'NATO's "Humanitarian War" over Kosovo', *Survival*, 41 (3).

—— (1995/6), 'From San Francisco to Sarajevo: The UN and the Use of Force', *Survival*, 37 (4).

—— (1994), 'The Crisis in UN Peacekeeping', *Survival*, 36 (3).

—— (1993), 'The United Nations and International Security', *Survival*, 35 (2).

Roberts, B. (1995) (ed.), *Order and Disorder after the Cold War: A Washington Quarterly Reader* (Cambridge, Mass.).

Rosecrance, R. (1992), 'A New Concert of Powers', *Foreign Affairs*, 71 (2).

Rosenau, J. N. (1997), *Along the Domestic-Foreign Frontier: Exploring Governance in a Turbulent World* (Cambridge).

—— (1992), 'Governance, Order, and Change in World Politics', in Rosenau and Czempiel (1992).

—— and Czempiel, E.-O. (1992) (eds.), *Governance without Government: Order and Change in World Politics* (Cambridge).

Ross, R. S. (1999), 'The Geography of the Peace: East Asia in the Twenty-first Century', *International Security*, 23 (4).

Rotfeld, A. D., and Stutzle, W. (1991) (eds.), *Germany and Europe in Transition* (Oxford).

Ruggie, J. G. (1998), *Constructing the World Polity: Essays on International Institutionalization* (London).

—— (1996), *Winning the Peace: America and World Order in the New Era* (New York).

—— (1995), 'At Home Abroad, Abroad at Home: International Liberalisation and Domestic Stability in the New World Economy', *Millennium*, 24 (3).

—— (1993*a*) (ed.), *Multilateralism Matters: The Theory and Praxis of an Institutional Form* (New York).

—— (1993*b*), 'Multilateralism: The Anatomy of an Institution', in Ruggie (1993*a*).

Russell, J. G. (1986), *Peacemaking in the Renaissance* (London).

Russett, B. (1998), 'A Neo-Kantian Perspective: Democracy, Interdependence, and International Organizations in Building Security Communities', in Adler and Barnett (1998).

—— (1993), *Grasping the Democratic Peace: Principles for a Post-Cold War World* (Princeton).

—— and Sutterlin, J. (1991), 'The UN in a New World Order', *Foreign Affairs*, 70 (2).

Rutland, P. (1999), 'Mission Impossible? The IMF and the Failure of the Market Transition in Russia', *Review of International Studies*, 25 (Special Issue).

Sabelnikov, L. (1996), 'Russia on the Way to the World Trade Organization', *International Affairs*, 72 (2).

SANDERS, J. W. (1991), 'Retreat from World Order: The Perils of Triumphalism', *World Policy Journal,* 8 (2).

SASSEN, S. (1996), *Losing Control? Sovereignty in an Age of Globalization* (New York).

SCHOLTE, J. A. (2000), *Globalization: A Critical Introduction* (Houndmills).

—— (1997), 'The Globalization of World Politics', in Baylis and Smith (1997).

SCHROEDER, P. W. (1995), 'A New World Order: A Historical Perspective', in B. Roberts (1995).

—— (1992), 'Did the Vienna Settlement Rest on a Balance of Power?', *American Historical Review,* 97 (June).

SCHWARZ, B. (1997), 'Permanent Interests, Endless Threats: Cold War Continuities and NATO Enlargement', *World Policy Journal,* 14 (3).

SCHWENNINGER, S. R. (1999), 'World Order Lost: American Foreign Policy in the Post-Cold War World' , *World Policy Journal,* 16 (2).

SEGAL, G. (1998), 'The Asia-Pacific: What Kind of Challenge?', in McGrew and Brook (1998).

SELF, P. (2000), *Rolling back the Market: Economic Dogma and Political Choice* (Houndmills).

SELLERS, M. (1996) (ed.), *The New World Order: Sovereignty, Human Rights and the Self-Determination of Peoples* (Oxford).

SHARP, A. (1997), 'Reflections on the Remaking of Europe: 1815, 1919, 1945, post-1989', *Irish Studies in International Affairs,* 8.

—— (1991), *The Versailles Settlement: Peacemaking in Paris, 1919* (Houndmills).

SHAW, M. (1997), 'The State of Globalization: Towards a Theory of State Transformation', *Review of International Political Economy,* 4 (3).

SHEARMAN, P. (1995*a*) (ed.), *Russian Foreign Policy since 1990* (Boulder, Colo.)

—— (1995*b*), 'Russian Policy toward the United States', in Shearman (1995*a*).

SINGER, M., and WILDAVSKY, A. (1993), *The Real World Order: Zones of Peace, Zones of Turmoil* (Chatham, NJ).

SJOLANDER, C. T. (1996), 'The Rhetoric of Globalization: What's in a Wor(l)d?', *International Journal,* 51 (4).

SKED, A. (1979) (ed.), *Europe's Balance of Power* (London).

SKIDELSKY, R. (1995), *The World after Communism: A Polemic for our Times* (London).

SMITH, M. J. (1998), 'Humanitarian Intervention: An Overview of the Ethical Issues', *Ethics and International Affairs,* 12.

SMITH, S. (1999), 'Is the Truth out There? Eight Questions about International Order', in Paul and Hall (1999).

SNOW, D. M. (1997), *Distant Thunder: Patterns of Conflict in the Developing World* (2nd edn.) (Armonk, NY).

SORENSEN, G. (1998), 'International Relations Theory after the Cold War', in Dunne, Cox, and Booth (1998).

STARKEY, B. (1996), 'Post-Cold War Security in the GCC Region: Continuity and Change in the 1990s', in Ahrari (1996*a*).

Starr, H. (1999), *Anarchy, Order, and Integration: How to Manage Interdependence* (Ann Arbor).

Steel, R. (1998), 'Prologue: 1919-1945-1989', in Boemeke, Feldman, and Glaser (1998).

Stephanson, A. (1998), 'Rethinking Cold War History', *Review of International Studies*, 24 (1).

Stevenson, D. (1998), 'French War Aims and Peace Planning', in Boemeke, Feldman, and Glaser (1998).

Strange, S. (1996), *The Retreat of the State: The Diffusion of Power in the World Economy* (Cambridge).

Stubbs, R., and Underhill, G. R. D. (1994) (eds.), *Political Economy and the Changing Global Order* (London).

Thomas, C. (1999), 'Where is the Third World Now?', in Cox, Booth, and Dunne (1999a).

—— (1997), 'Globalization and the South', in Thomas and Wilkin (1997).

—— and Wilkin P. (1997) (eds.), *Globalization and the South* (Houndmills).

Thompson, J. (1998), 'Community, Identity and World Citizenship', in Archibugi, Held, and Kohler (1998).

Thompson, K. W. (1994) (ed.), *Community, Diversity, and a New World Order: Essays in Honor of Inis L. Claude, Jr* (Lanham, Md.).

Towle, P. (1997), *Enforced Disarmament: From the Napoleonic Campaigns to the Gulf War* (Oxford).

Townsend, C. (1995), 'The Fin De Siècle', in Danchev (1995a).

Trachtenberg, M. (1999), *A Constructed Peace: The Making of the European Settlement 1945–1963* (Princeton).

Tucker, R. W. (1990), '1989 and All That', *Foreign Affairs*, 69 (4).

—— and Hendrickson, D. C. (1992), *The Imperial Temptation: The New World Order and America's Purpose* (New York).

Tussie, D., and Woods, N. (2000), 'Trade, Regionalism and the Threat to Multilateralism', in Woods (2000a).

Underhill, G. R. D. (1997), *The New World Order in International Finance* (Houndmills).

US Department of State (1989), 'Eastern Europe: Regional Brief', Oct.

US Information Service (1991), *The New World Order: An Analysis and Document Collection* (London).

Van Creveld, M. (1999), *The Rise and Decline of the State* (Cambridge).

Vayrynen, R. (1999) (ed.), *Globalization and Global Governance* (Oxford).

Vincent, J. (1990), 'Order in International Politics', in Miller and Vincent (1990).

Von Laue, T. H. (1987), *The World Revolution of Westernization: The Twentieth Century in Global Perspective* (New York).

Wallace, W. (1999), 'Europe after the Cold War: Interstate Order or Post-Sovereign Regional System?', in Cox, Booth, and Dunne (1999a).

Waltz, K. N. (2000), 'Structural Realism after the Cold War', *International Security*, 25 (1).

WALTZ, K. N. (1993), 'The Emerging Structure of International Politics', *International Security*, 18 (2).

WATTANAYAGORN, P., and BALL, D. (1996), 'A Regional Arms Race?', in Ball (1996a).

WEBER, S. (1997), 'Institutions and Change', in Doyle and Ikenberry (1997).

WEISS, L. (1999), 'Globalization and National Governance: Antinomy or Interdependence', in Cox, Booth, and Dunne (1999a).

WEISS, T. G. (1993) (ed.), *Collective Security in a Changing World* (Boulder, Colo.).

—— and HOLGATE, L. S. H. (1993), 'Opportunities and Obstacles for Collective Security after the Cold War', in Dewitt, Haglund, and Kirton (1993).

WEISSKOPF, T. E. (1995), 'Russia in Transition: Perils of the Fast Track to Capitalism', in Frieden and Lake (1995).

WELLER, M. (1999/2000), 'The US, Iraq and the Use of Force in a Unipolar World', *Survival*, 41 (4).

WHEELER, N. J. (2000), *Saving Strangers: Humanitarian Intervention in International Society* (Oxford).

WIENER, J. (1995), 'Leadership, the United Nations, and the New World Order', in Bourantanis and Wiener (1995).

WILLIAMS, A. J. (1999), 'Ideas and the Creation of Successive World Orders', in Chan and Wiener (1999).

—— (1998), *Failed Imagination? New World Order of the Twentieth Century* (Manchester).

WILLIAMS, J. (1996), 'Nothing Succeeds like Success? Legitimacy and International Relations', in Holden (1996a).

WILLIAMS, P. (1995), 'Multilateralism: Critique and Appraisal', in Brenner (1995a).

WOHLFORTH, W. C. (1999), 'The Stability of a Unipolar World', *International Security*, 24 (1).

WOODS, N. (2000a), *The Political Economy of Globalization* (Houndmills).

—— (2000b), 'The Political Economy of Globalization', in Woods (2000a).

—— (2000c), 'Globalization and International Institutions', in Woods (2000a).

ZAGORSKI, A. (1994), 'Russia and the CIS', in Miall (1994).

ZELIKOW, P., and RICE, C. (1995), *Germany Unified and Europe Transformed: A Study in Statecraft* (Cambridge, Mass.).

ZUBOK, V. M. (1995), 'Russia: Between Peace and Conflict', in Holm and Sorensen (1995a).

INDEX